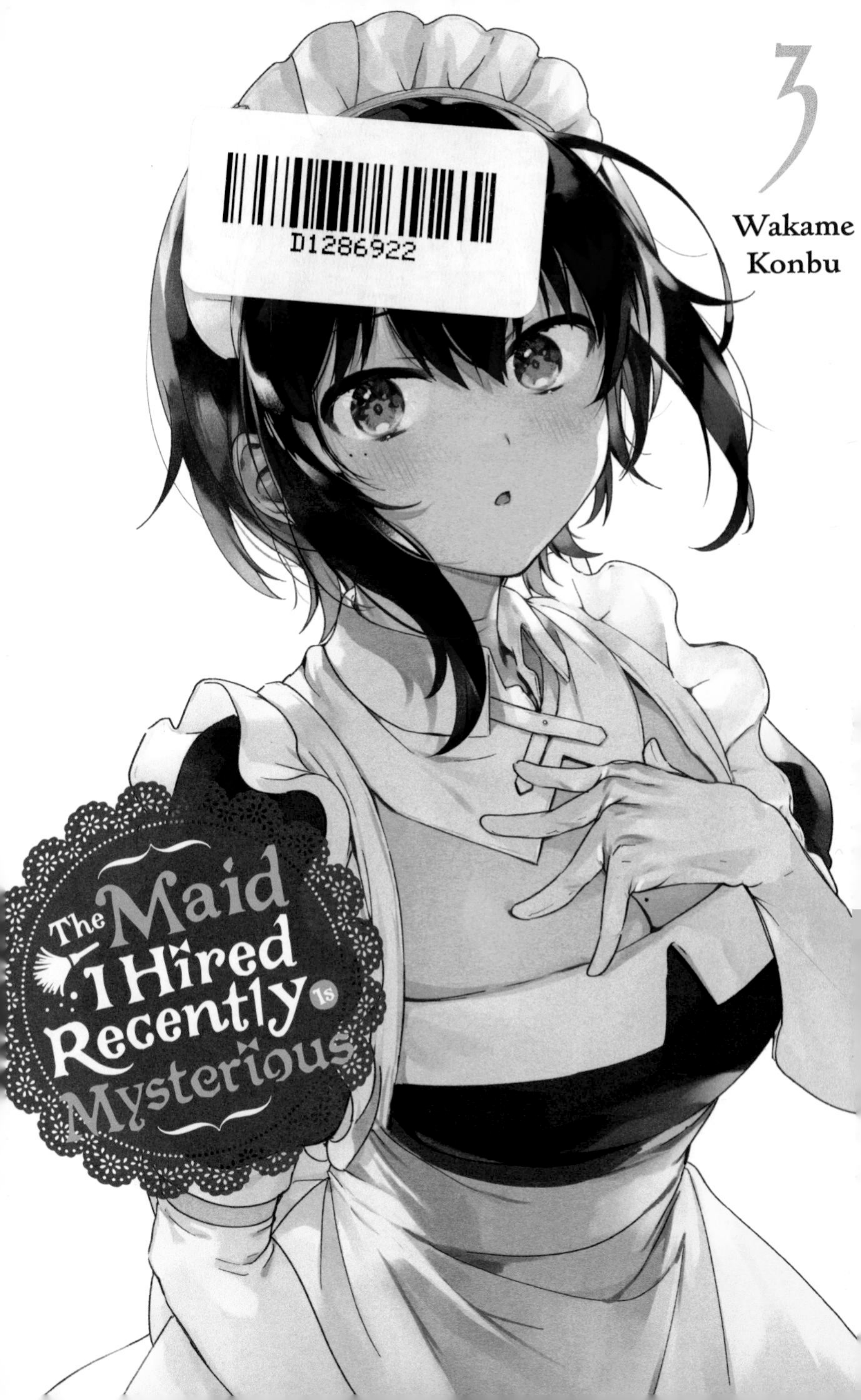
3
Wakame
Konbu
The Maid I Hired Recently Is Mysterious

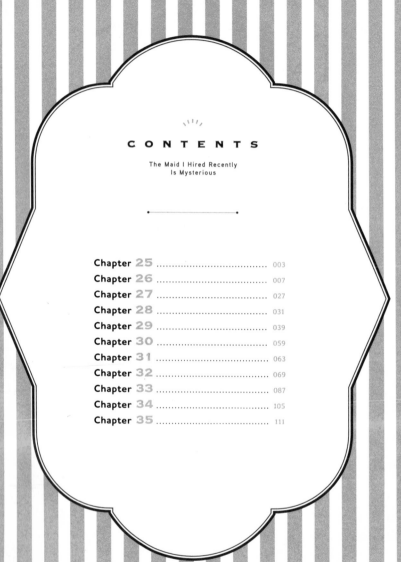

CONTENTS

The Maid I Hired Recently
Is Mysterious

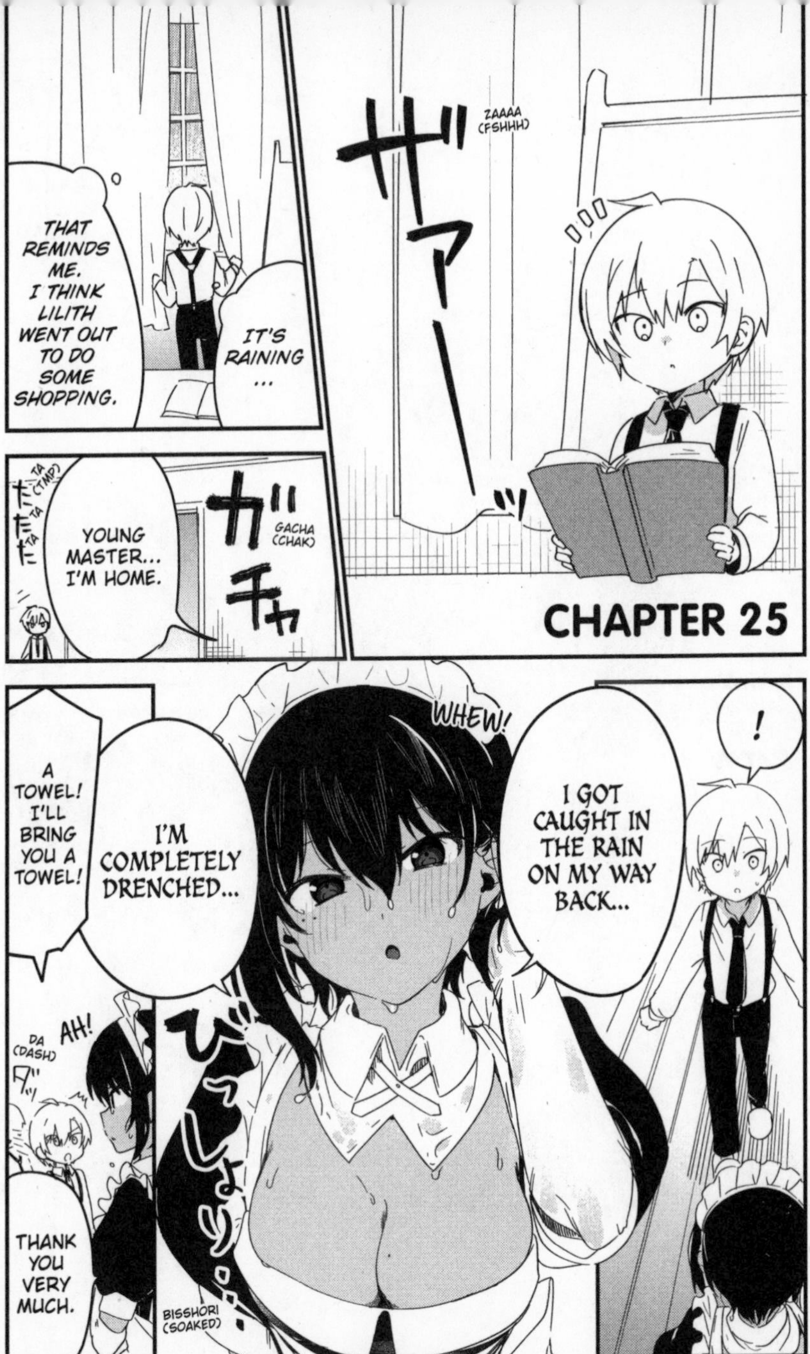
ZAAAA (FSHHH)
CHAPTER 25
IT'S RAINING ...
THAT REMINDS ME. I THINK LILITH WENT OUT TO DO SOME SHOPPING.
GACHA (CHAK)
YOUNG MASTER... I'M HOME.
TA TA TA (TMP)
!
I GOT CAUGHT IN THE RAIN ON MY WAY BACK...
WHEW!
I'M COMPLETELY DRENCHED...
BISSHORI (SOAKED)
A TOWEL! I'LL BRING YOU A TOWEL!
AH!
DA (DASH)
THANK YOU VERY MUCH.

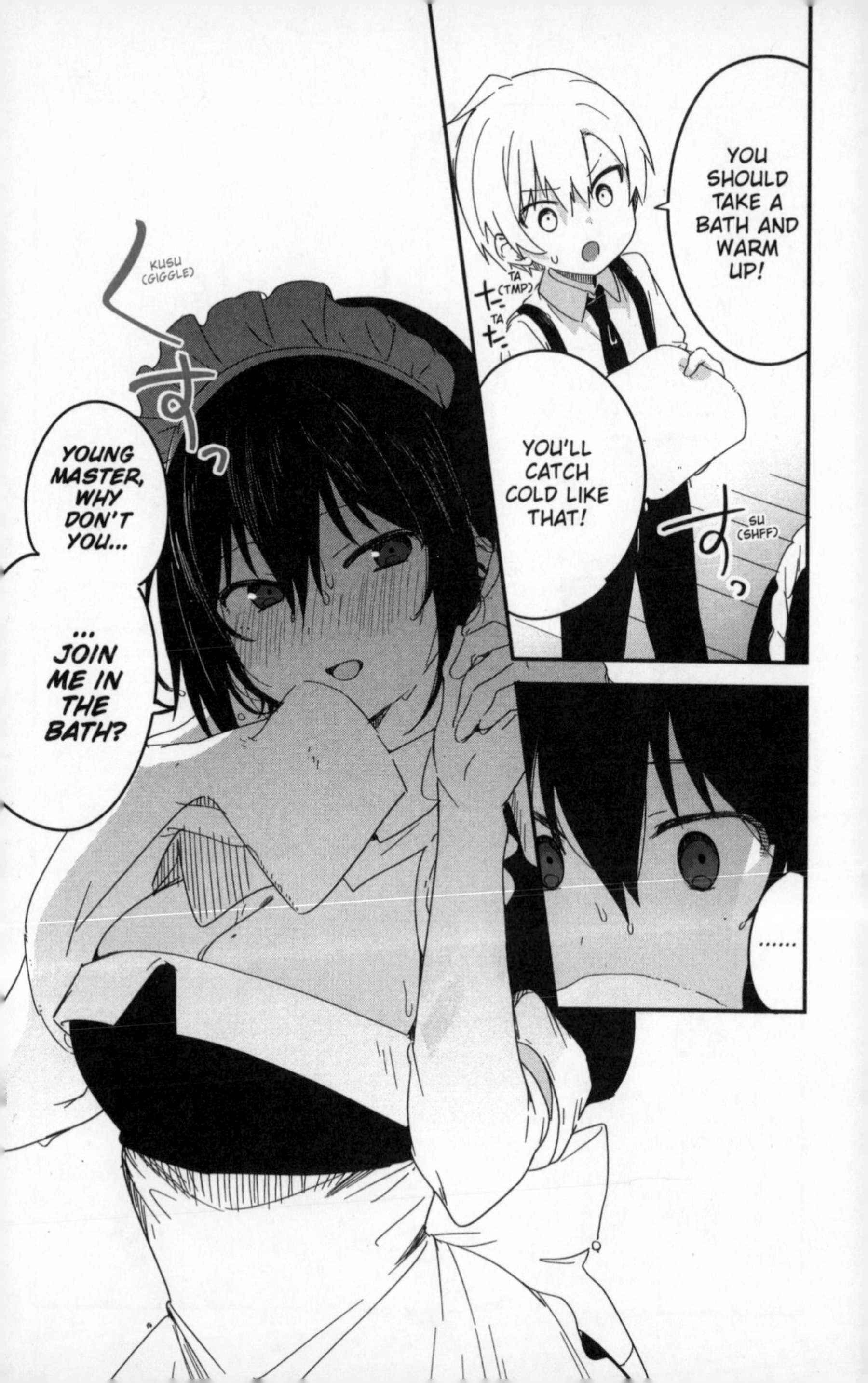
YOU SHOULD TAKE A BATH AND WARM UP!
TA (TMP) TA
YOU'LL CATCH COLD LIKE THAT!
SU (SHFF)
KUSU (GIGGLE)
YOUNG MASTER, WHY DON'T YOU...
...JOIN ME IN THE BATH?
......

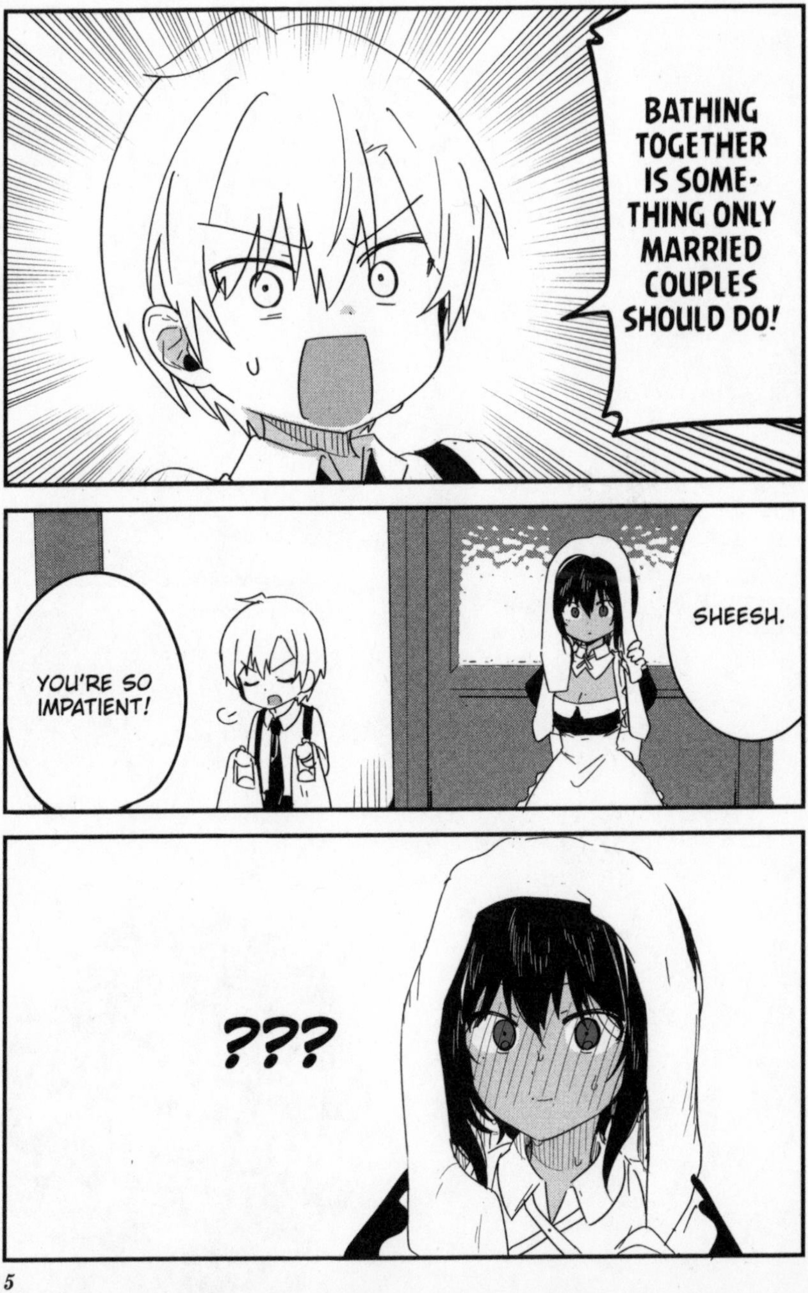
BATHING TOGETHER IS SOME-THING ONLY MARRIED COUPLES SHOULD DO!
SHEESH.
YOU'RE SO IMPATIENT!
???

The Maid I Hired Recently Is Mysterious

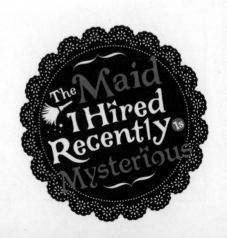

CHAPTER 26

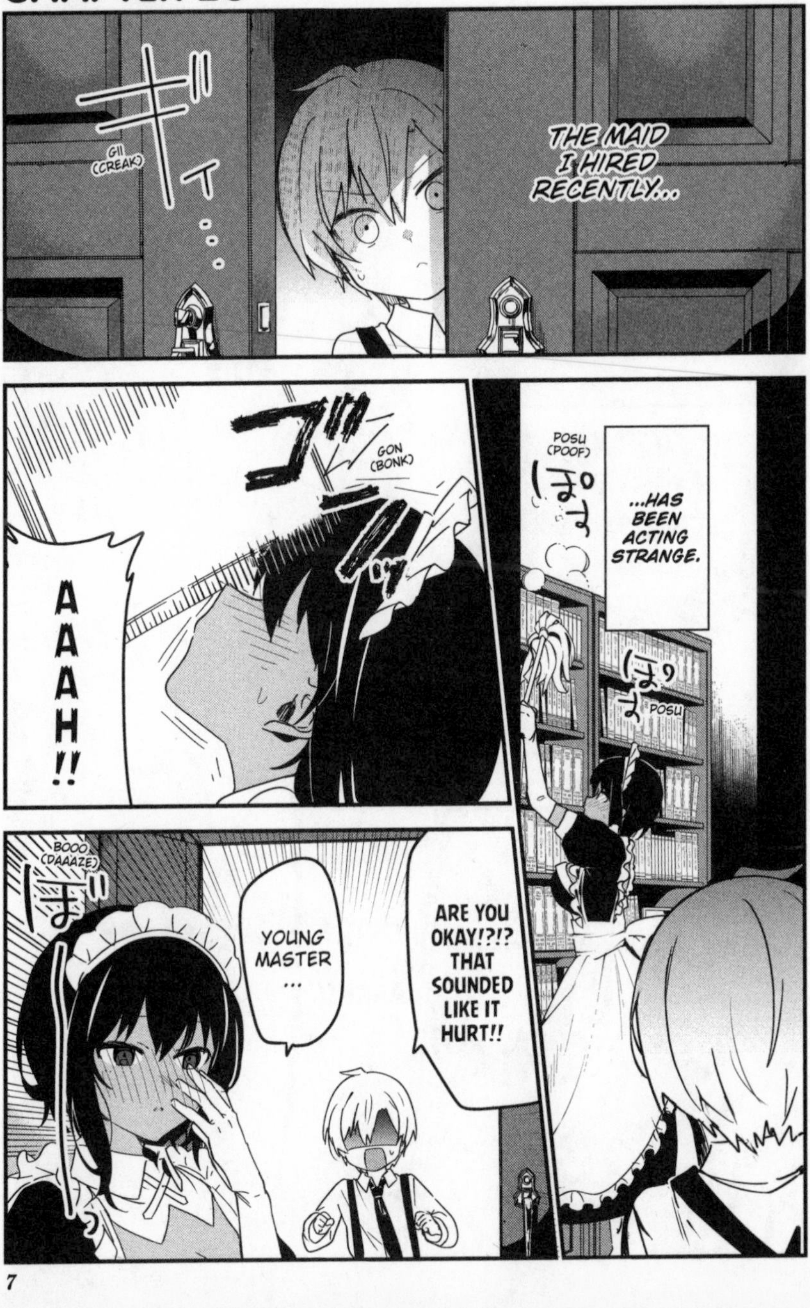

THE MAID I HIRED RECENTLY...
GII (CREAK)
POSU (POOF)
...HAS BEEN ACTING STRANGE.
POSU
GON (BONK)
AAAAH!!
ARE YOU OKAY!?!? THAT SOUNDED LIKE IT HURT!!
YOUNG MASTER ...
BOOO (DAAAZE)

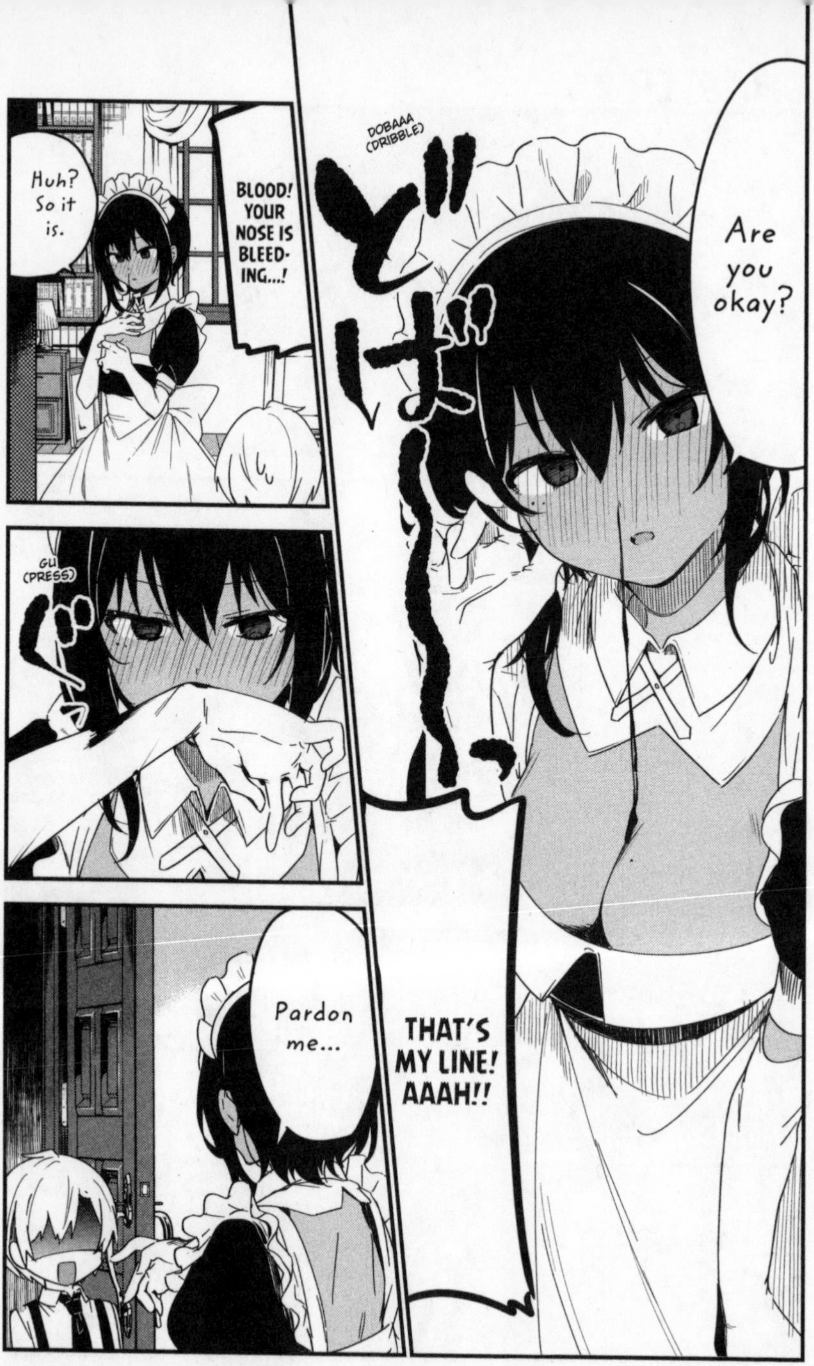
Are you okay?
DOBAAA (DRIBBLE)
THAT'S MY LINE! AAAH!!
BLOOD! YOUR NOSE IS BLEEDING...!
Huh? So it is.
GU (PRESS)
Pardon me...

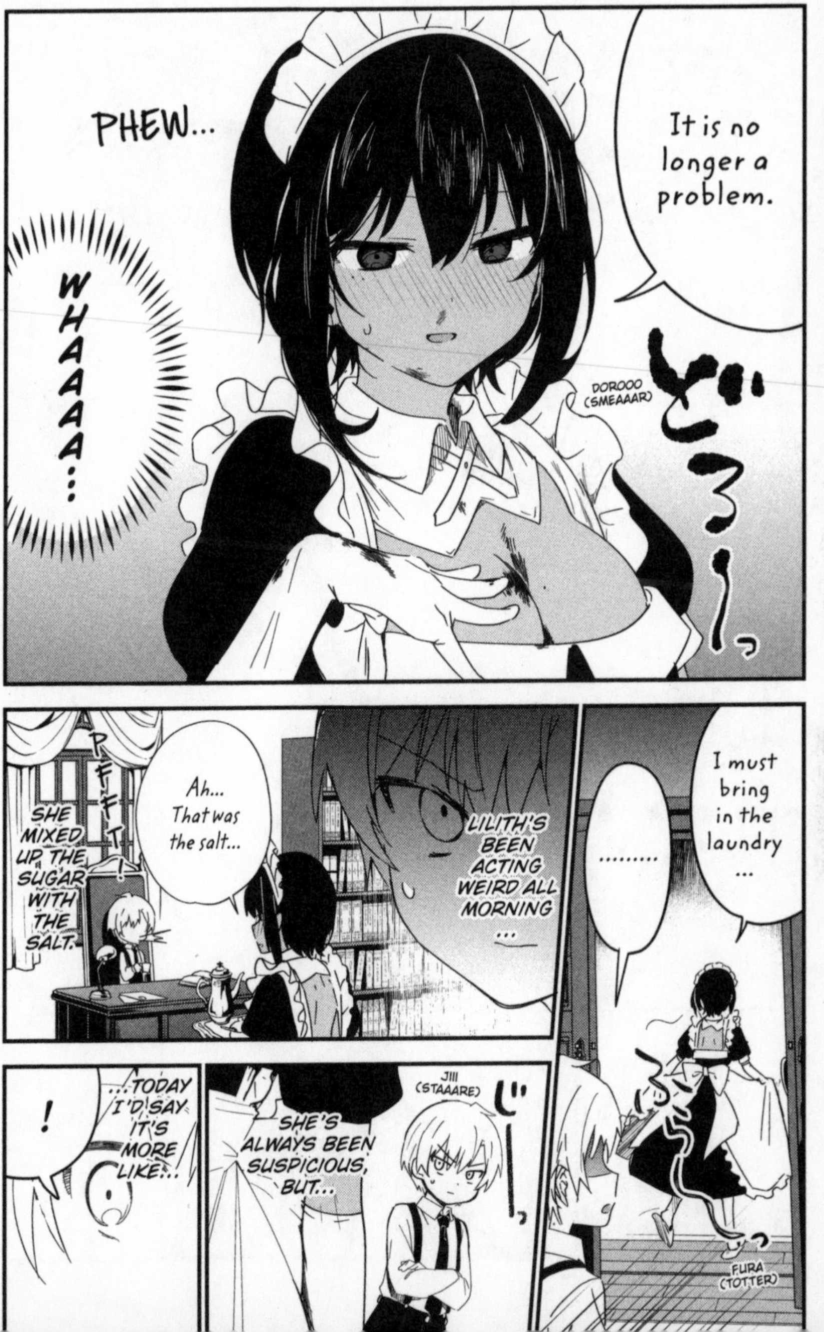
It is no longer a problem.
DOROOO (SMEAAAR)
PHEW...
WHAAAAA...
I must bring in the laundry ...
....
FURA (TOTTER)
LILITH'S BEEN ACTING WEIRD ALL MORNING ...
Ah... That was the salt...
PFFT!
SHE MIXED UP THE SUGAR WITH THE SALT.
JIII (STAAARE)
SHE'S ALWAYS BEEN SUSPICIOUS, BUT...
...TODAY I'D SAY IT'S MORE LIKE...
!

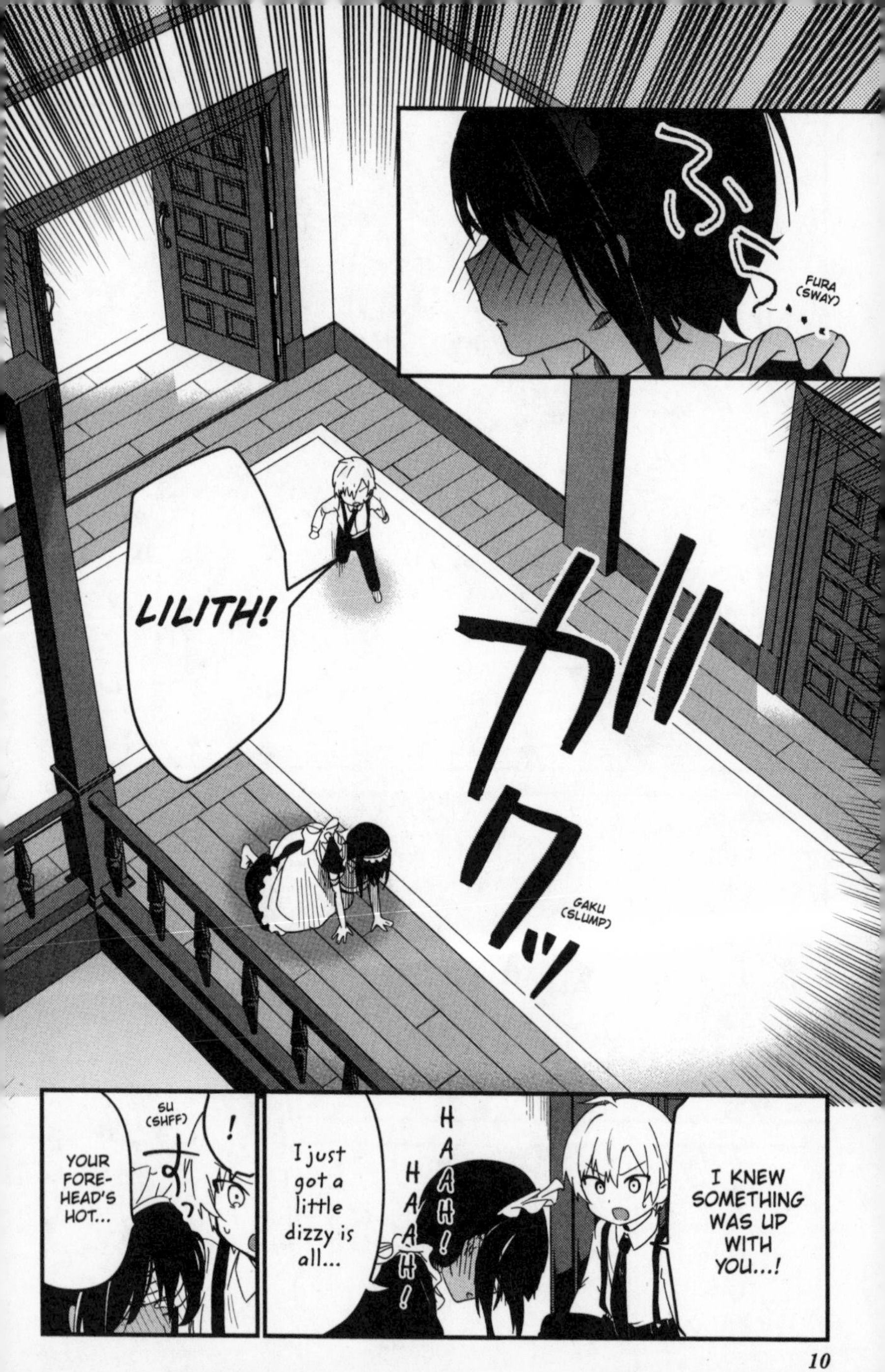
ふら
FURA (SWAY)
LILITH!
ガクッ
GAKU (SLUMP)
I KNEW SOMETHING WAS UP WITH YOU...!
HAAH! HAAAH!
I just got a little dizzy is all...
す
SU (SHFF)
!
YOUR FORE-HEAD'S HOT...

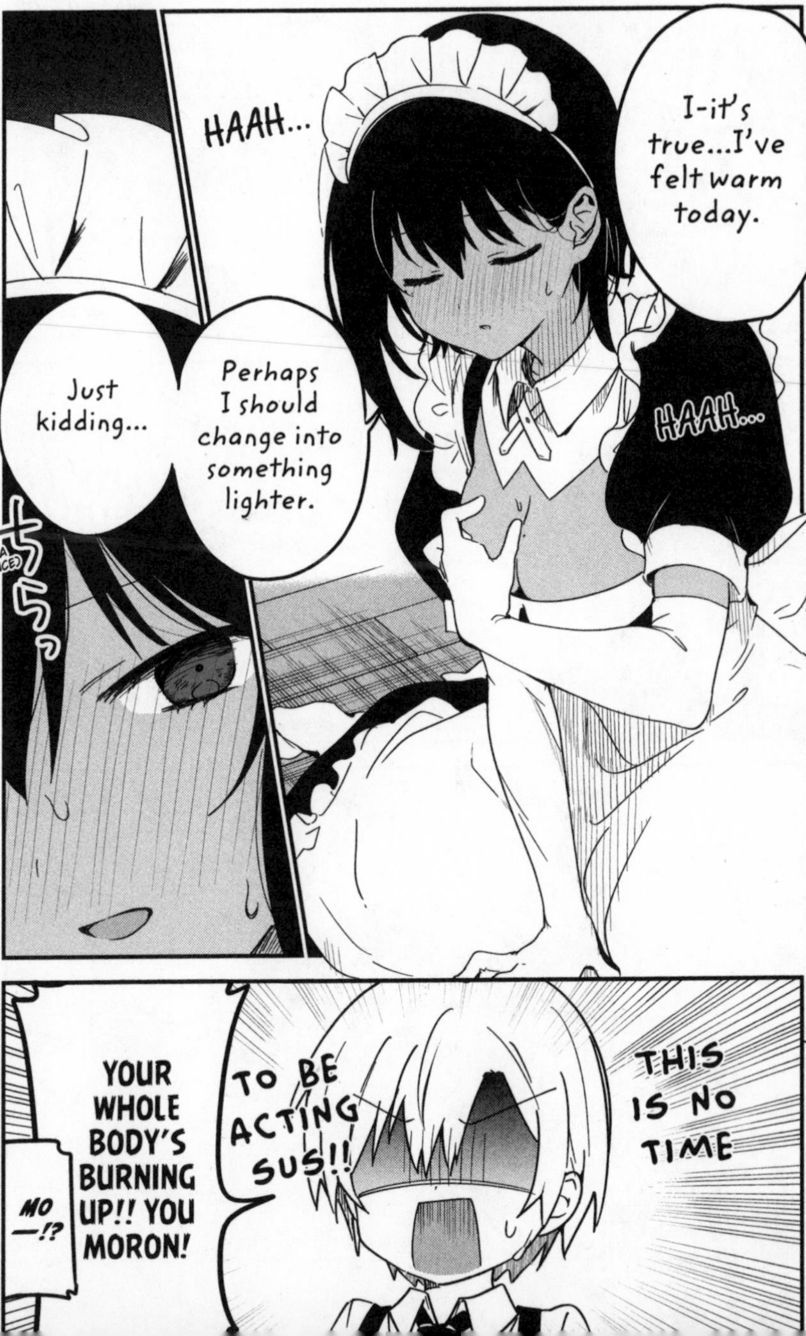
I-it's true...I've felt warm today.
HAAH...
HAAH...
Perhaps I should change into something lighter.
Just kidding...
CHIRA (GLANCE)
THIS IS NO TIME
TO BE ACTING SUS!!
YOUR WHOLE BODY'S BURNING UP!! YOU MORON!
MO—!?

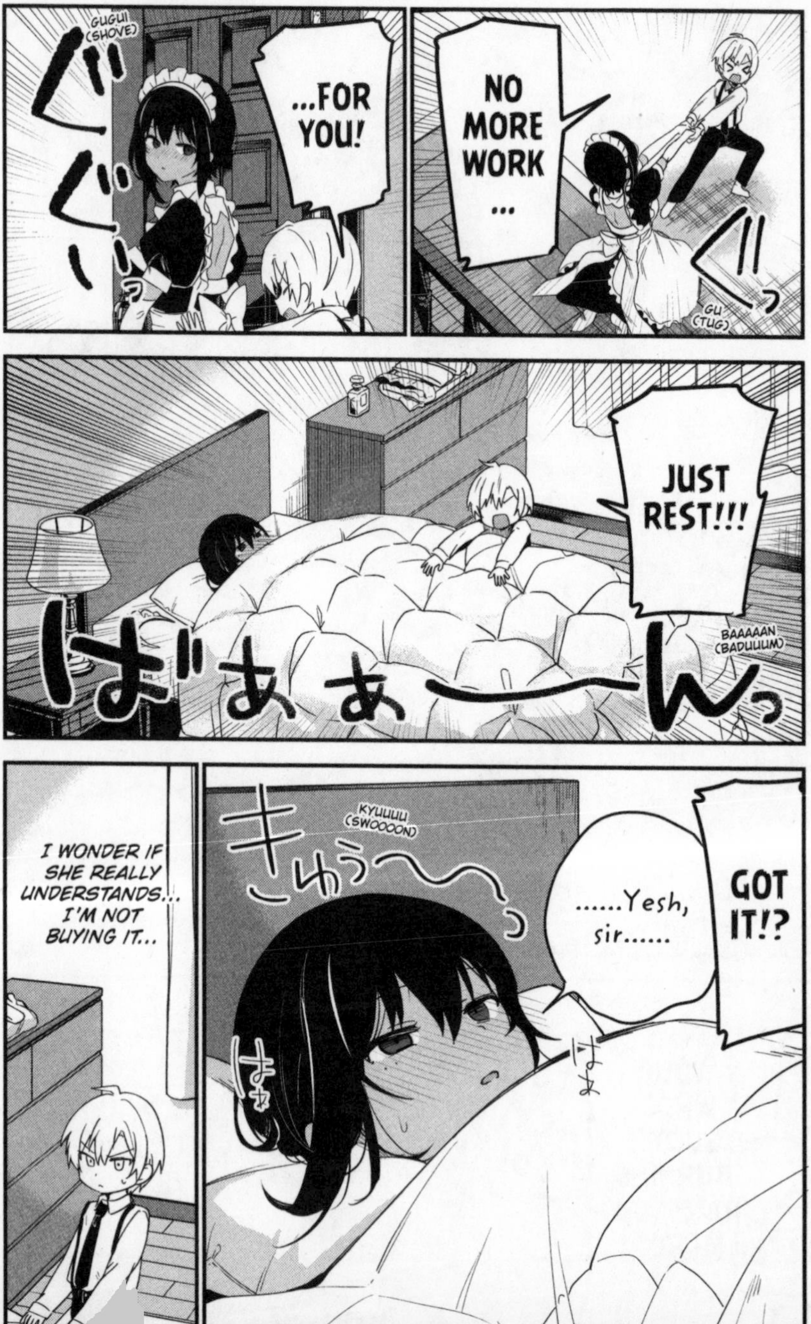
NO MORE WORK ...
GU (TUG)
GUGUI (SHOVE)
...FOR YOU!
JUST REST!!!
BAAAAAN (BADUUUM)
GOT IT!?
......Yesh, sir......
KYUUUU (SWOOOON)
I WONDER IF SHE REALLY UNDERSTANDS... I'M NOT BUYING IT...

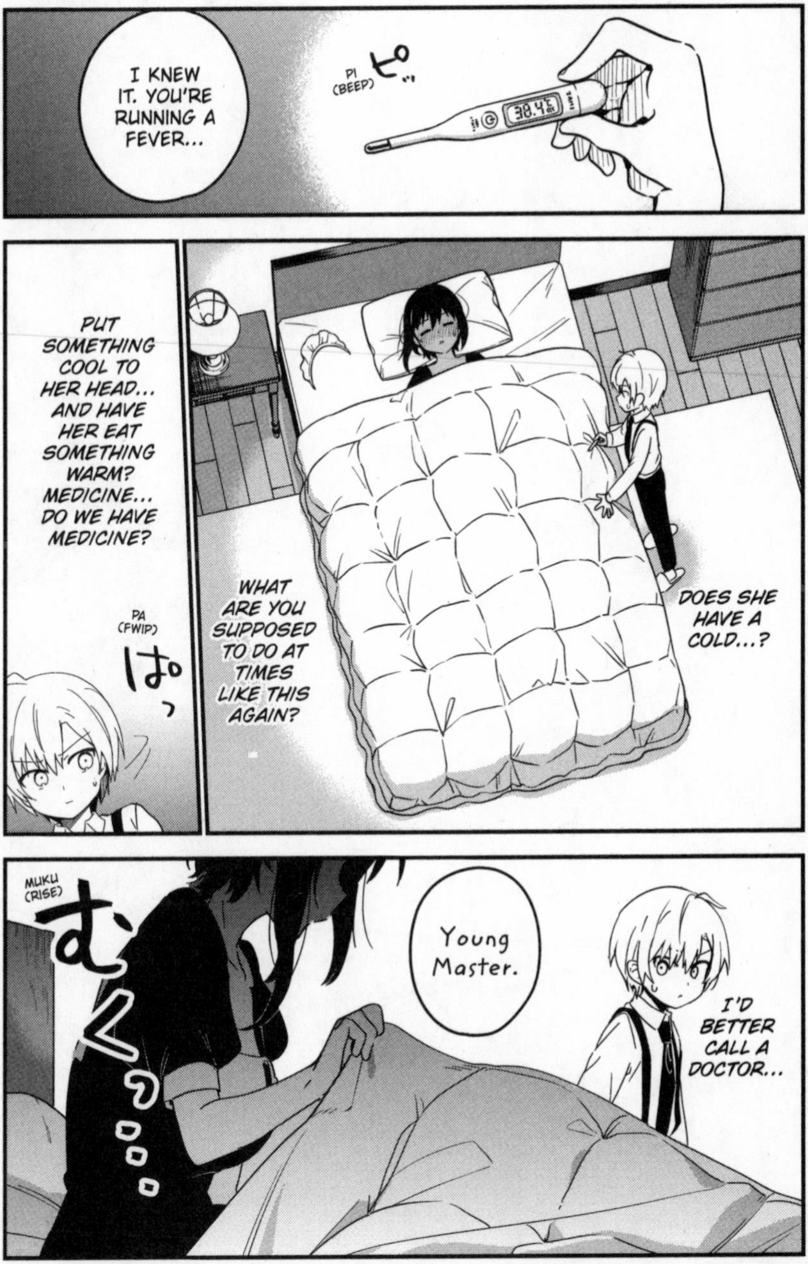
PI (BEEP) ピッ
I KNEW IT. YOU'RE RUNNING A FEVER...
DOES SHE HAVE A COLD...?
WHAT ARE YOU SUPPOSED TO DO AT TIMES LIKE THIS AGAIN?
PA (FWIP) ぱっ
PUT SOMETHING COOL TO HER HEAD... AND HAVE HER EAT SOMETHING WARM? MEDICINE... DO WE HAVE MEDICINE?
I'D BETTER CALL A DOCTOR...
Young Master.
MUKU (RISE) むくっ。。。

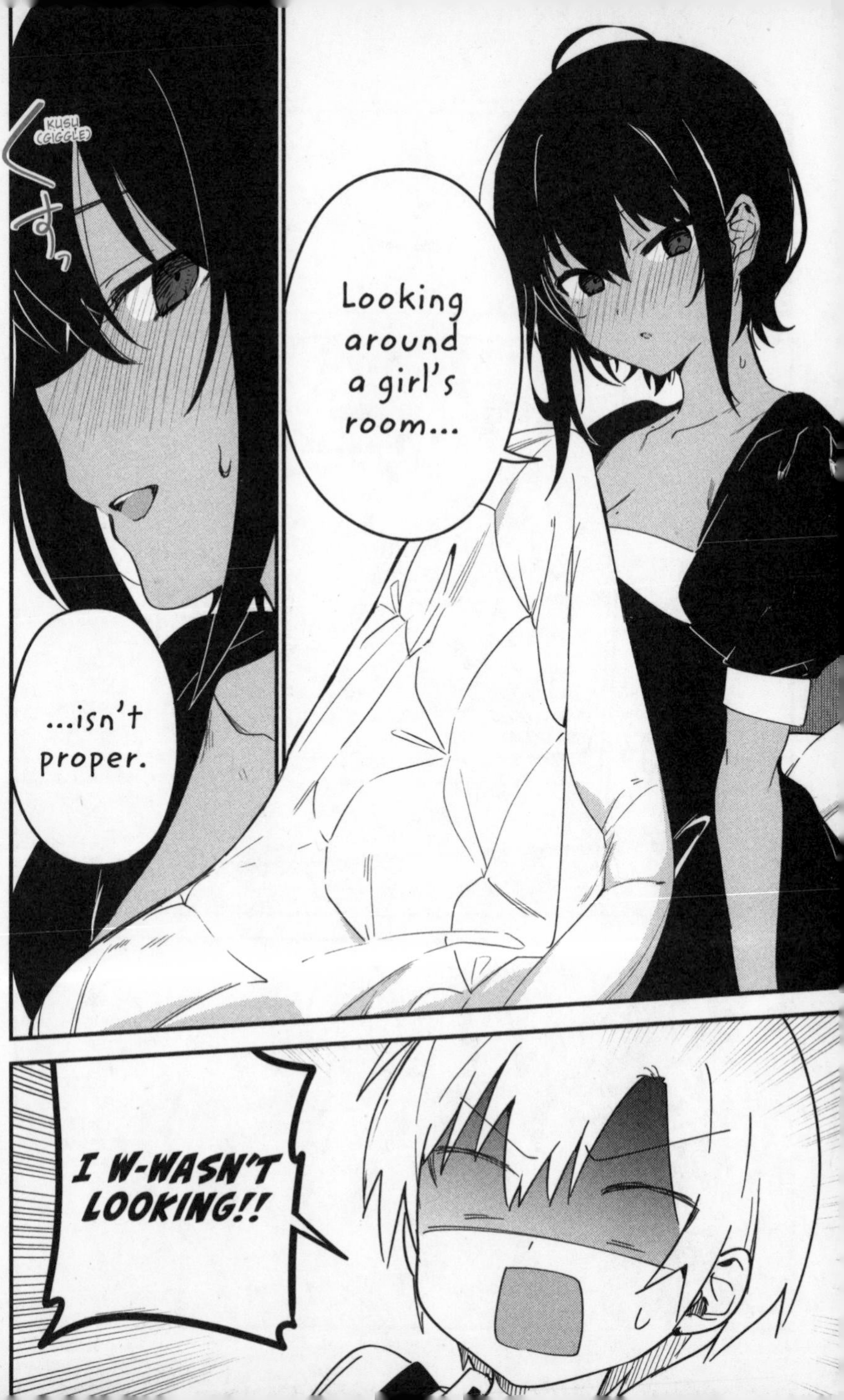
Looking around a girl's room...
くすっ
KUSU (GIGGLE)
...isn't proper.
I W-WASN'T LOOKING!!

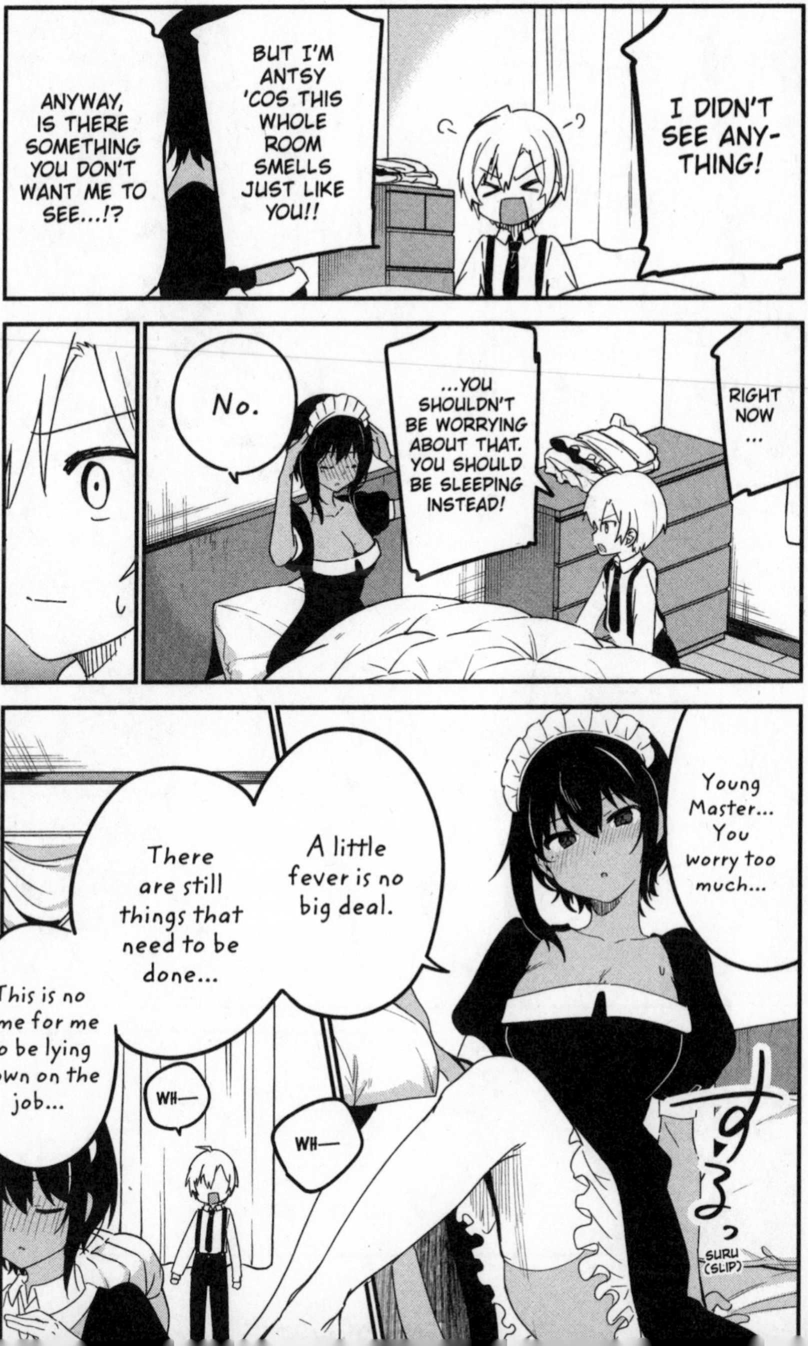
I DIDN'T SEE ANY-THING!
BUT I'M ANTSY 'COS THIS WHOLE ROOM SMELLS JUST LIKE YOU!!
ANYWAY, IS THERE SOMETHING YOU DON'T WANT ME TO SEE...!?
RIGHT NOW ...
...YOU SHOULDN'T BE WORRYING ABOUT THAT. YOU SHOULD BE SLEEPING INSTEAD!
No.
Young Master... You worry too much...
A little fever is no big deal.
There are still things that need to be done...
This is no time for me to be lying down on the job...
WH—
WH—
SURU (SLIP)

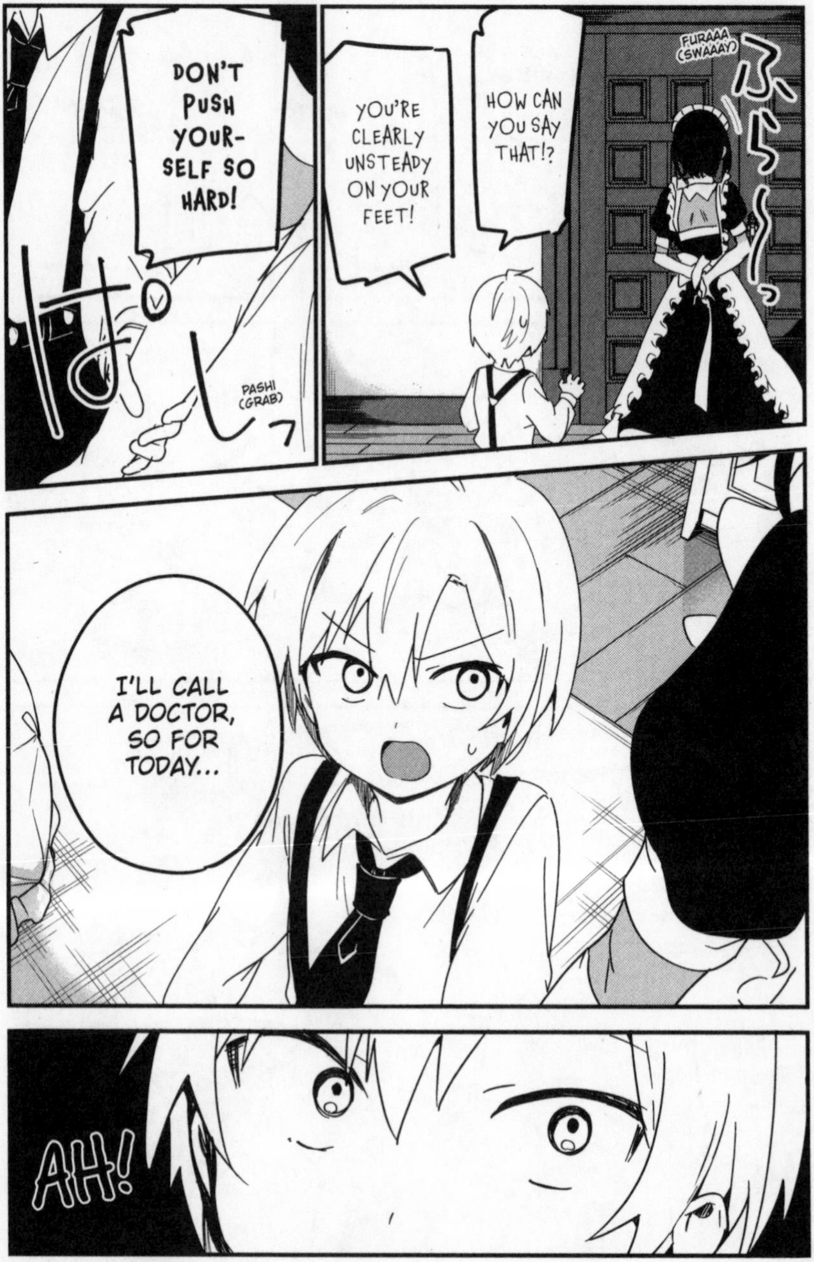
FURAAA (SWAAAY)
HOW CAN YOU SAY THAT!?
YOU'RE CLEARLY UNSTEADY ON YOUR FEET!
DON'T PUSH YOUR-SELF SO HARD!
PASHI (GRAB)
I'LL CALL A DOCTOR, SO FOR TODAY...
AH!

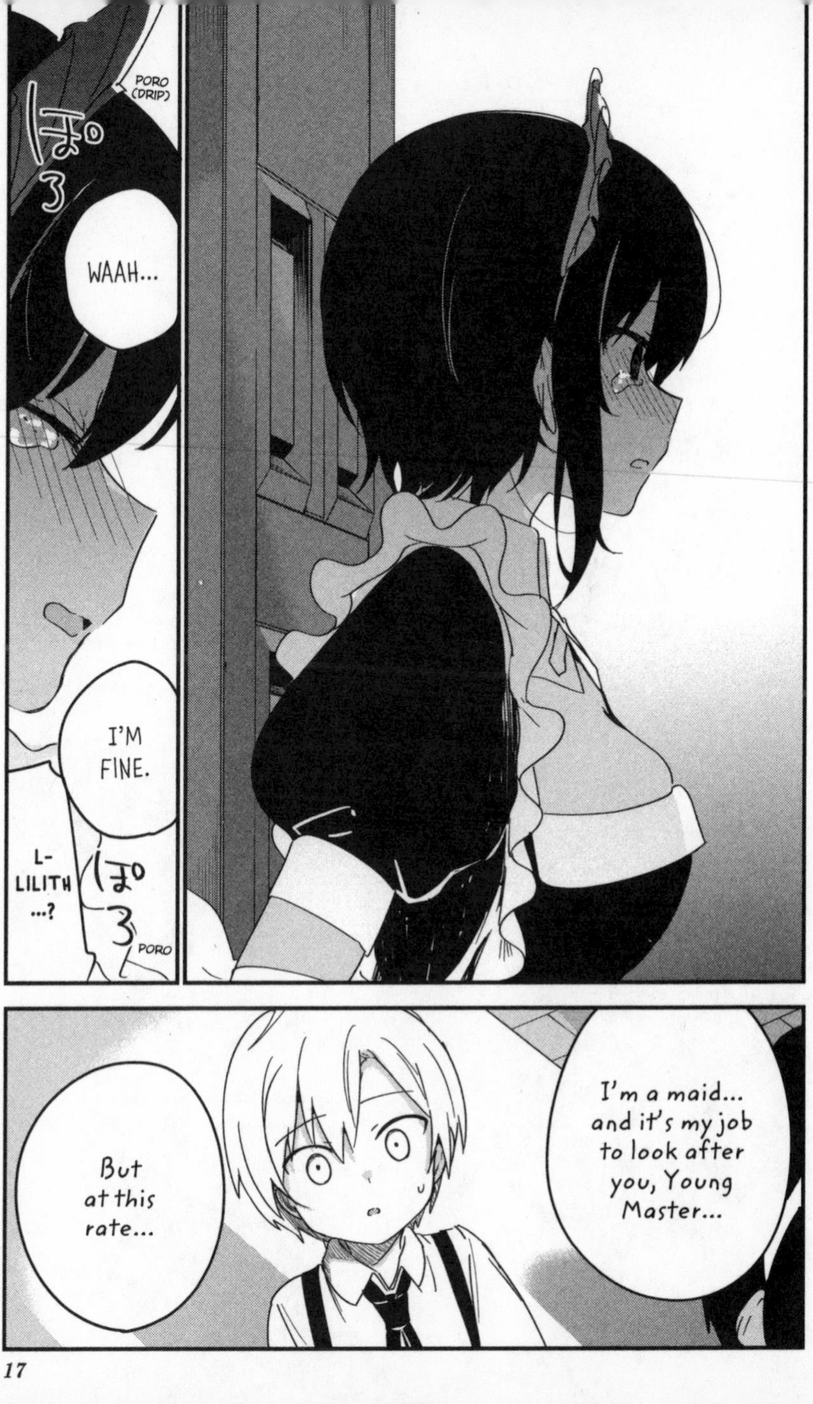
ぽろ
PORO (DRIP)
WAAH...
I'M FINE.
L- LILITH ...?
ぽろ
PORO
I'm a maid... and it's my job to look after you, Young Master...
But at this rate...

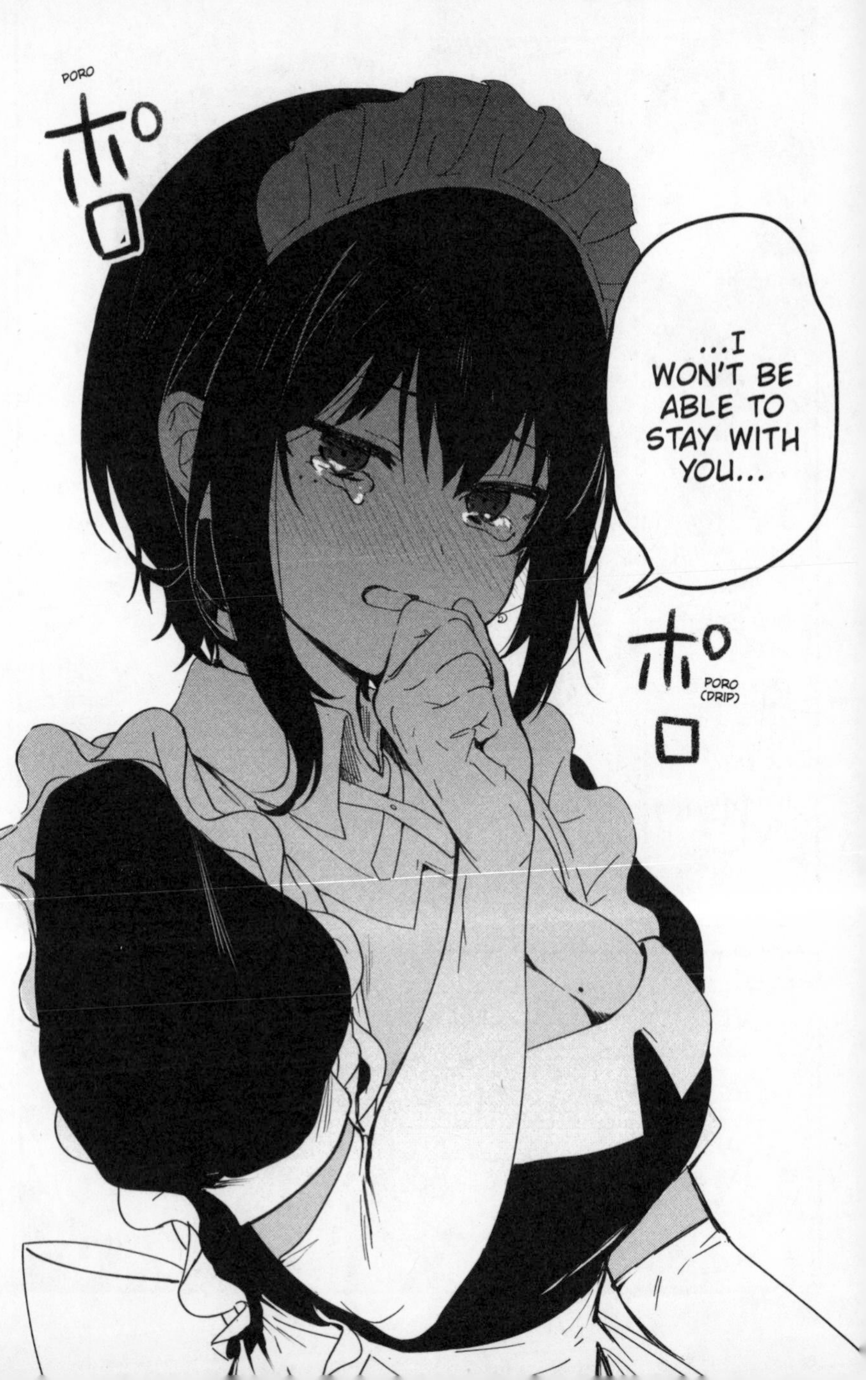
PORO
ホロ
...I WON'T BE ABLE TO STAY WITH YOU...
ホロ
PORO (DRIP)

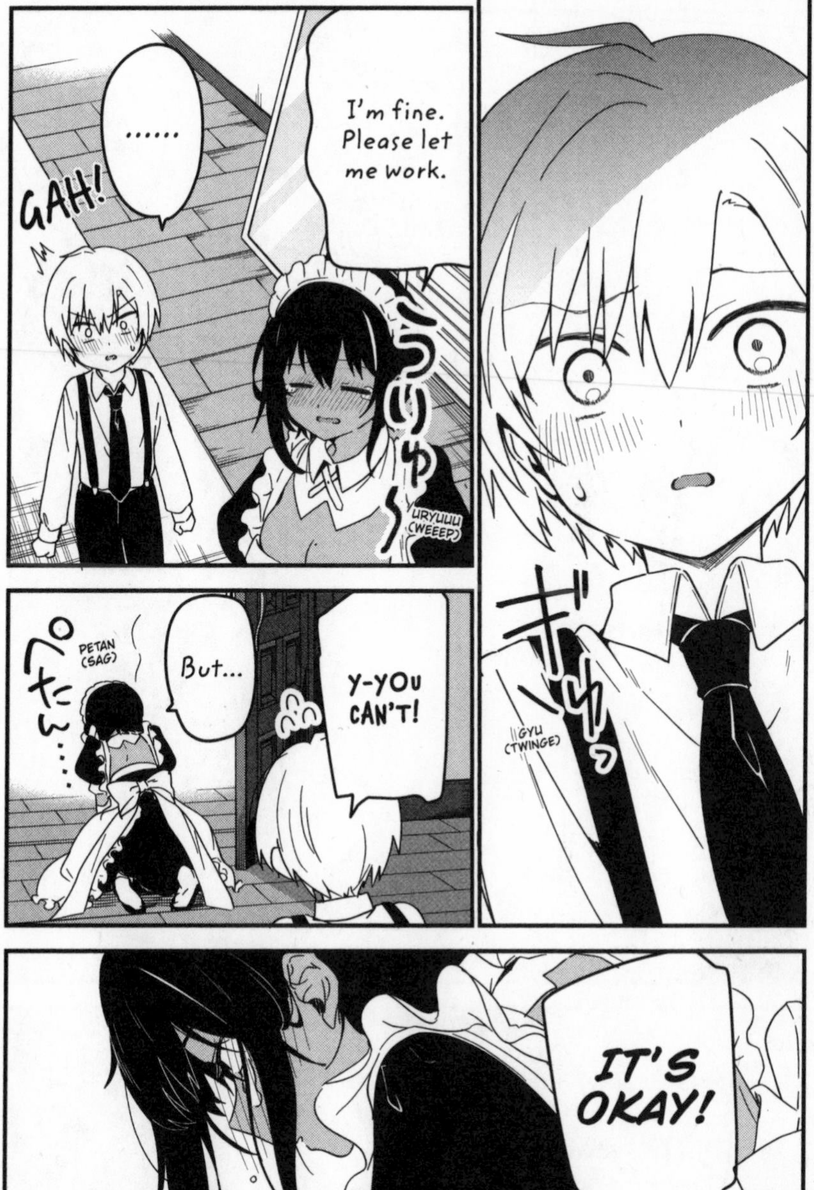
GYU (TWINGE)
I'm fine. Please let me work.
......
GAH!
URYUUU (WEEEP)
Y-YOU CAN'T!
But...
PETAN (SAG)
IT'S OKAY!

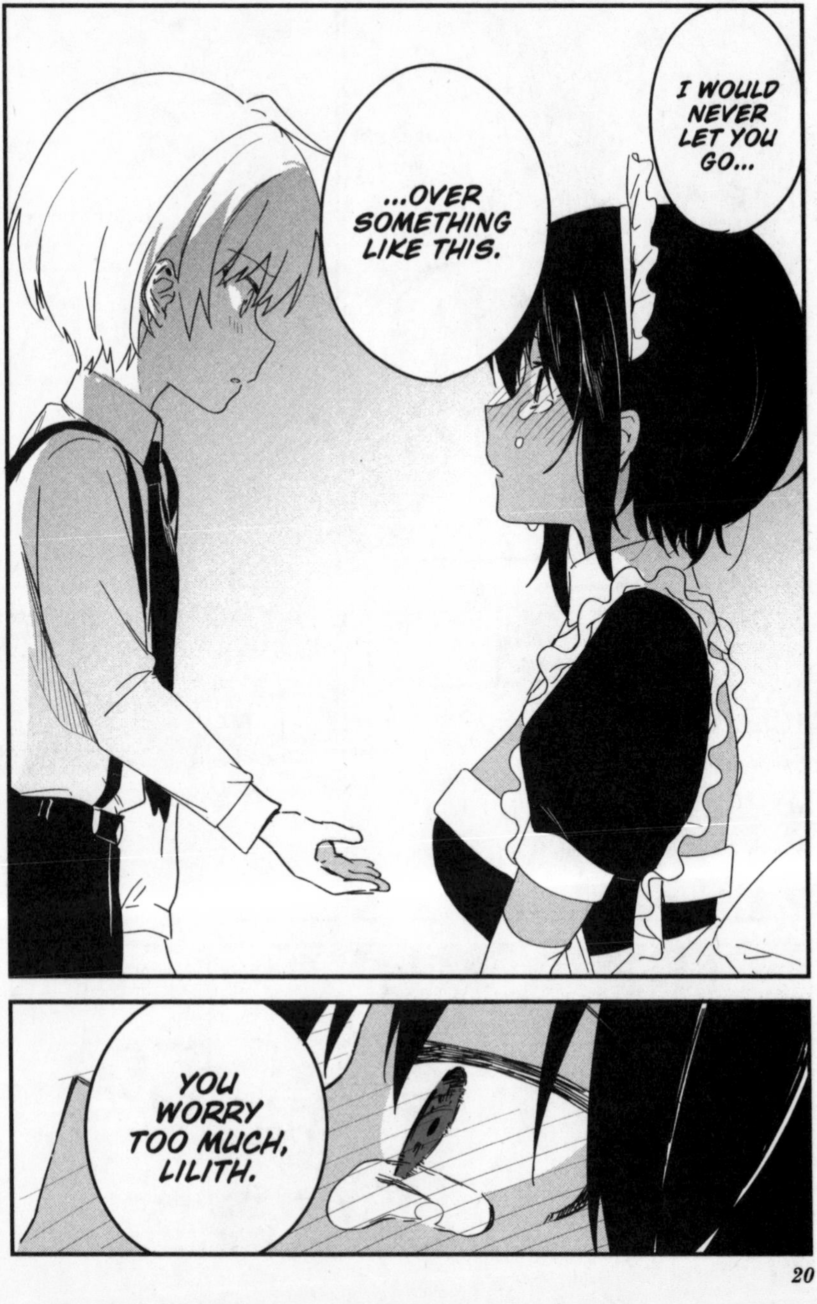
I WOULD NEVER LET YOU GO...
...OVER SOMETHING LIKE THIS.
YOU WORRY TOO MUCH, LILITH.

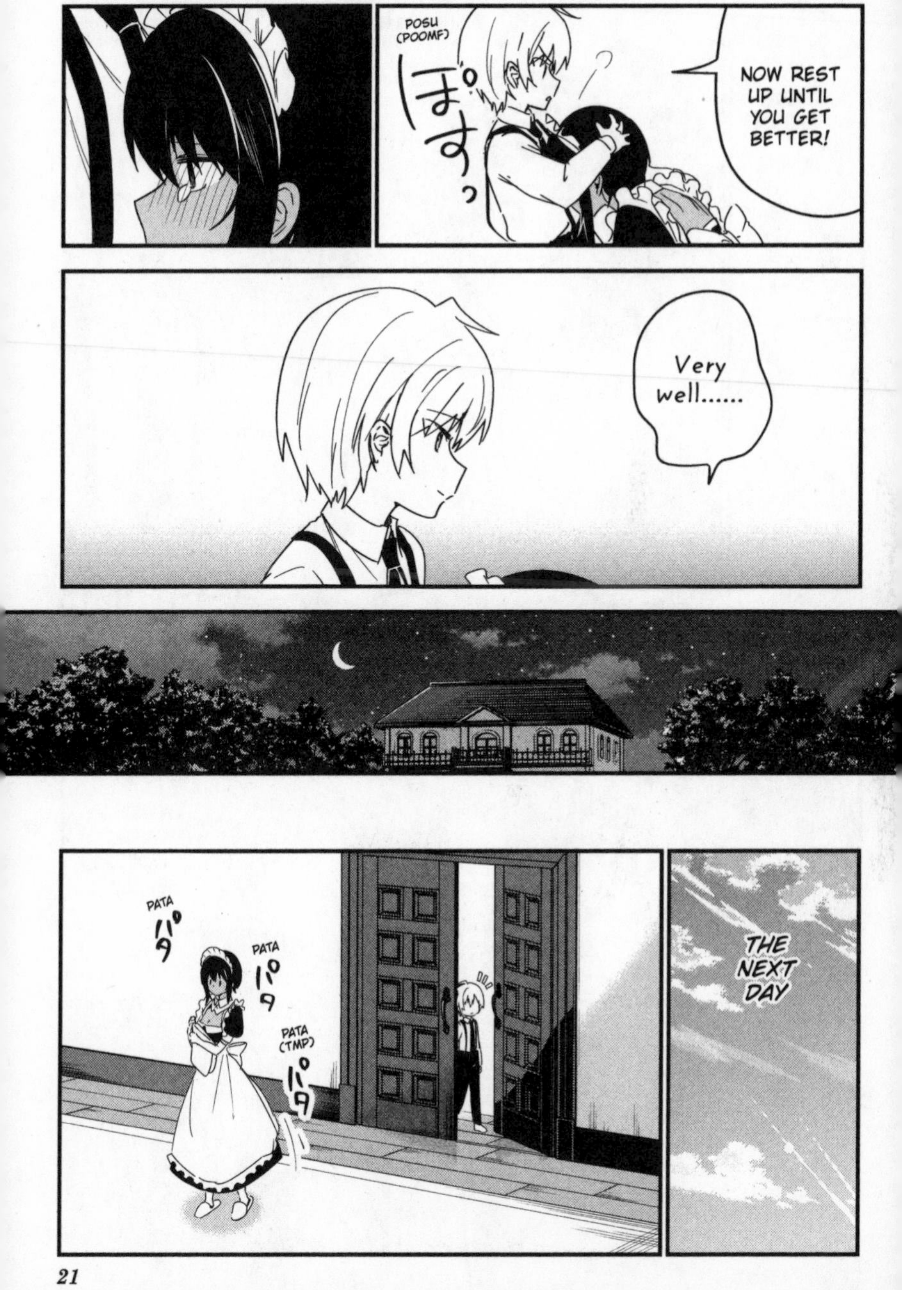
NOW REST UP UNTIL YOU GET BETTER!
POSU (POOMF)
ぽすっ
Very well......
THE NEXT DAY
PATA
パタ
PATA
パタ
PATA (TMP)
パタ

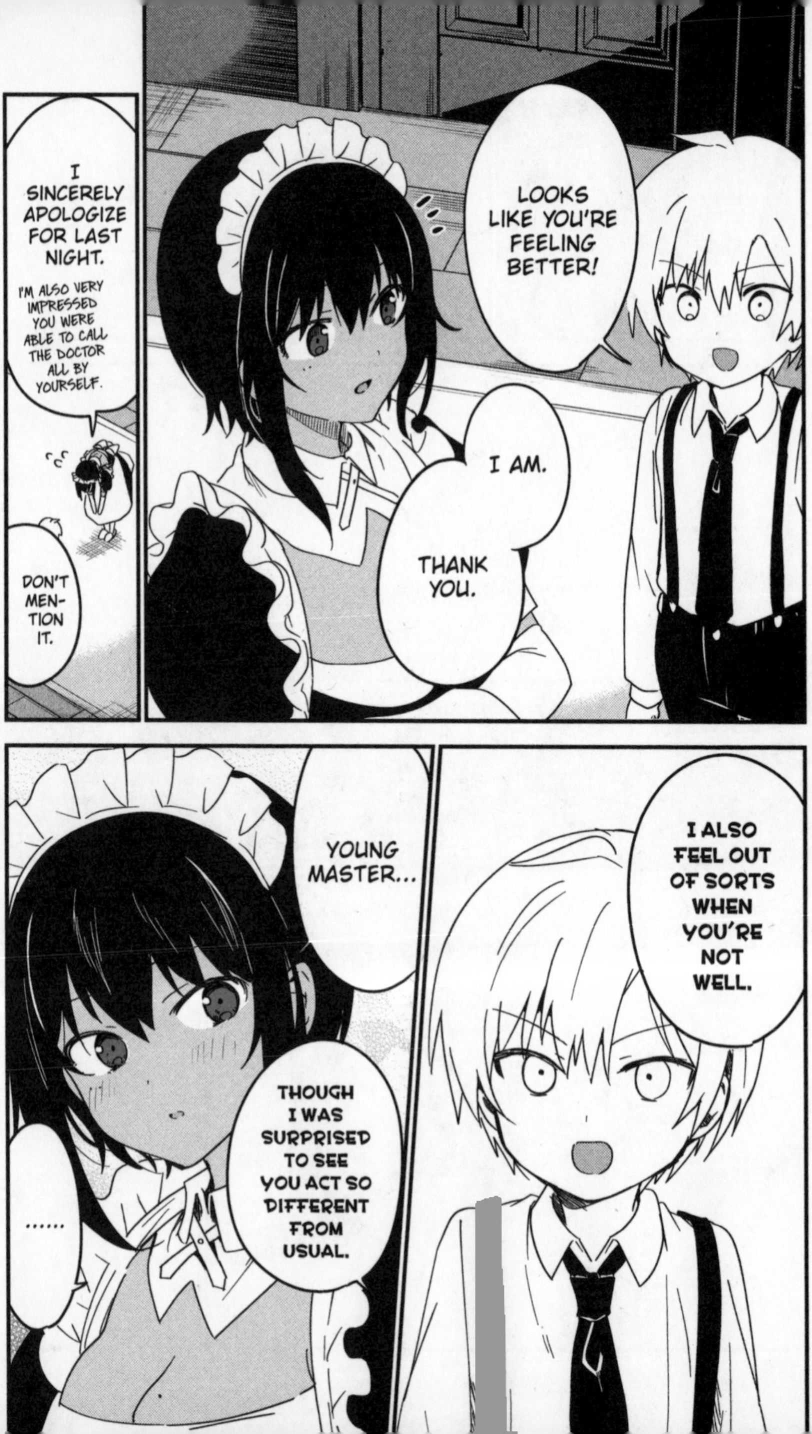
LOOKS LIKE YOU'RE FEELING BETTER!
I AM.
THANK YOU.
I SINCERELY APOLOGIZE FOR LAST NIGHT.
I'M ALSO VERY IMPRESSED YOU WERE ABLE TO CALL THE DOCTOR ALL BY YOURSELF.
DON'T MEN-TION IT.
I ALSO FEEL OUT OF SORTS WHEN YOU'RE NOT WELL.
YOUNG MASTER...
THOUGH I WAS SURPRISED TO SEE YOU ACT SO DIFFERENT FROM USUAL.
......

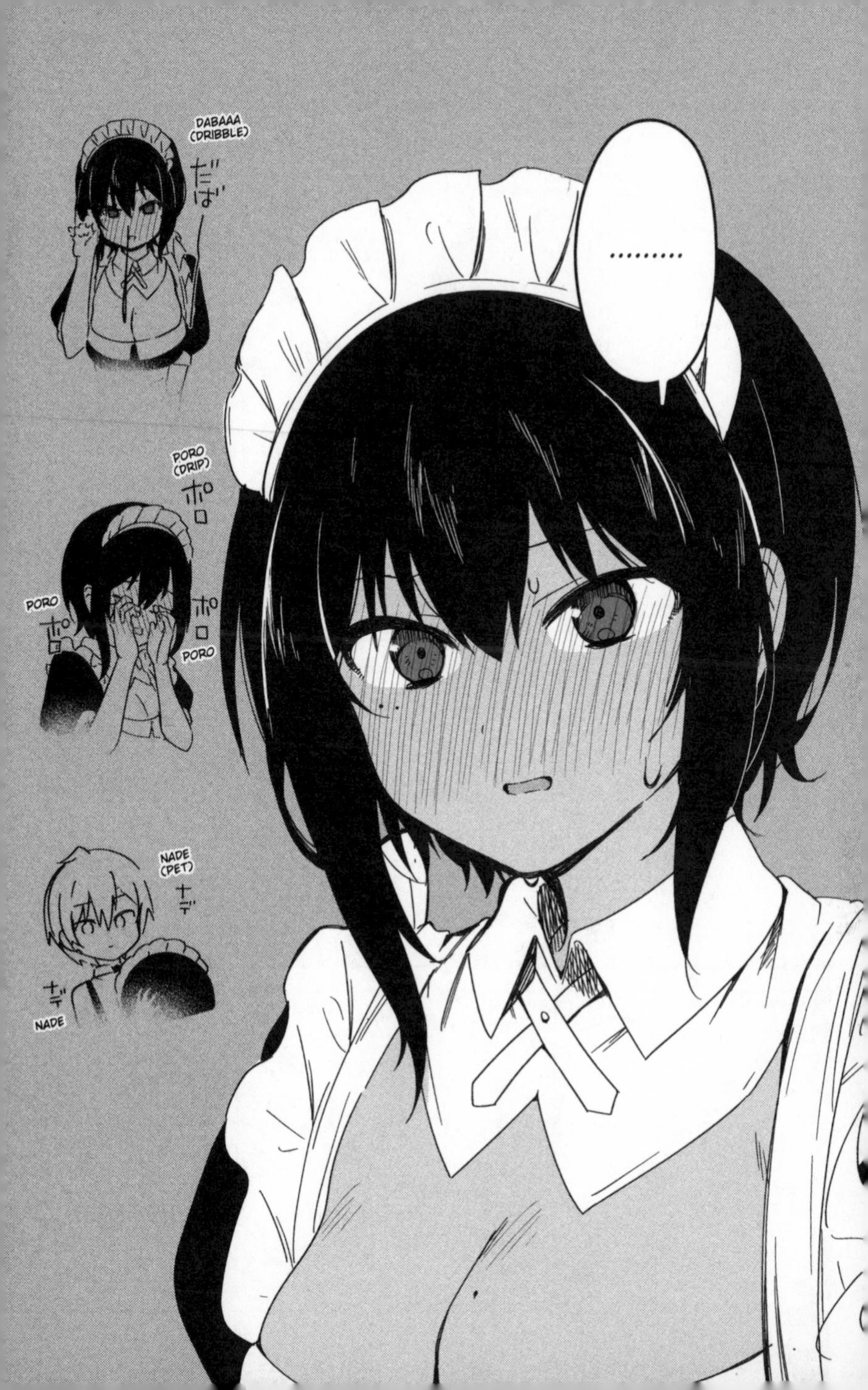

....
DABAAA (DRIBBLE)
だば
PORO (DRIP)
ポロ
ポロ
PORO
PORO
ポロ
NADE (PET)
ナデ
ナデ
NADE

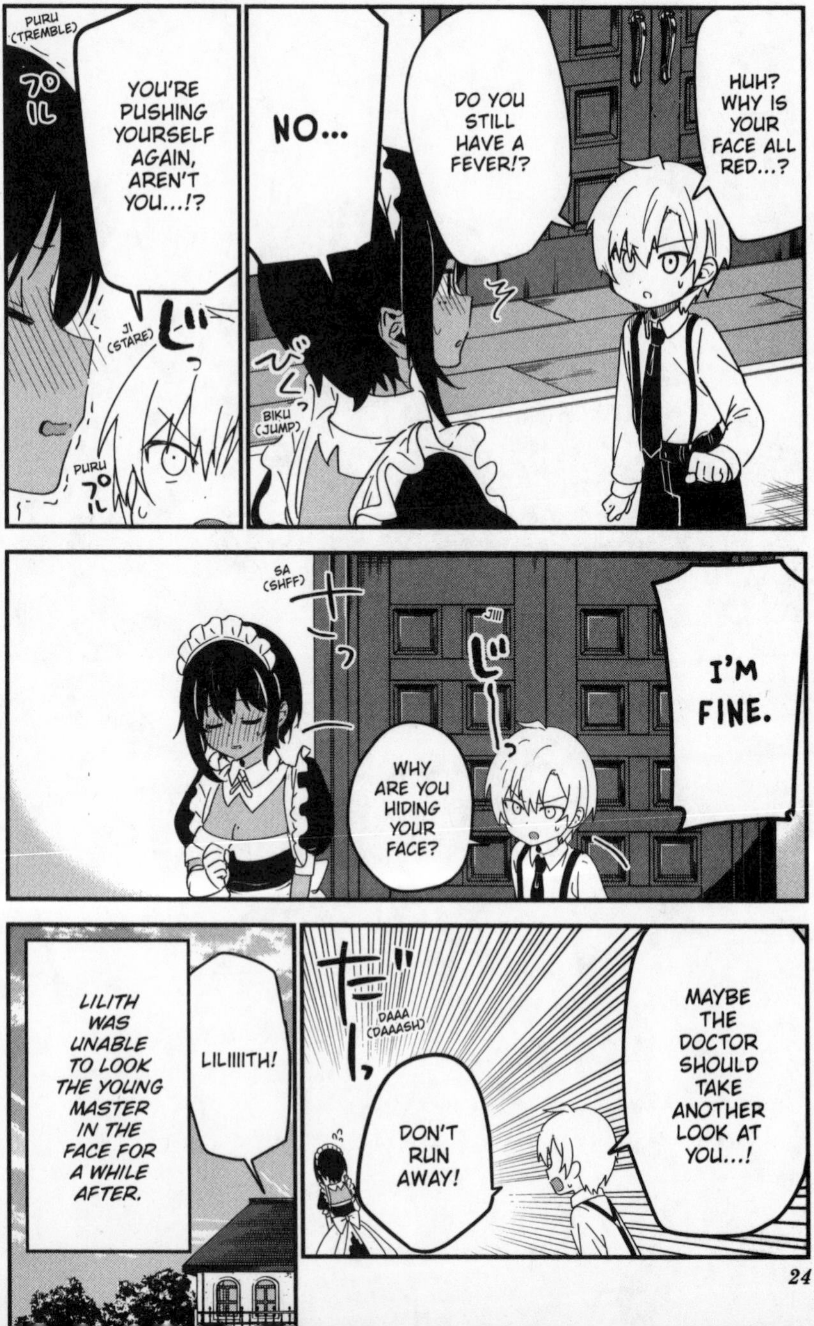
HUH? WHY IS YOUR FACE ALL RED...?
DO YOU STILL HAVE A FEVER!?
NO...
BIKU (JUMP)
PURU (TREMBLE)
YOU'RE PUSHING YOURSELF AGAIN, AREN'T YOU...!?
JI (STARE)
PURU
I'M FINE.
JIII
WHY ARE YOU HIDING YOUR FACE?
SA (SHFF)
MAYBE THE DOCTOR SHOULD TAKE ANOTHER LOOK AT YOU...!
DAAA (DAAASH)
DON'T RUN AWAY!
LILIIIITH!
LILITH WAS UNABLE TO LOOK THE YOUNG MASTER IN THE FACE FOR A WHILE AFTER.

The Maid I Hired Recently Is Mysterious

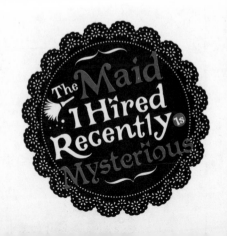

CHAPTER 27

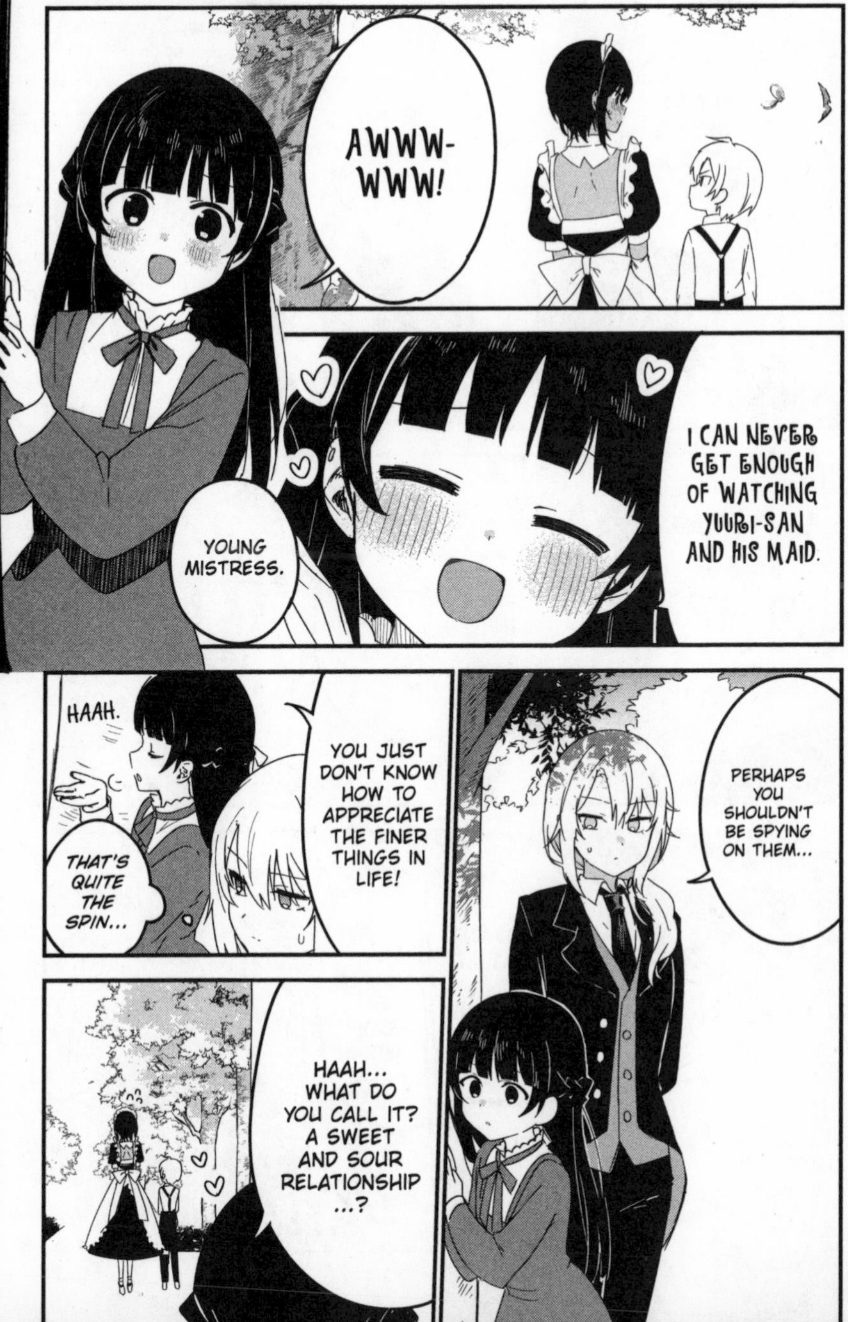
AWWW-WWW!
I CAN NEVER GET ENOUGH OF WATCHING YUURI-SAN AND HIS MAID.
YOUNG MISTRESS.
PERHAPS YOU SHOULDN'T BE SPYING ON THEM...
HAAH.
YOU JUST DON'T KNOW HOW TO APPRECIATE THE FINER THINGS IN LIFE!
THAT'S QUITE THE SPIN...
HAAH... WHAT DO YOU CALL IT? A SWEET AND SOUR RELATIONSHIP ...?

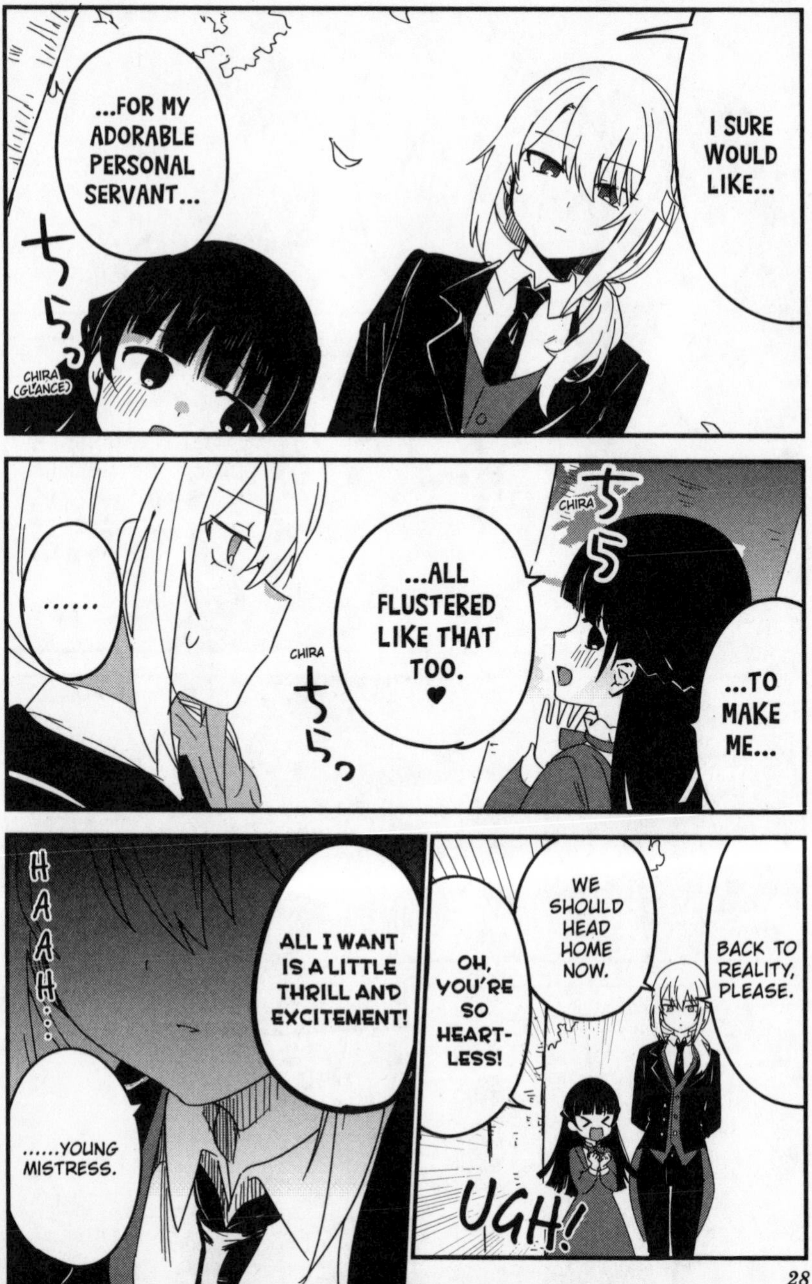

I SURE WOULD LIKE...
...FOR MY ADORABLE PERSONAL SERVANT...
ちらっ
CHIRA (GLANCE)
...TO MAKE ME...
ち
CHIRA
...ALL FLUSTERED LIKE THAT TOO. ♥
ちらっ
CHIRA
......
BACK TO REALITY, PLEASE.
WE SHOULD HEAD HOME NOW.
OH, YOU'RE SO HEART-LESS!
UGH!
ALL I WANT IS A LITTLE THRILL AND EXCITEMENT!
HAAAH...
......YOUNG MISTRESS.

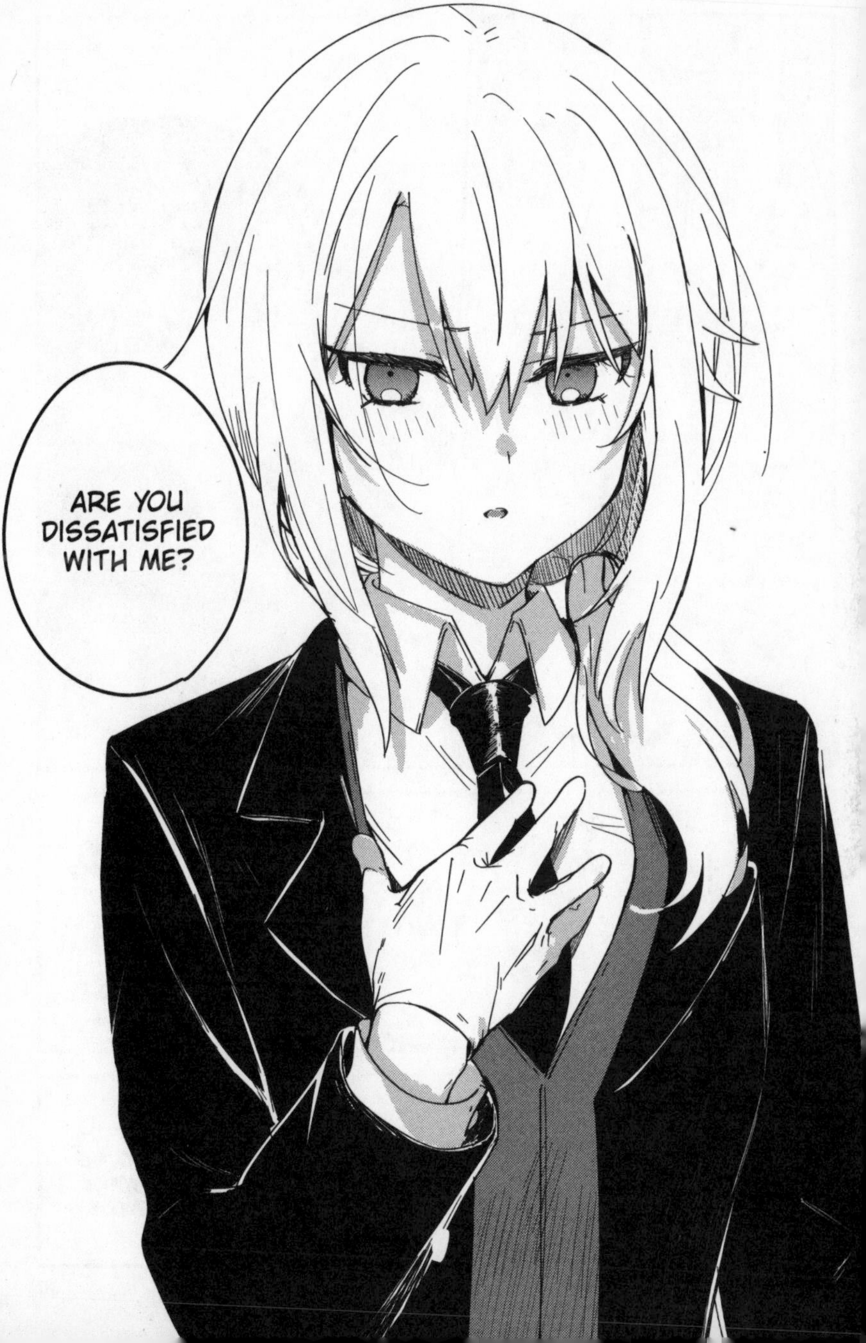
ARE YOU DISSATISFIED WITH ME?

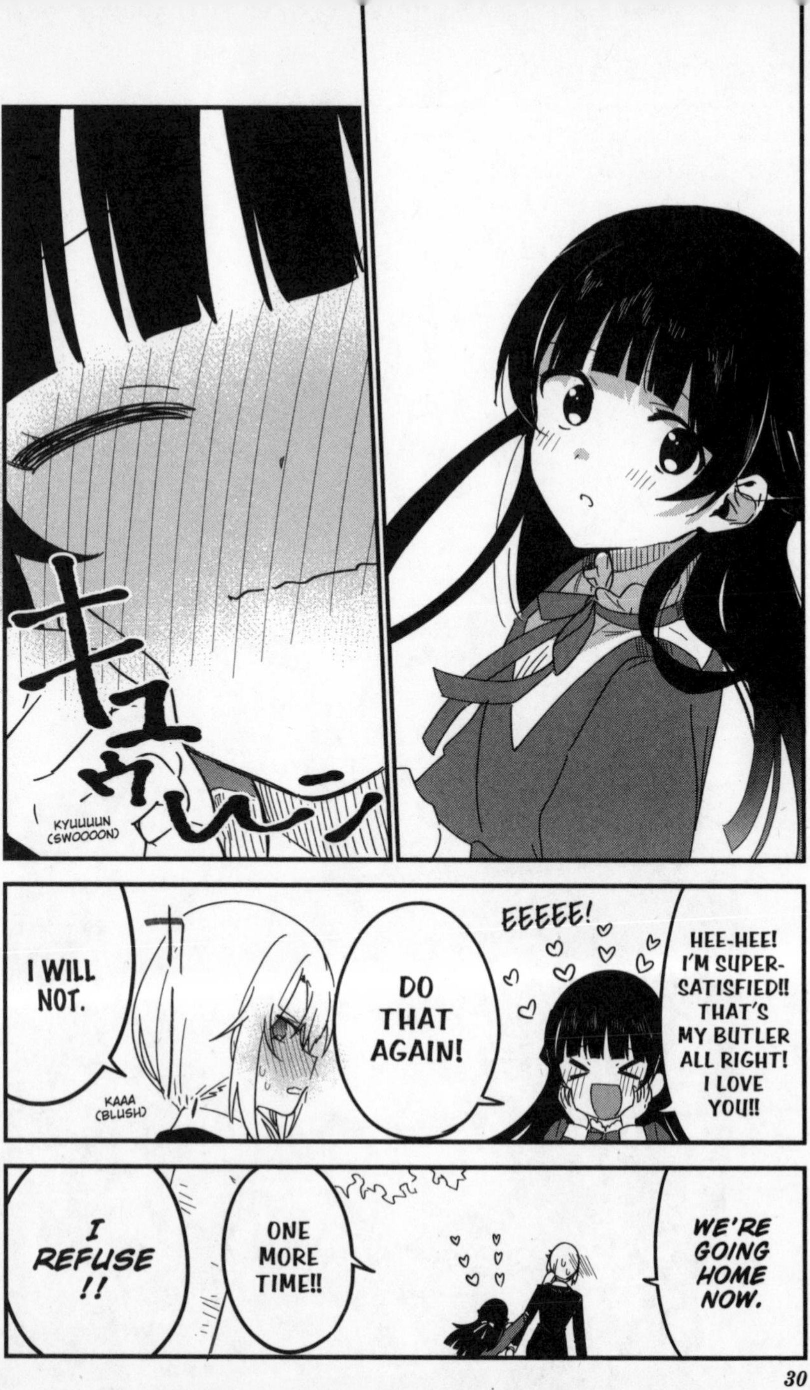
KYUUUUN (SWOOOON)
HEE-HEE! I'M SUPER-SATISFIED!! THAT'S MY BUTLER ALL RIGHT! I LOVE YOU!!
EEEEE!
DO THAT AGAIN!
KAAA (BLUSH)
I WILL NOT.
WE'RE GOING HOME NOW.
ONE MORE TIME!!
I REFUSE !!

CHAPTER 28

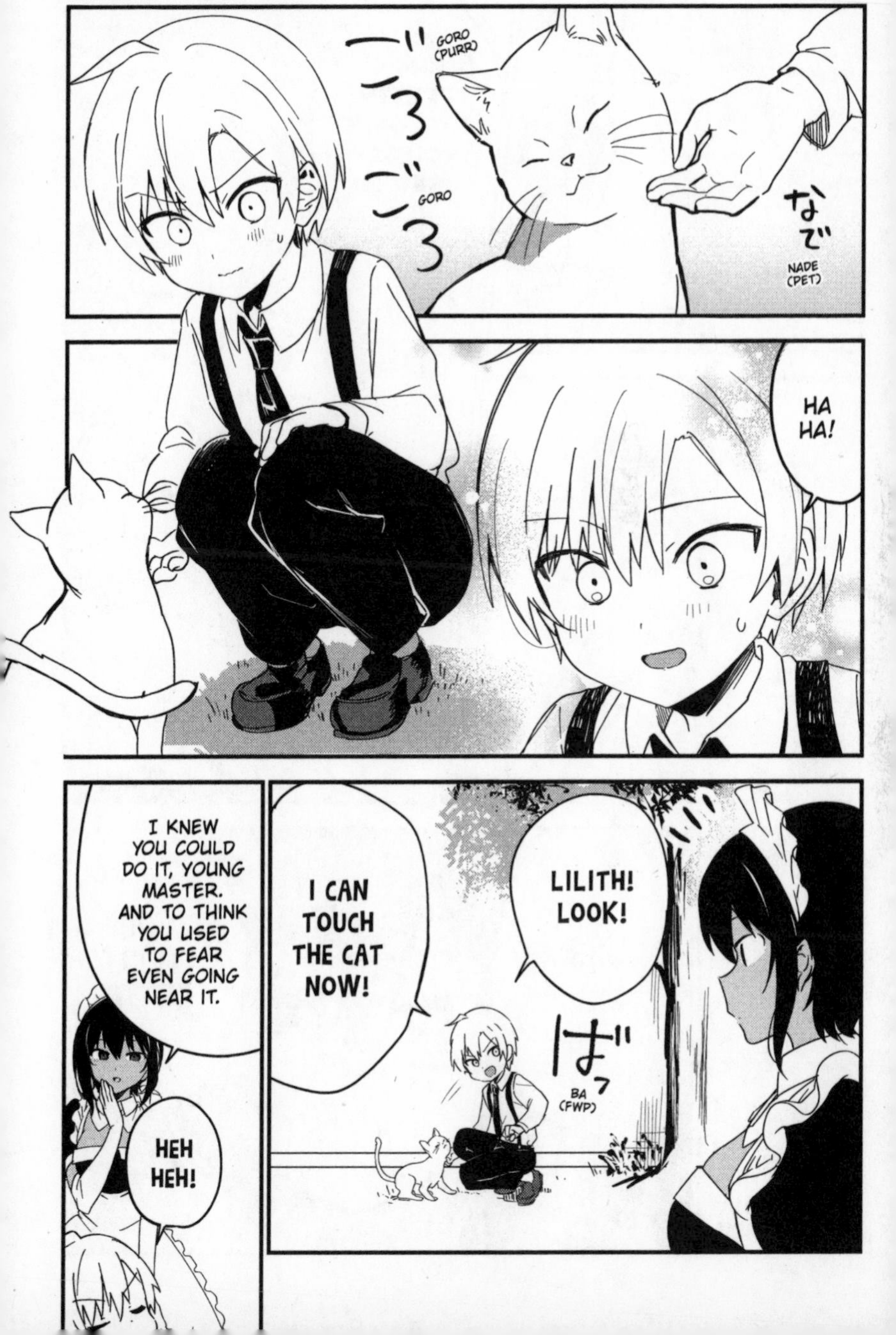
なで
NADE (PET)
ごろ
GORO (PURR)
ごろ
GORO
HA HA!
LILITH! LOOK!
ばっ
BA (FWP)
I CAN TOUCH THE CAT NOW!
I KNEW YOU COULD DO IT, YOUNG MASTER. AND TO THINK YOU USED TO FEAR EVEN GOING NEAR IT.
HEH HEH!

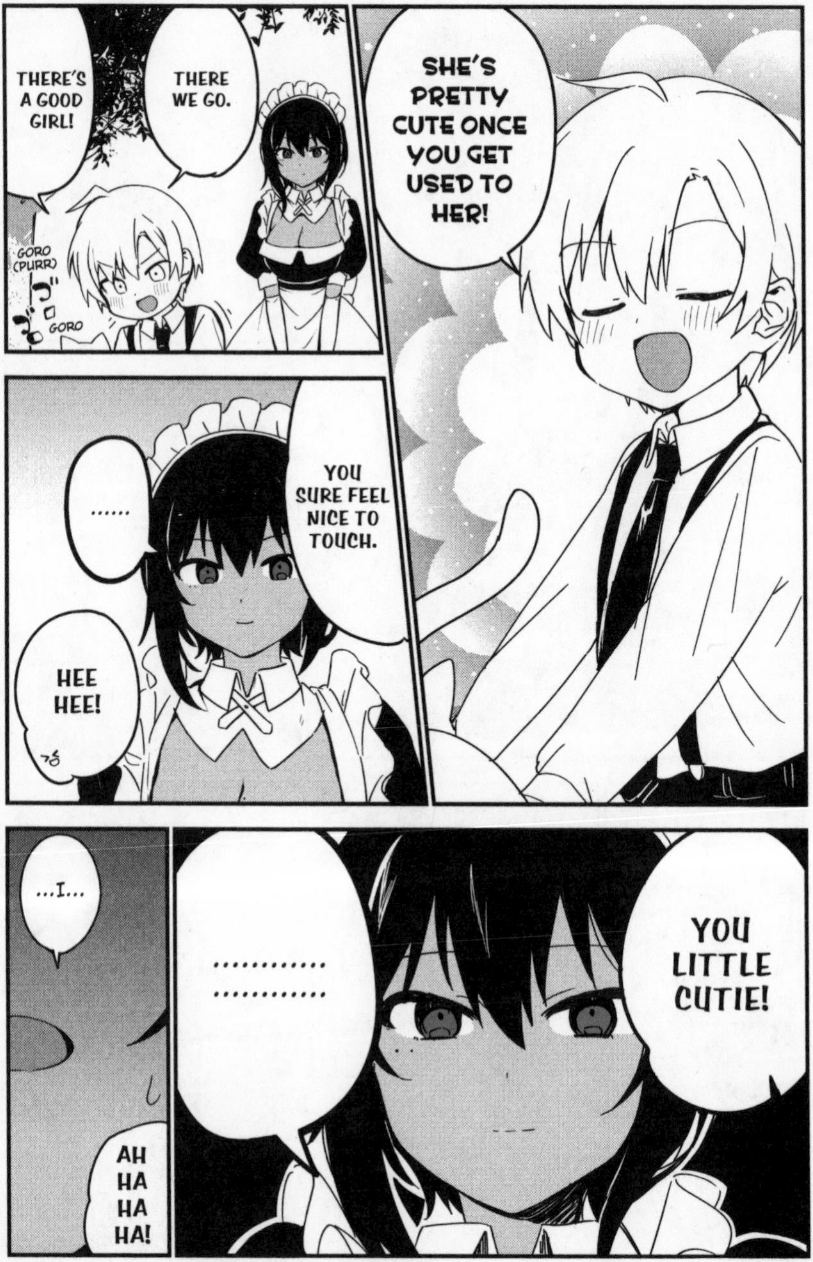

SHE'S PRETTY CUTE ONCE YOU GET USED TO HER!
THERE WE GO.
THERE'S A GOOD GIRL!
GORO (PURR)
GORO
YOU SURE FEEL NICE TO TOUCH.
......
HEE HEE!
YOU LITTLE CUTIE!
....
...I...
AH HA HA HA!

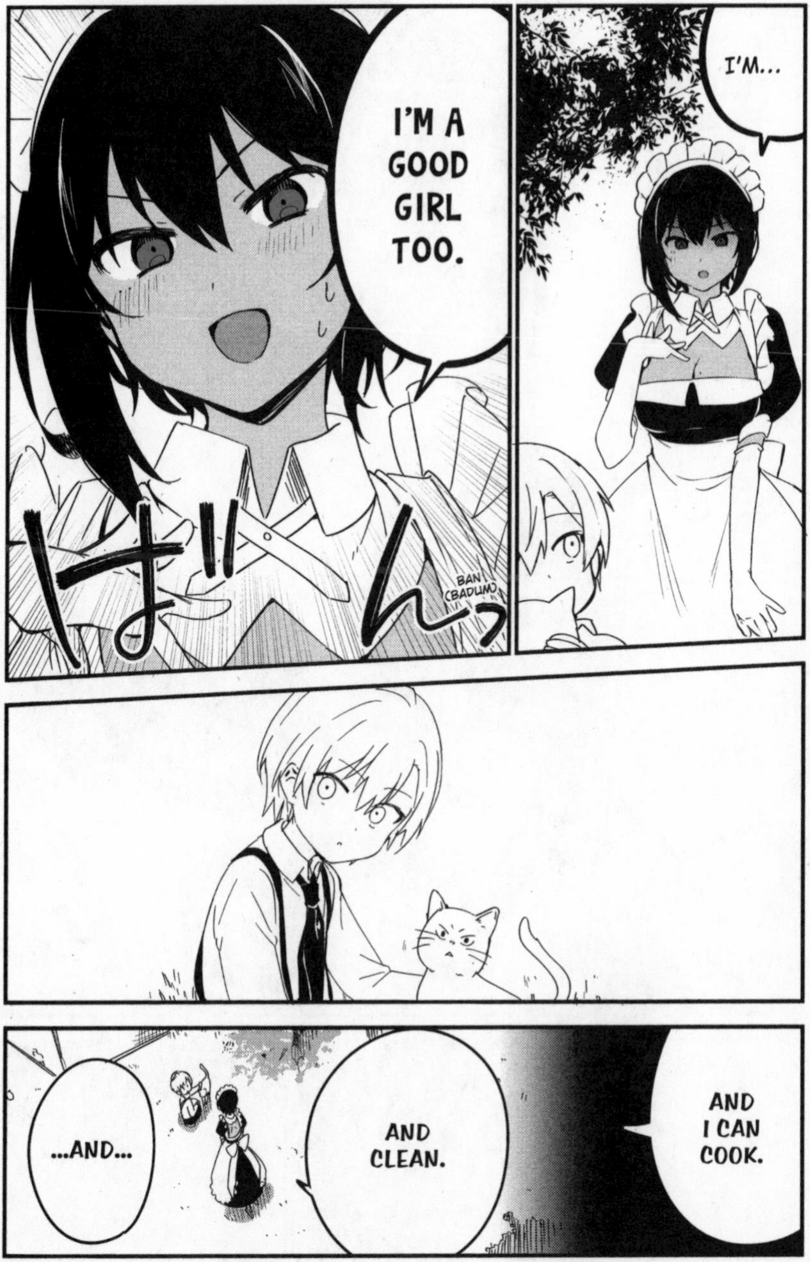
I'M...
I'M A GOOD GIRL TOO.
ばんっ
BAN (BADUM)
AND I CAN COOK.
AND CLEAN.
...AND...

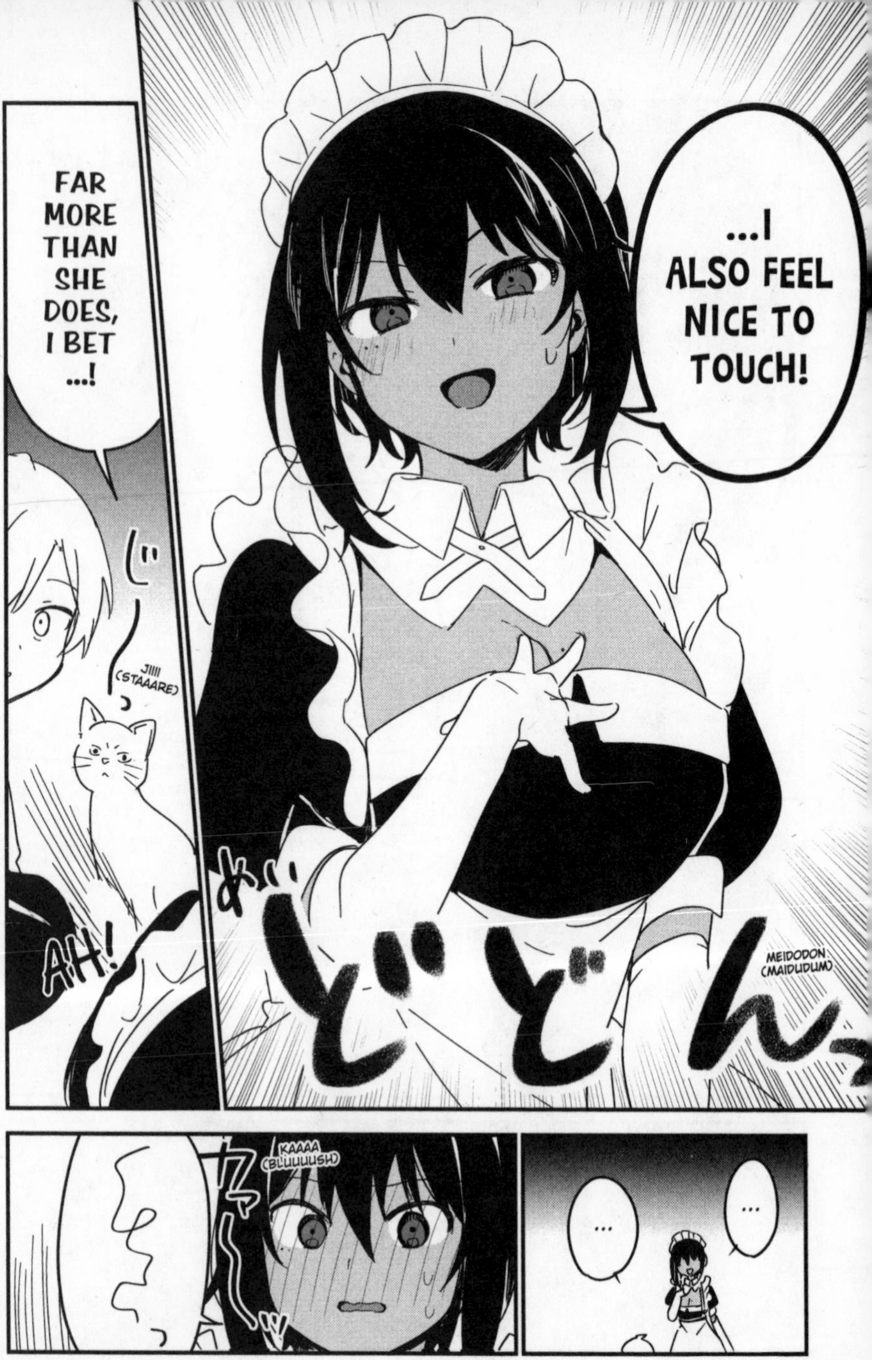
...I ALSO FEEL NICE TO TOUCH!
MEIDODON (MAIDUDUM)
FAR MORE THAN SHE DOES, I BET ...!
JIIII (STAAARE)
AH!
...
...
KAAAA (BLUUUUSH)

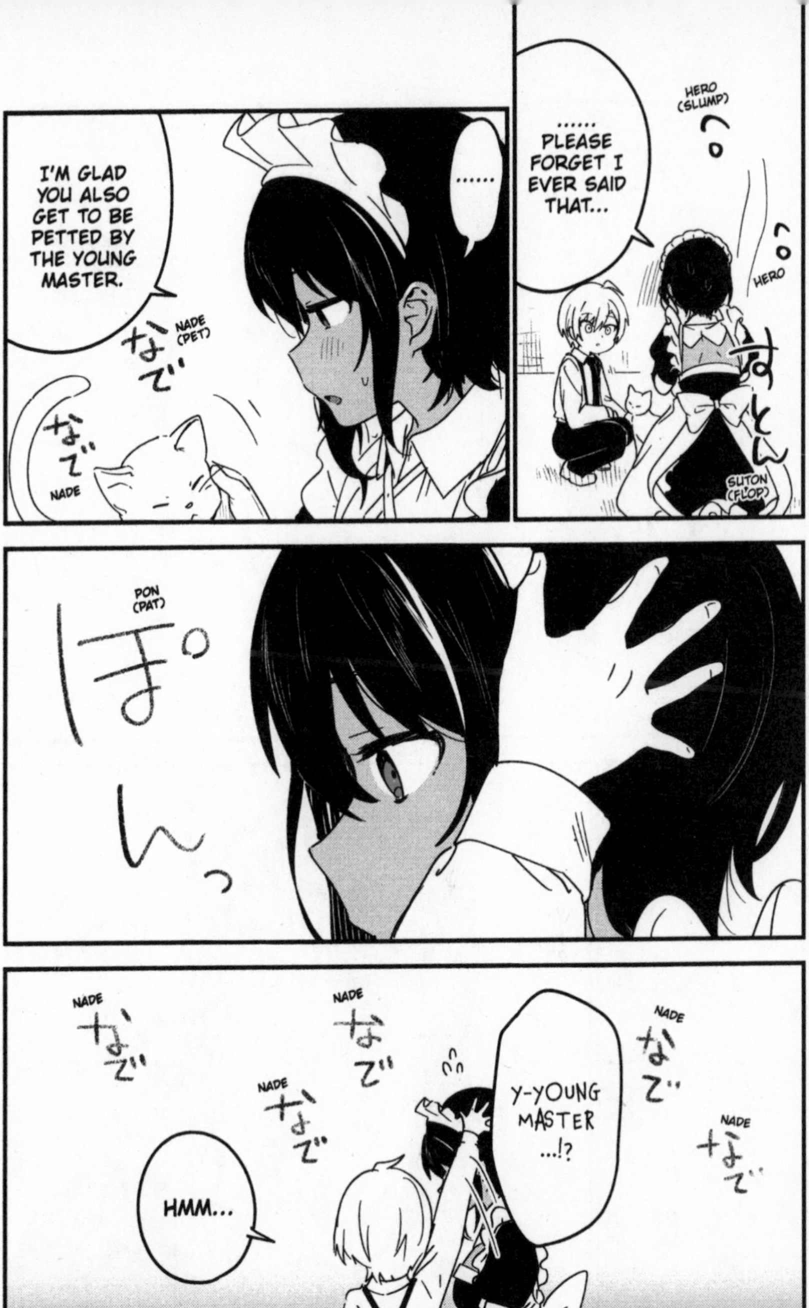

...... PLEASE FORGET I EVER SAID THAT...
HERO (SLUMP)
HERO
すとん
SUTON (FLOP)
I'M GLAD YOU ALSO GET TO BE PETTED BY THE YOUNG MASTER.
......
なで
NADE (PET)
なで
NADE
PON (PAT)
ぽんっ
NADE
なで
Y-YOUNG MASTER ...!?
NADE
なで
NADE
なで
NADE
なで
NADE
なで
HMM...

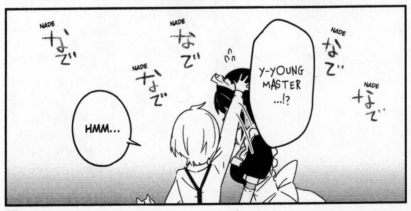

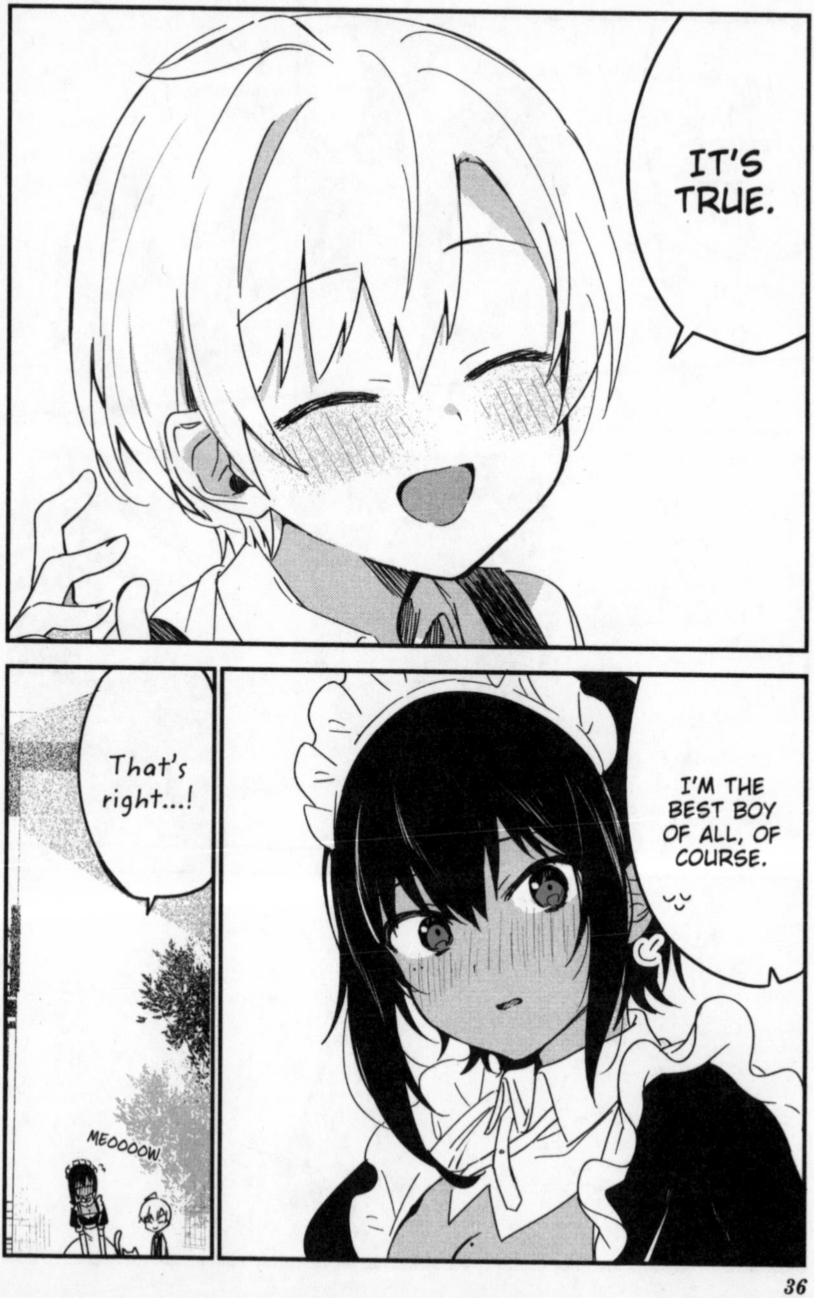
IT'S TRUE.
I'M THE BEST BOY OF ALL, OF COURSE.
That's right...!
MEOOOOW.

The Maid I Hired Recently Is Mysterious

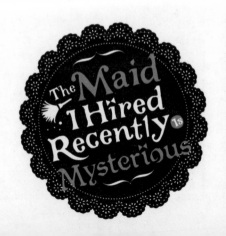

CHAPTER 29

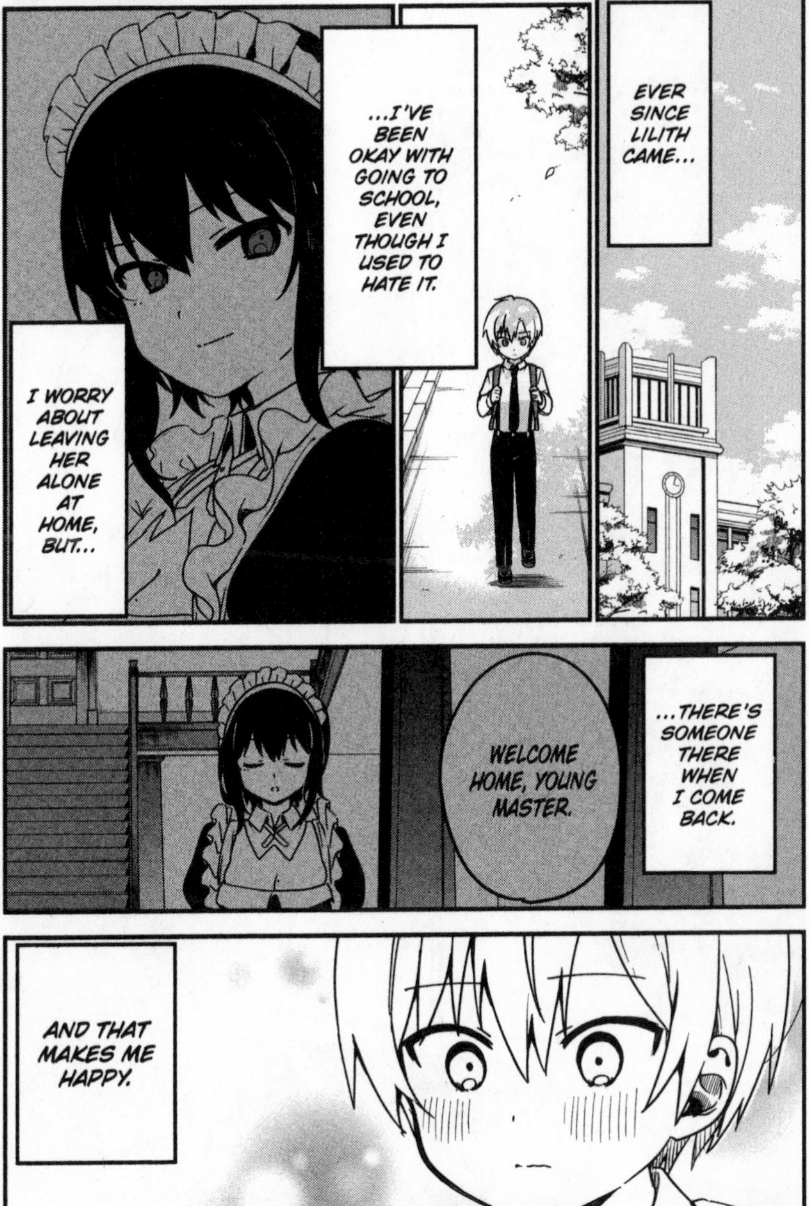
EVER SINCE LILITH CAME...
...I'VE BEEN OKAY WITH GOING TO SCHOOL, EVEN THOUGH I USED TO HATE IT.
I WORRY ABOUT LEAVING HER ALONE AT HOME, BUT...
...THERE'S SOMEONE THERE WHEN I COME BACK.
WELCOME HOME, YOUNG MASTER.
AND THAT MAKES ME HAPPY.

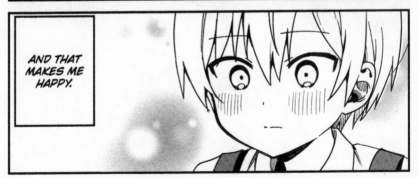

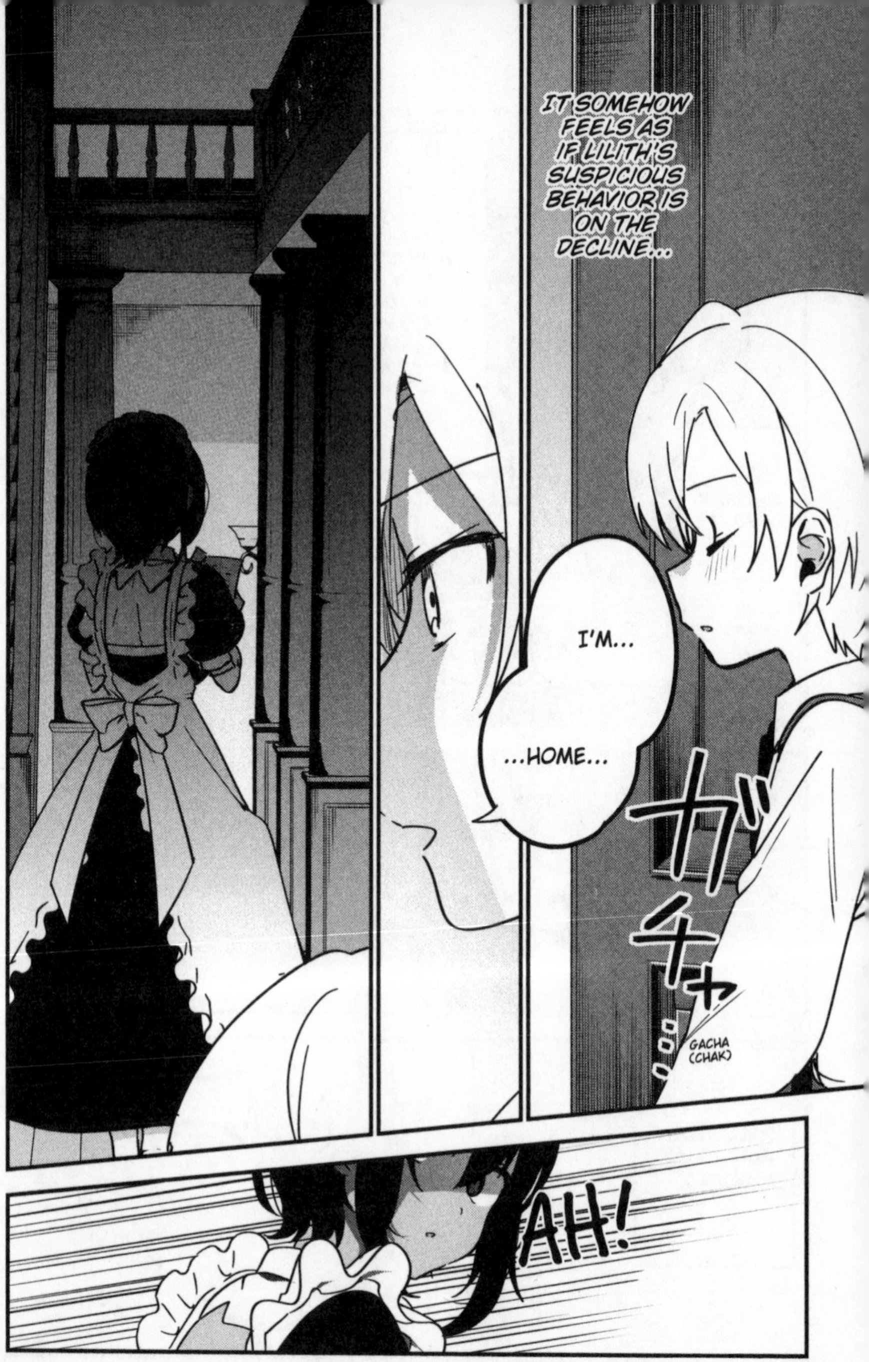
IT SOMEHOW FEELS AS IF LILITH'S SUSPICIOUS BEHAVIOR IS ON THE DECLINE...
GACHA (CHAK)
I'M...
...HOME...
AH!

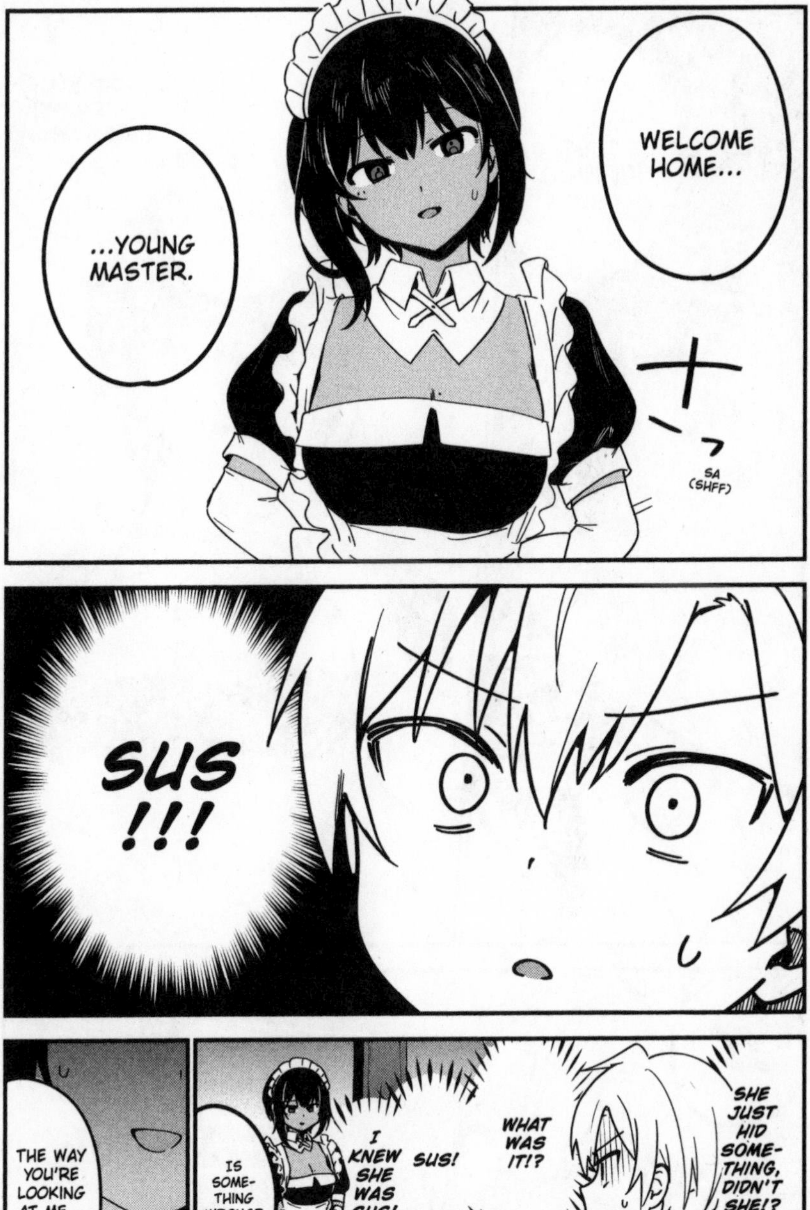
WELCOME HOME...
...YOUNG MASTER.
SA (SHFF)
SUS !!!
SHE JUST HID SOME-THING, DIDN'T SHE!?
WHAT WAS IT!?
SUS!
I KNEW SHE WAS SUS!
IS SOME-THING WRONG?
THE WAY YOU'RE LOOKING AT ME...

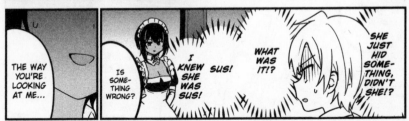

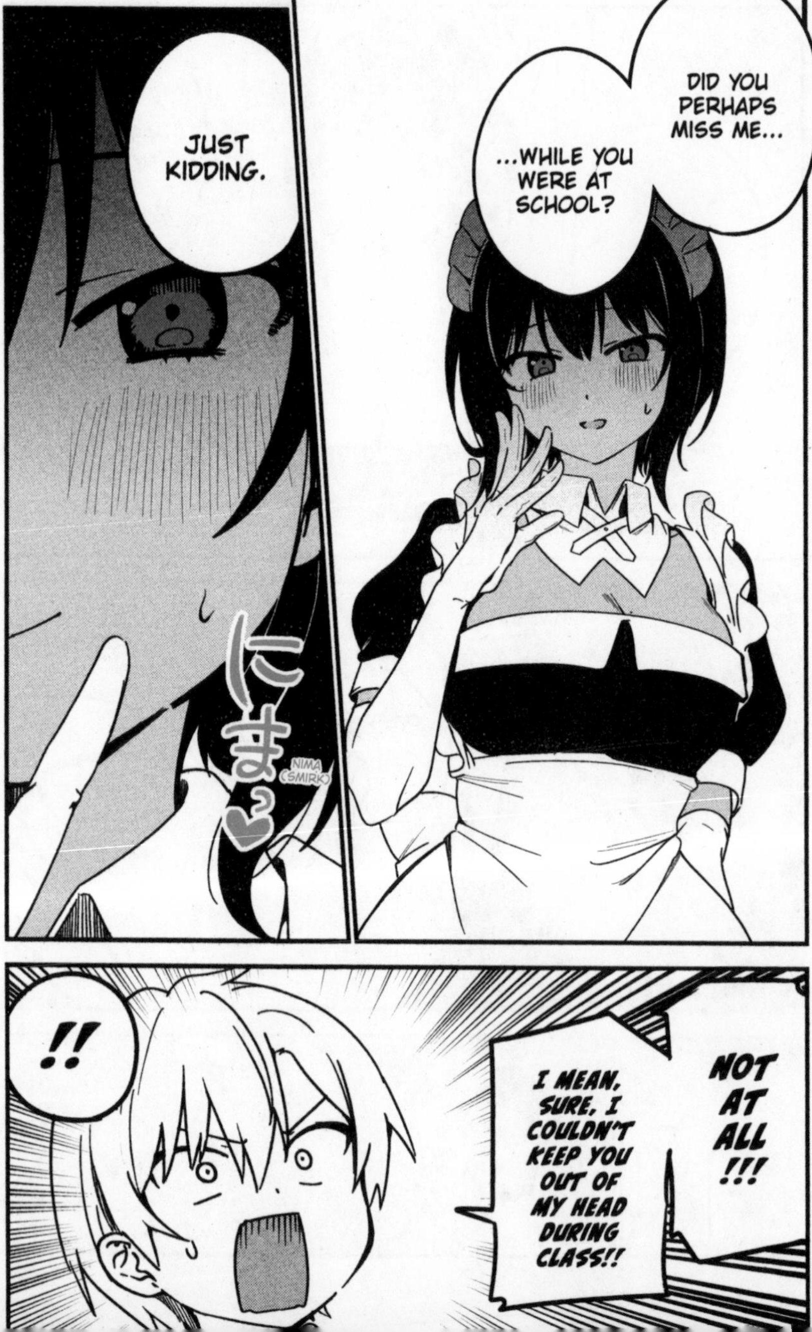
DID YOU PERHAPS MISS ME...
...WHILE YOU WERE AT SCHOOL?
JUST KIDDING.
にまっ
NIMA (SMIRK)
NOT AT ALL!!!
I MEAN, SURE, I COULDN'T KEEP YOU OUT OF MY HEAD DURING CLASS!!
!!

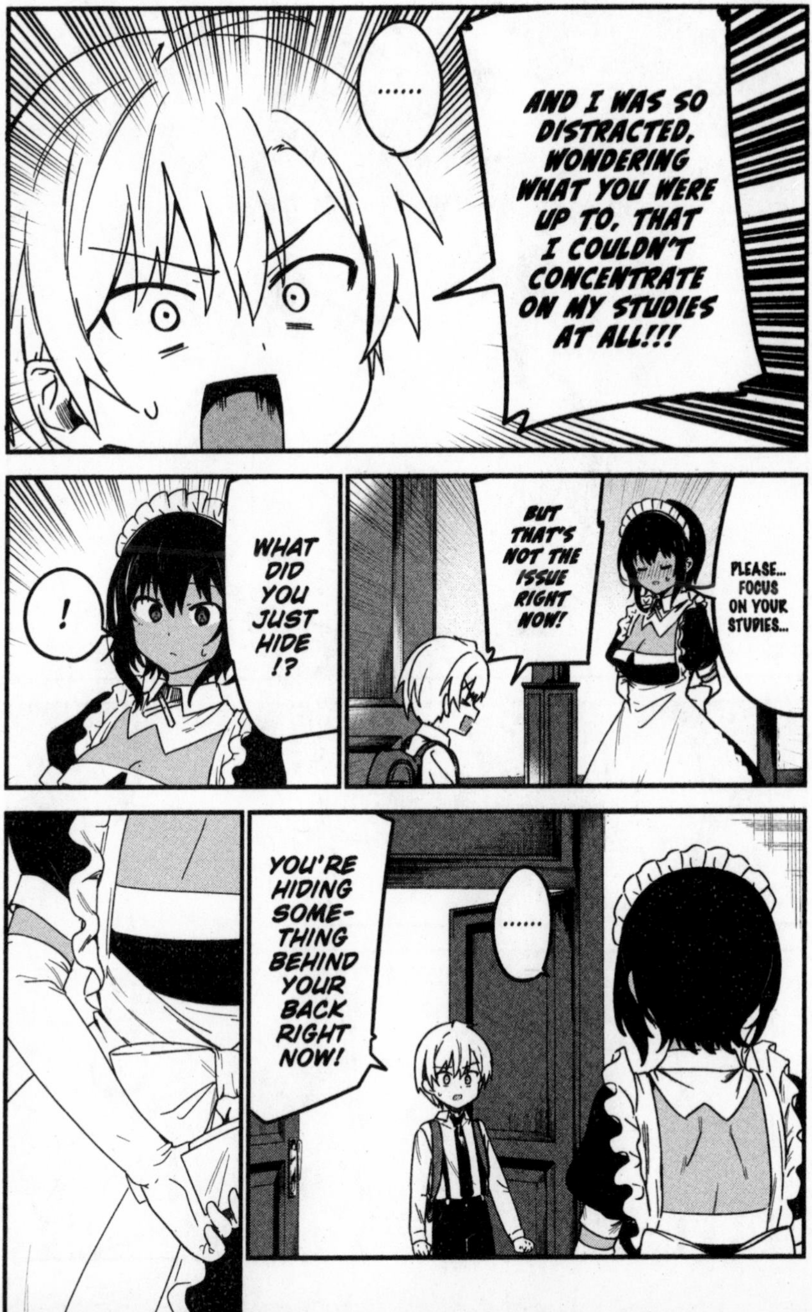
AND I WAS SO DISTRACTED, WONDERING WHAT YOU WERE UP TO, THAT I COULDN'T CONCENTRATE ON MY STUDIES AT ALL!!!
......
PLEASE... FOCUS ON YOUR STUDIES...
BUT THAT'S NOT THE ISSUE RIGHT NOW!
WHAT DID YOU JUST HIDE!?
!
......
YOU'RE HIDING SOME-THING BEHIND YOUR BACK RIGHT NOW!

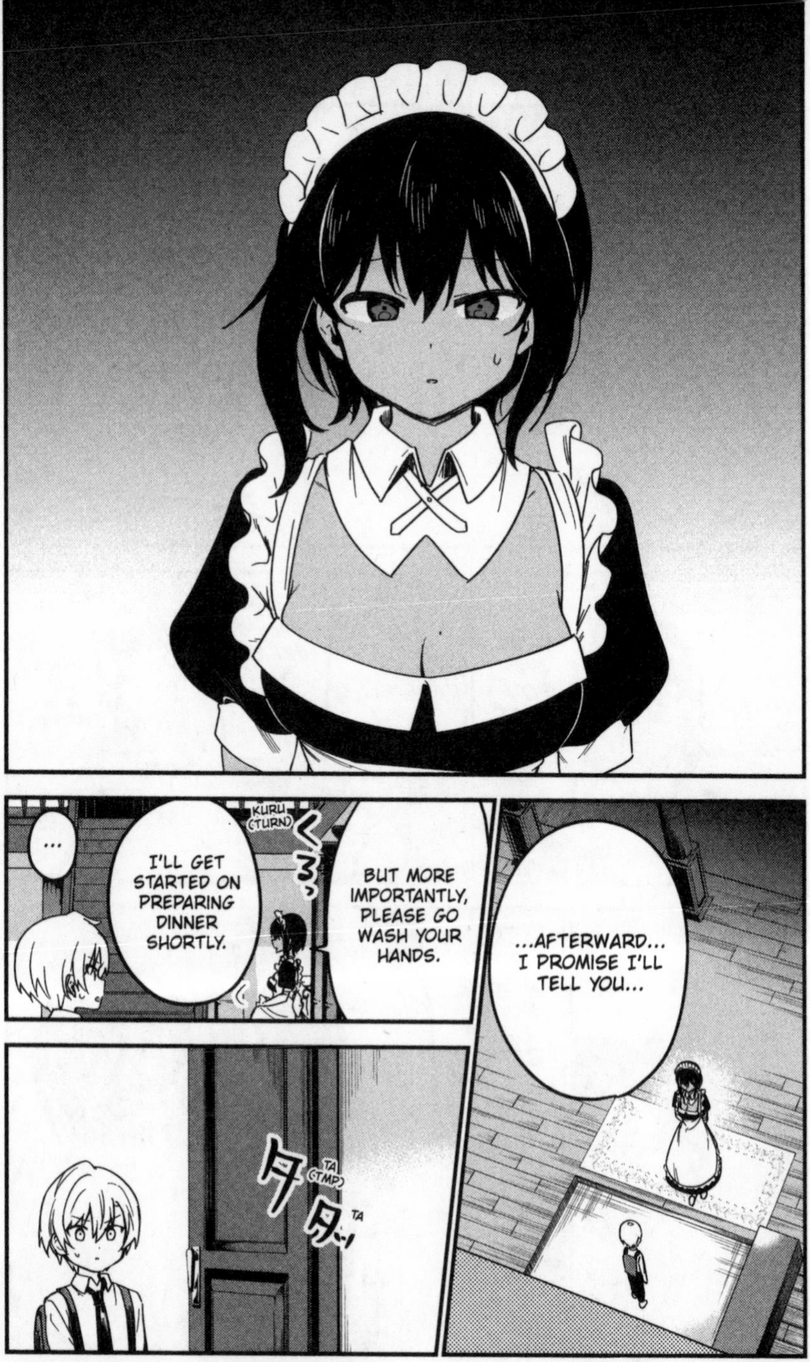
...AFTERWARD... I PROMISE I'LL TELL YOU...
BUT MORE IMPORTANTLY, PLEASE GO WASH YOUR HANDS.
KURU (TURN)
I'LL GET STARTED ON PREPARING DINNER SHORTLY.
...
TA (TMP)
TA

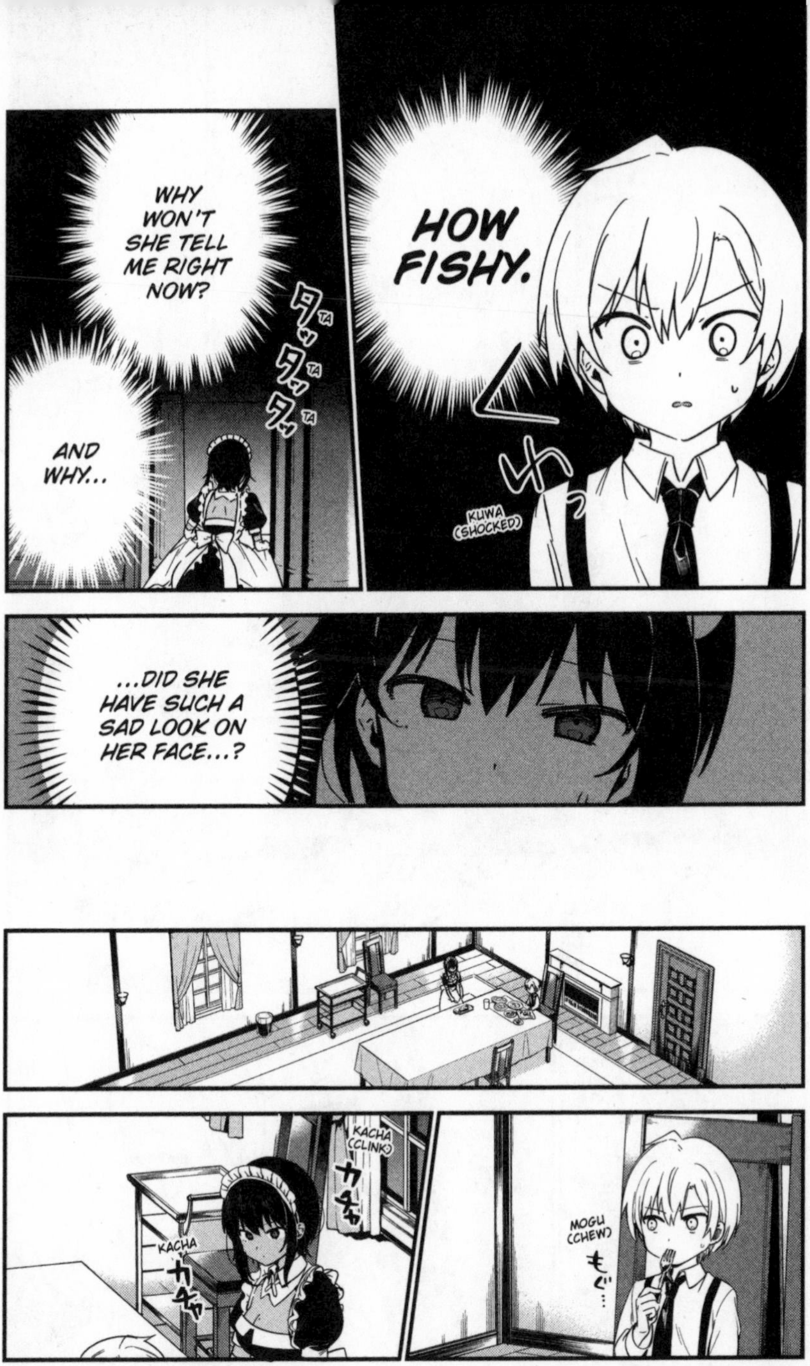
HOW FISHY.
くわっ
KUWA (SHOCKED)
WHY WON'T SHE TELL ME RIGHT NOW?
タッタッタッ
TA TA TA
AND WHY...
...DID SHE HAVE SUCH A SAD LOOK ON HER FACE...?
MOGU (CHEW)
もぐ…
KACHA (CLINK)
カチャ
KACHA
カチャ

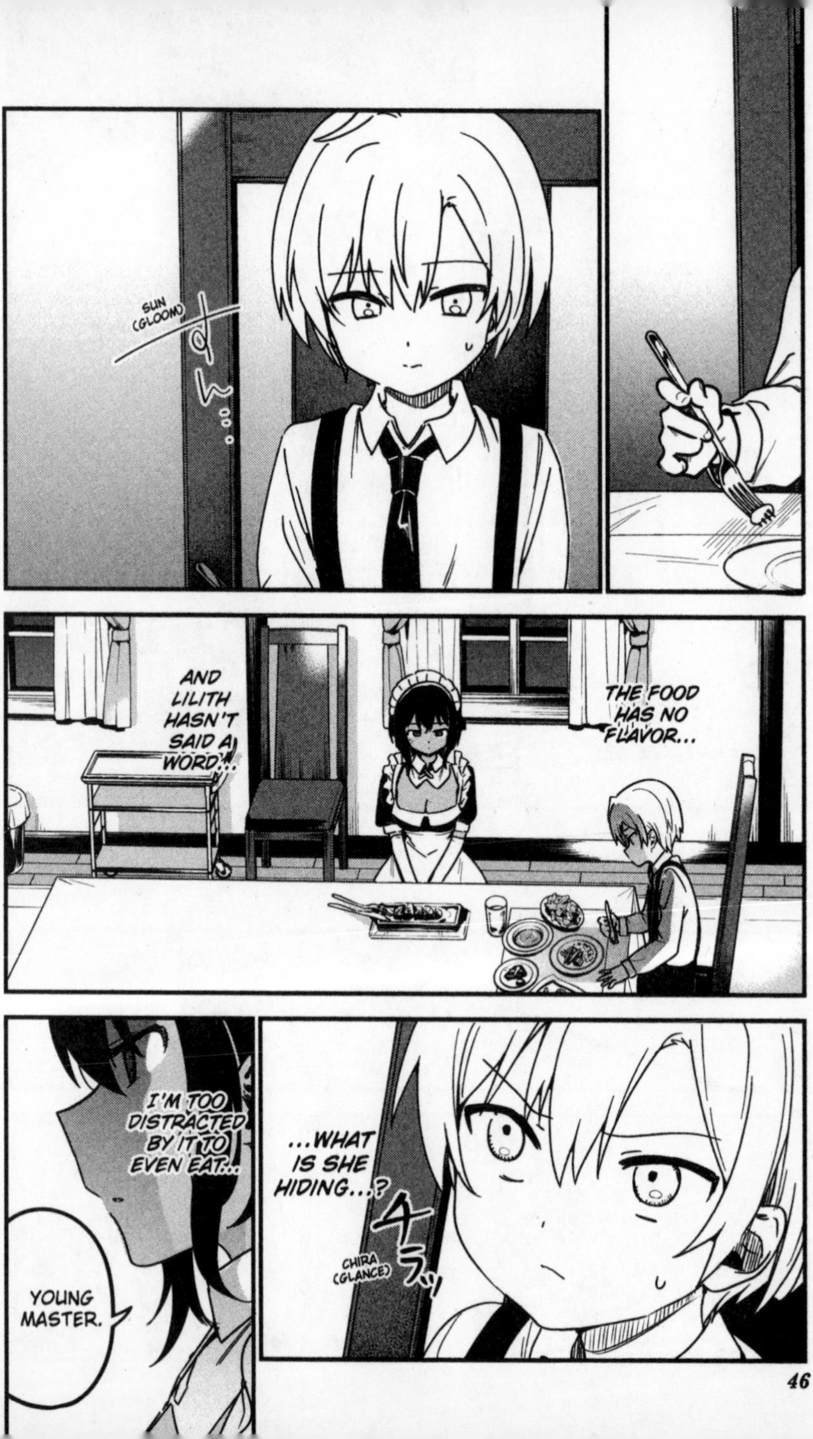
SUN (GLOOM)
THE FOOD HAS NO FLAVOR...
AND LILITH HASN'T SAID A WORD...
...WHAT IS SHE HIDING...?
CHIRA (GLANCE)
I'M TOO DISTRACTED BY IT TO EVEN EAT...
YOUNG MASTER.

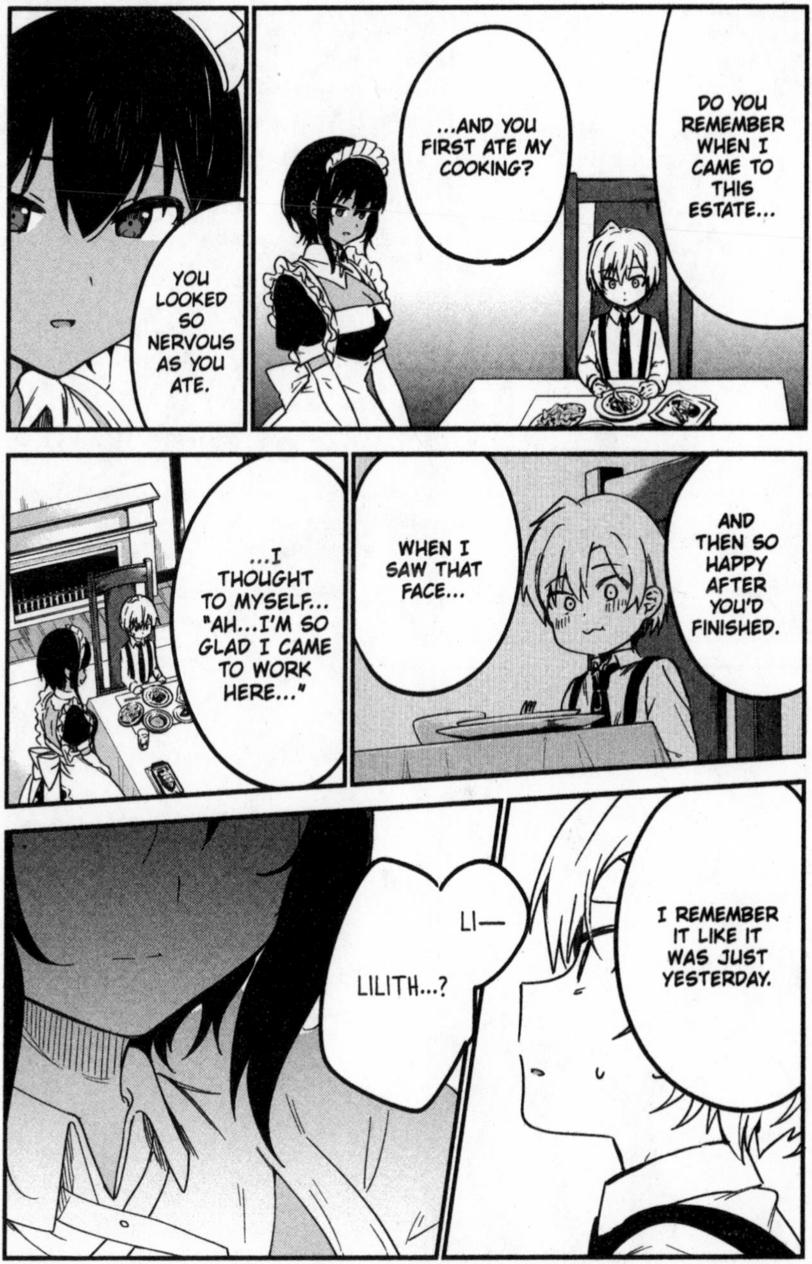
DO YOU REMEMBER WHEN I CAME TO THIS ESTATE...
...AND YOU FIRST ATE MY COOKING?
YOU LOOKED SO NERVOUS AS YOU ATE.
AND THEN SO HAPPY AFTER YOU'D FINISHED.
WHEN I SAW THAT FACE...
...I THOUGHT TO MYSELF... "AH...I'M SO GLAD I CAME TO WORK HERE..."
I REMEMBER IT LIKE IT WAS JUST YESTERDAY.
LI—
LILITH...?

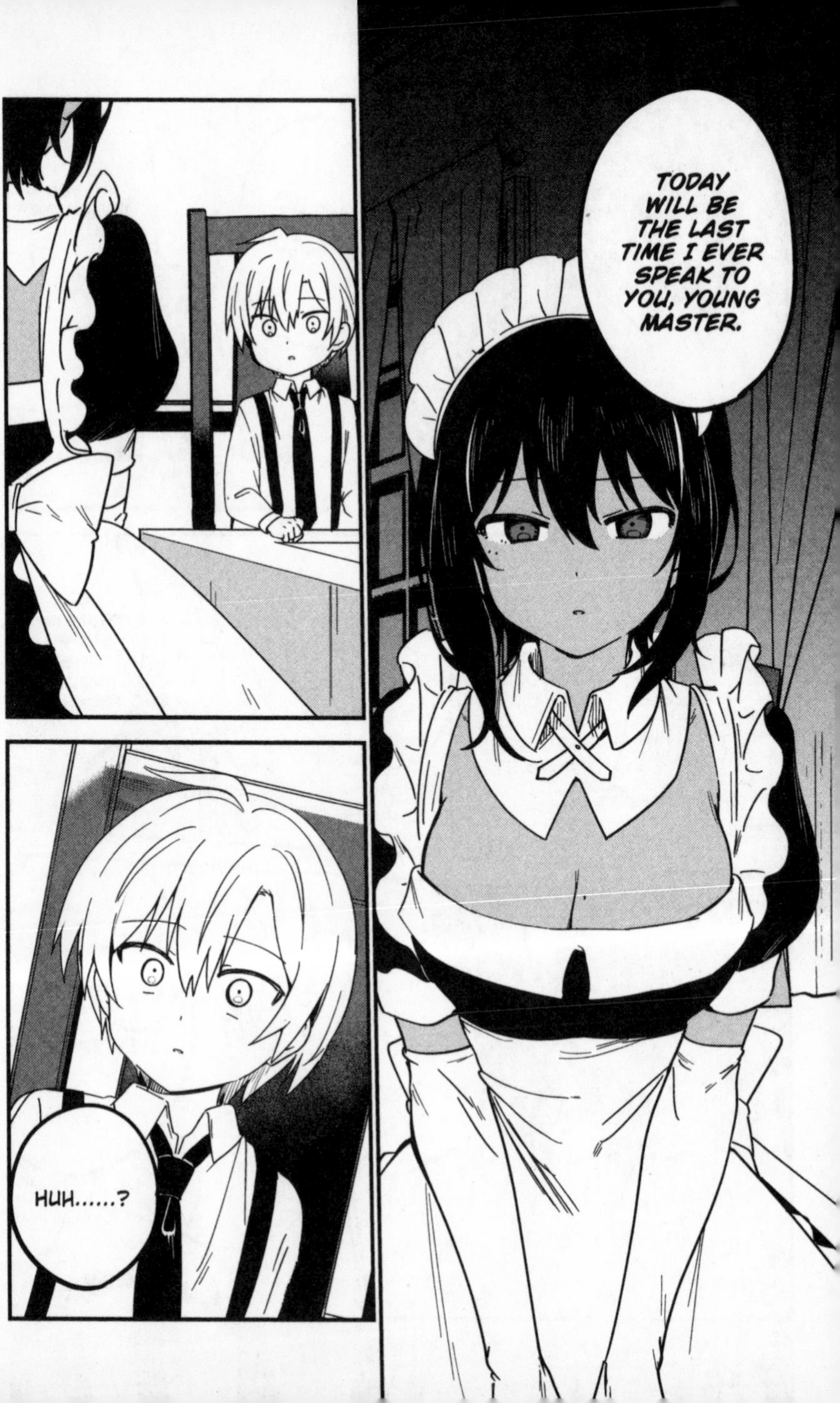
TODAY WILL BE THE LAST TIME I EVER SPEAK TO YOU, YOUNG MASTER.
HUH......?

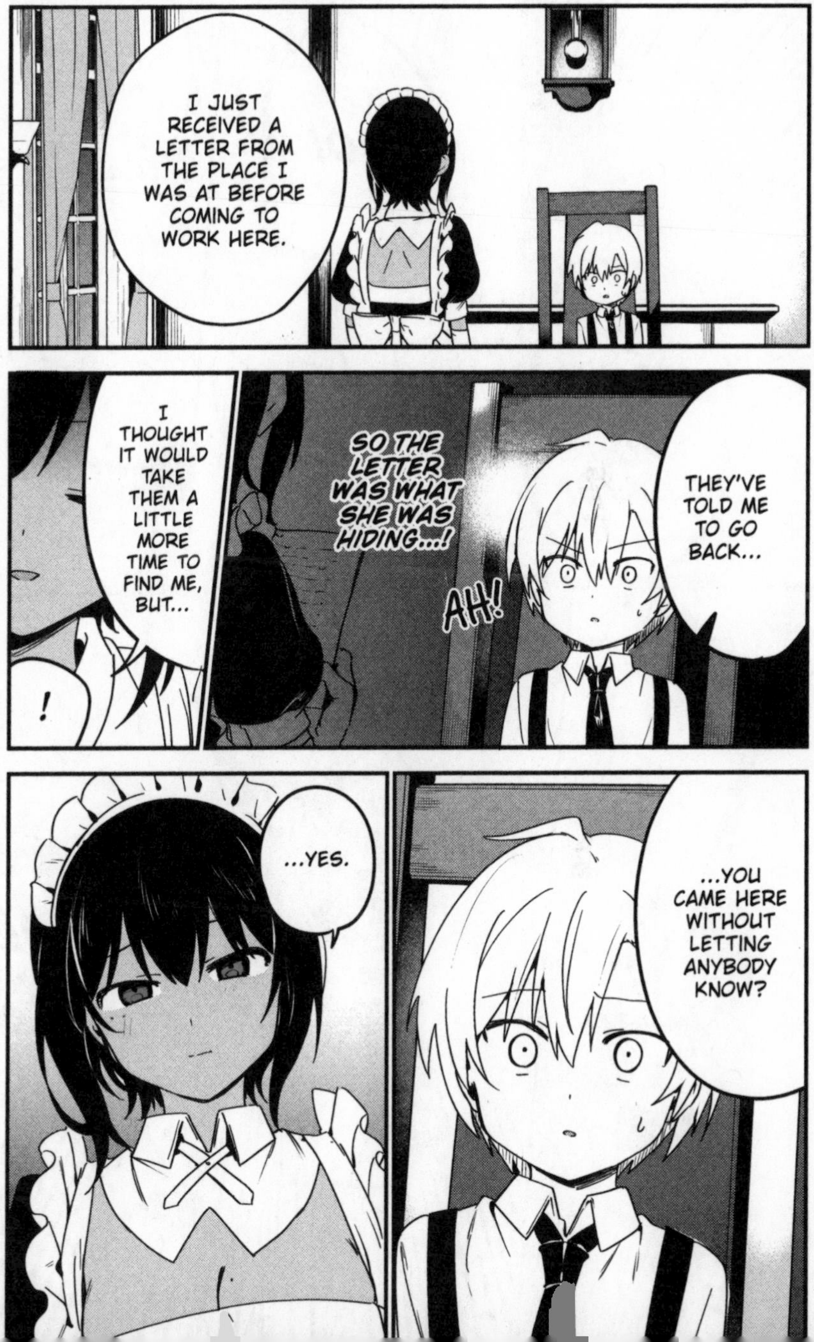
I JUST RECEIVED A LETTER FROM THE PLACE I WAS AT BEFORE COMING TO WORK HERE.
THEY'VE TOLD ME TO GO BACK...
AH!
SO THE LETTER WAS WHAT SHE WAS HIDING...!
I THOUGHT IT WOULD TAKE THEM A LITTLE MORE TIME TO FIND ME, BUT...
!
...YOU CAME HERE WITHOUT LETTING ANYBODY KNOW?
...YES.

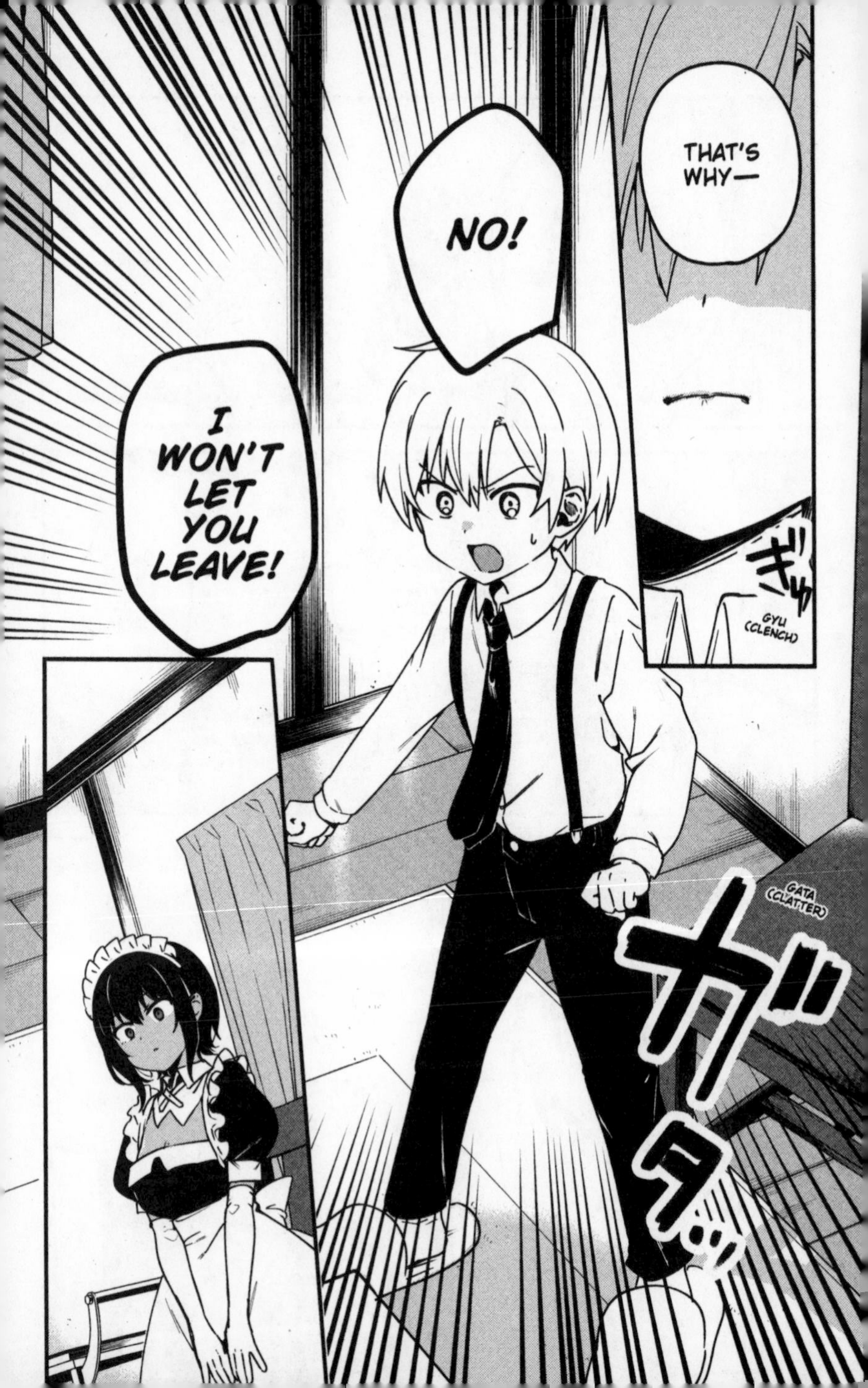
THAT'S WHY—
ギュ
GYU (CLENCH)
NO!
I WON'T LET YOU LEAVE!
ガタッ
GATA (CLATTER)

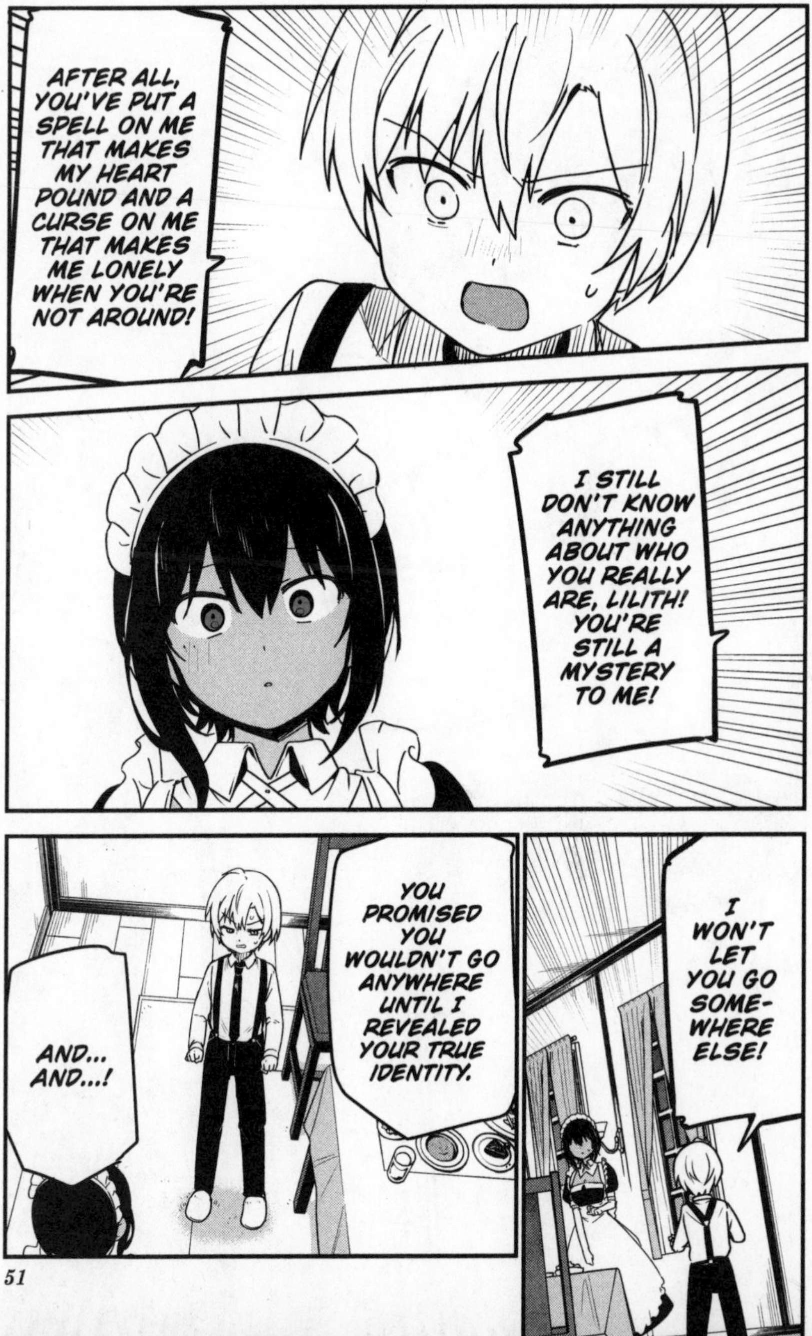
AFTER ALL, YOU'VE PUT A SPELL ON ME THAT MAKES MY HEART POUND AND A CURSE ON ME THAT MAKES ME LONELY WHEN YOU'RE NOT AROUND!
I STILL DON'T KNOW ANYTHING ABOUT WHO YOU REALLY ARE, LILITH! YOU'RE STILL A MYSTERY TO ME!
I WON'T LET YOU GO SOME-WHERE ELSE!
YOU PROMISED YOU WOULDN'T GO ANYWHERE UNTIL I REVEALED YOUR TRUE IDENTITY.
AND... AND...!

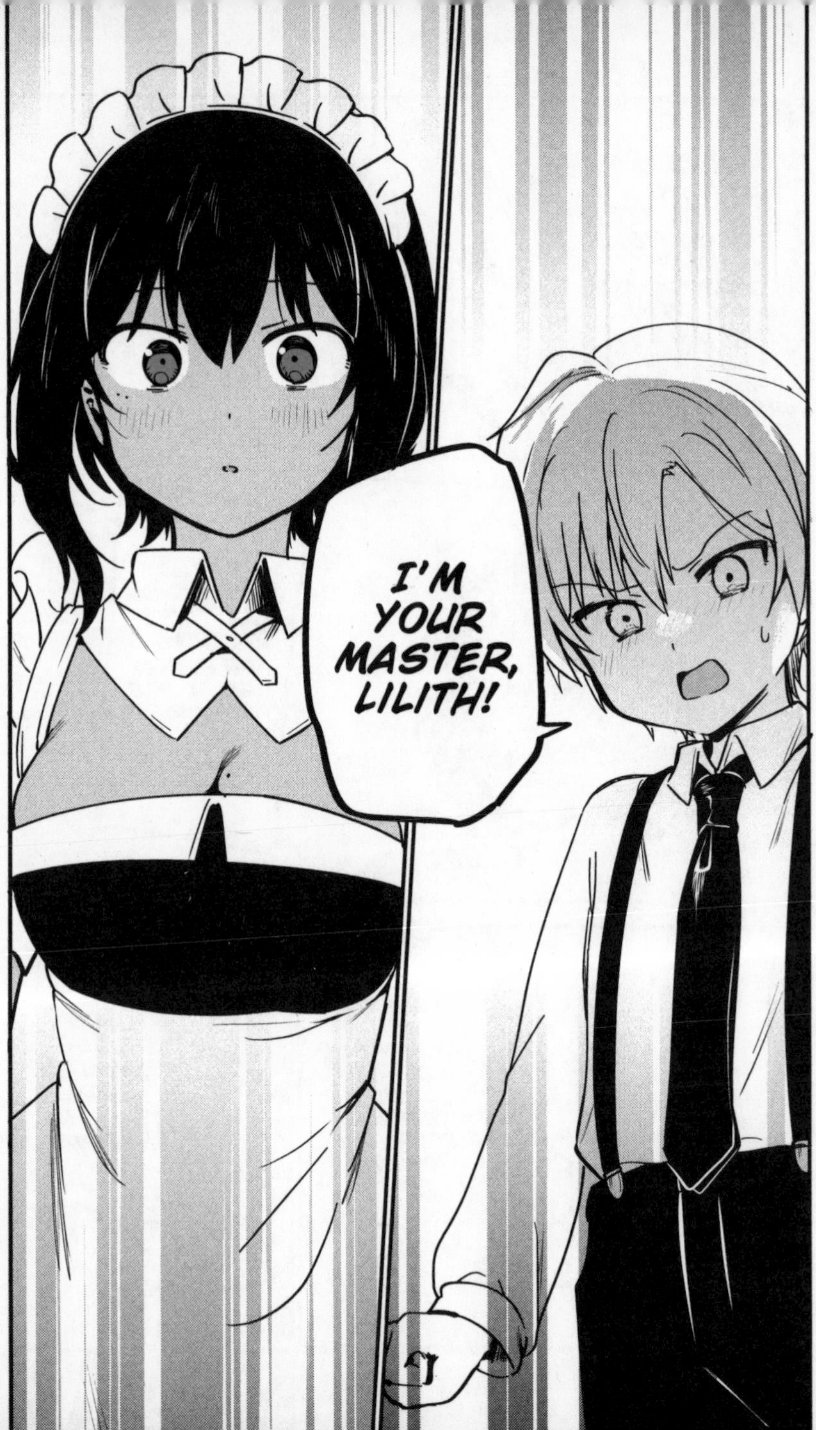
I'M YOUR MASTER, LILITH!

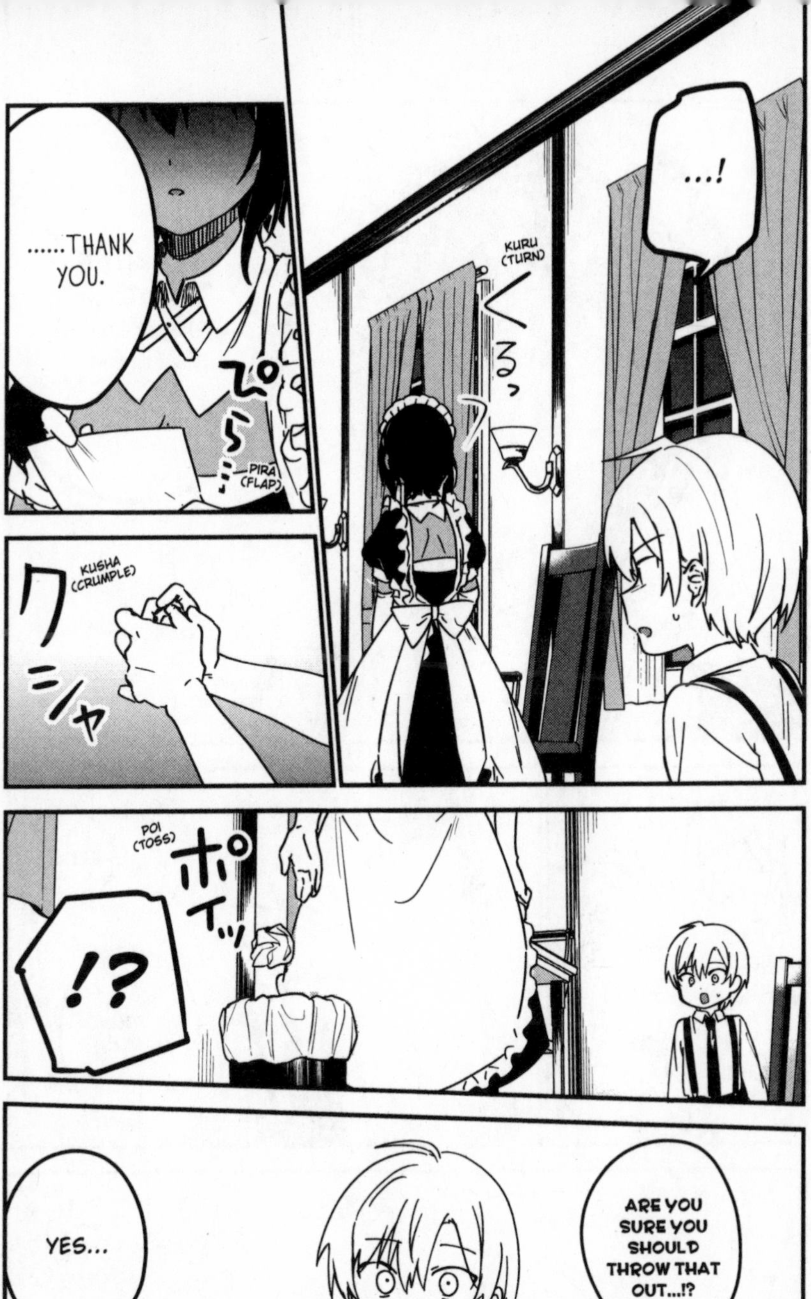
...!
KURU (TURN)
くるっ
......THANK YOU.
ぴら
PIRA (FLAP)
KUSHA (CRUMPLE)
クシャ
POI (TOSS)
ポイッ
!?
ARE YOU SURE YOU SHOULD THROW THAT OUT...!?
YES...

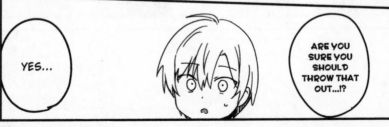

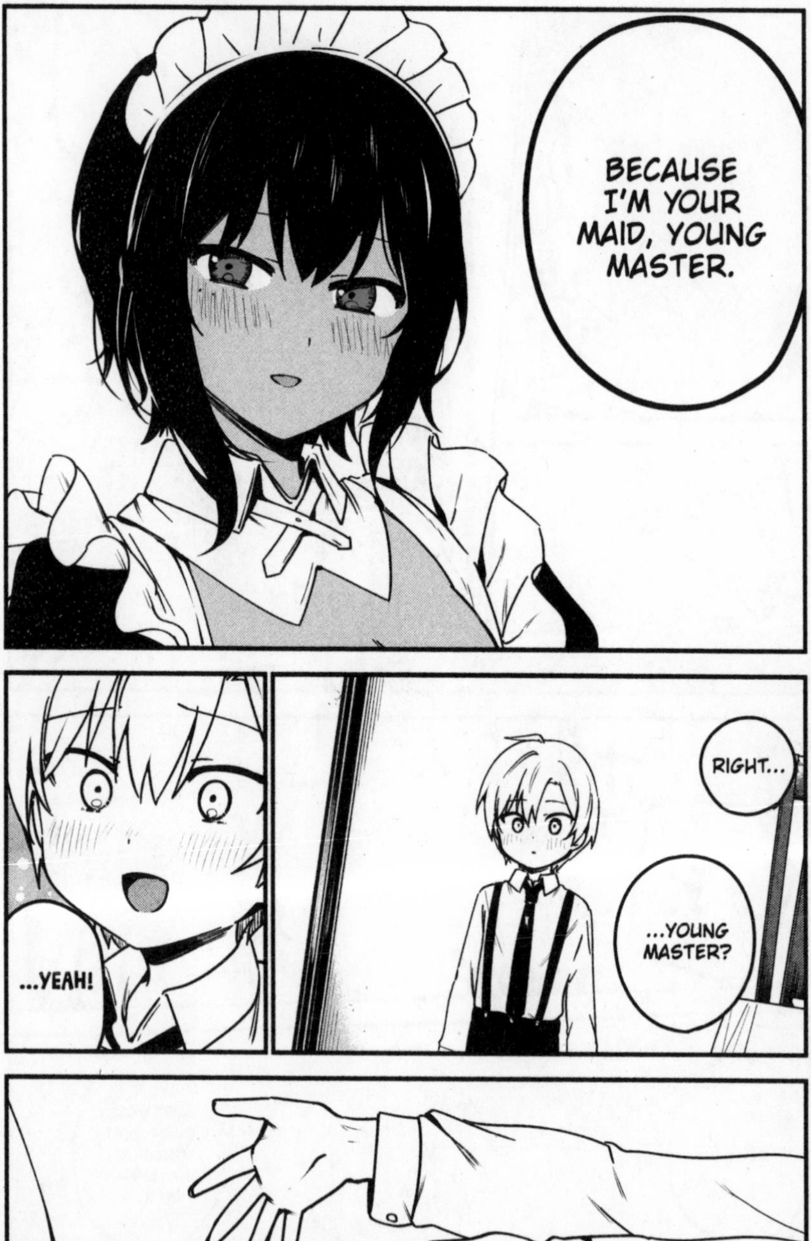
BECAUSE I'M YOUR MAID, YOUNG MASTER.
RIGHT...
...YOUNG MASTER?
...YEAH!

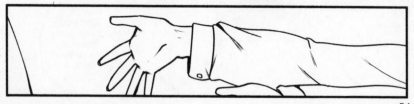

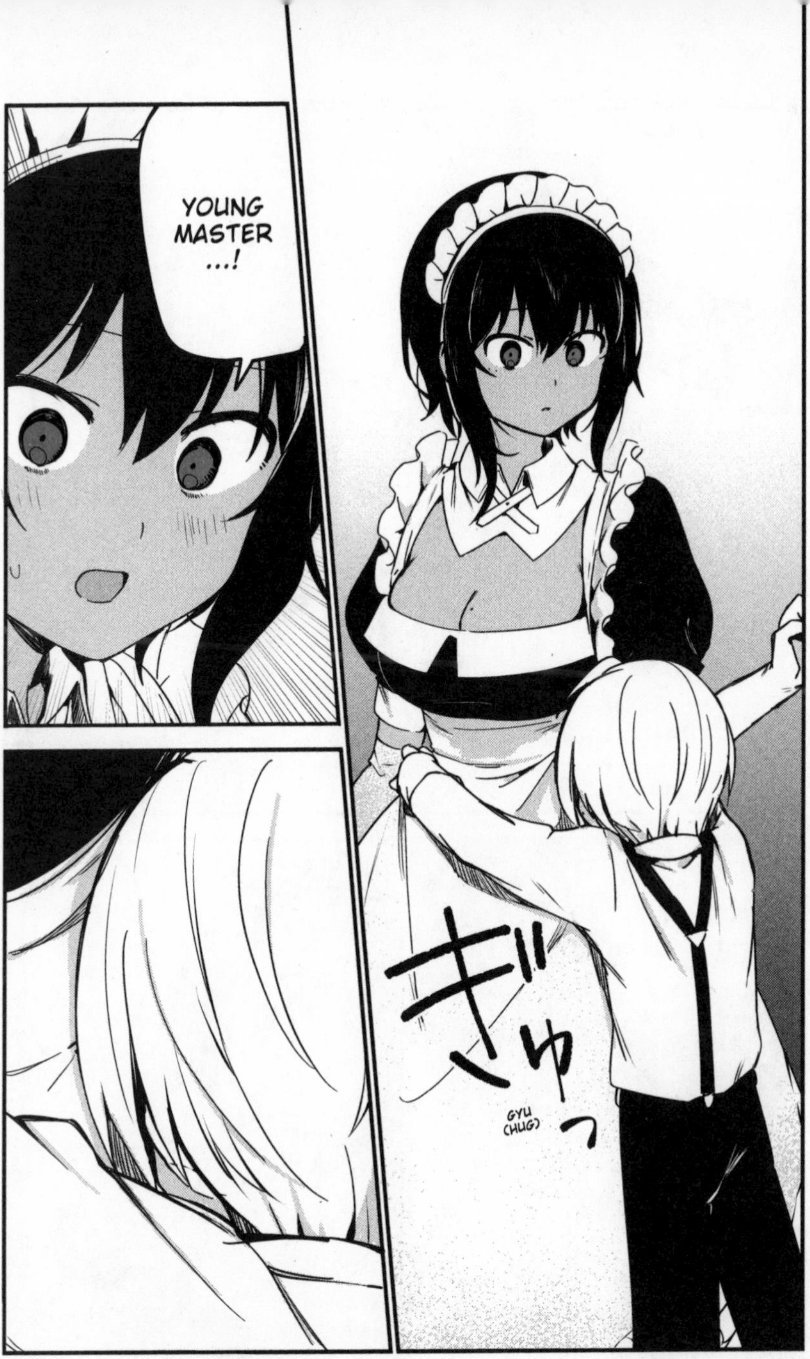
ぎゅっ
GYU (HUG)
YOUNG MASTER ...!

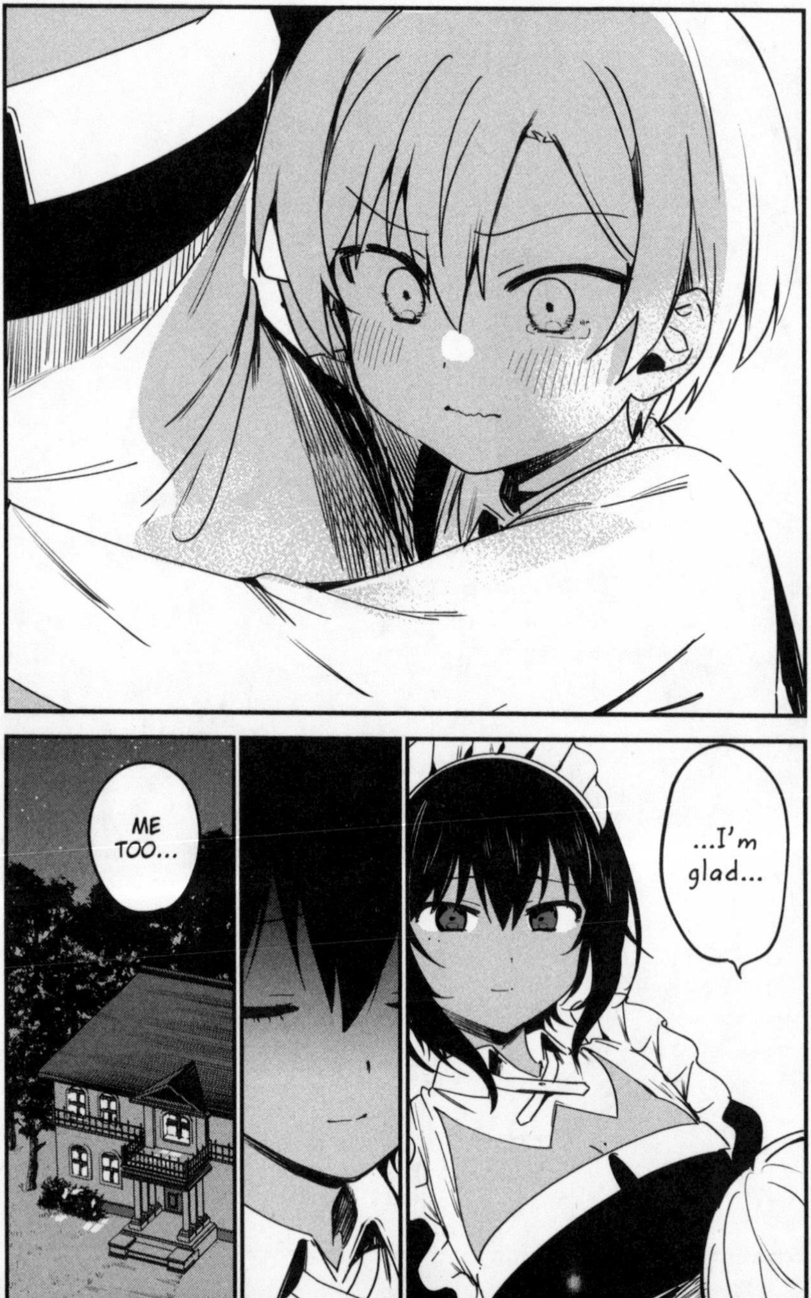
...I'm glad...
ME TOO...

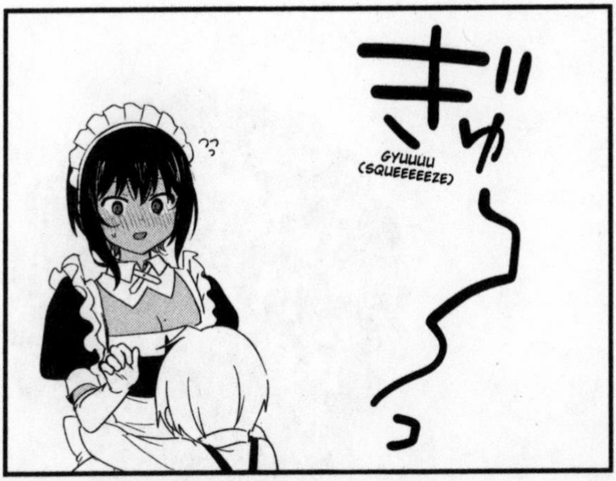
ぎゅううう
GYUUUU
(SQUEEEEEZE)

The Maid I Hired Recently Is Mysterious

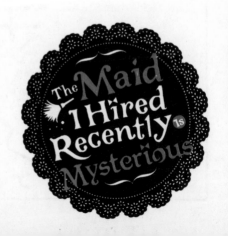

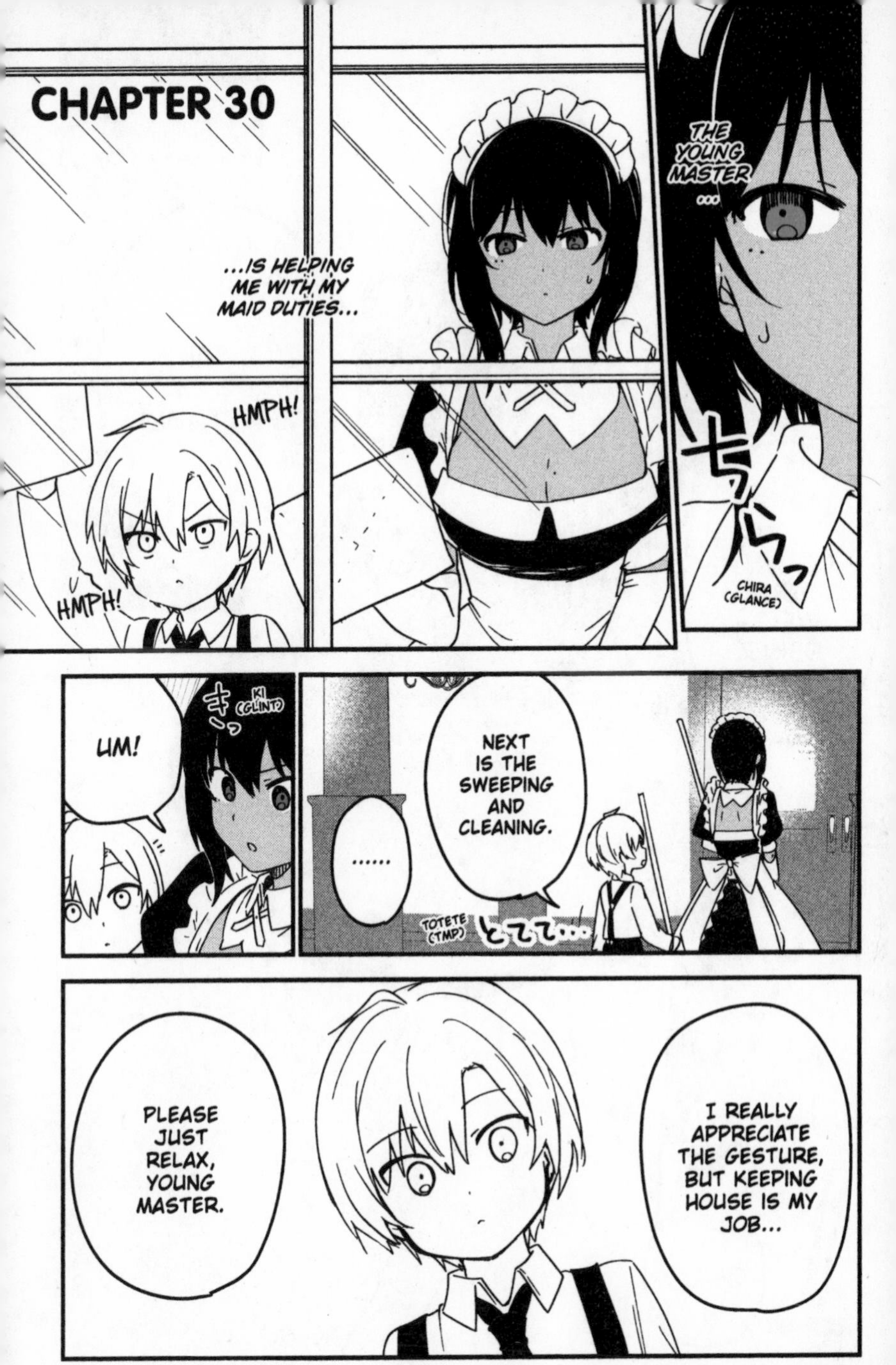
THE YOUNG MASTER...
ちらっ
CHIRA (GLANCE)
CHAPTER 30
...IS HELPING ME WITH MY MAID DUTIES...
HMPH!
HMPH!
NEXT IS THE SWEEPING AND CLEANING.
......
とてて…
TOTETE (TMP)
UM!
きっ
KI (GLINT)
I REALLY APPRECIATE THE GESTURE, BUT KEEPING HOUSE IS MY JOB...
PLEASE JUST RELAX, YOUNG MASTER.

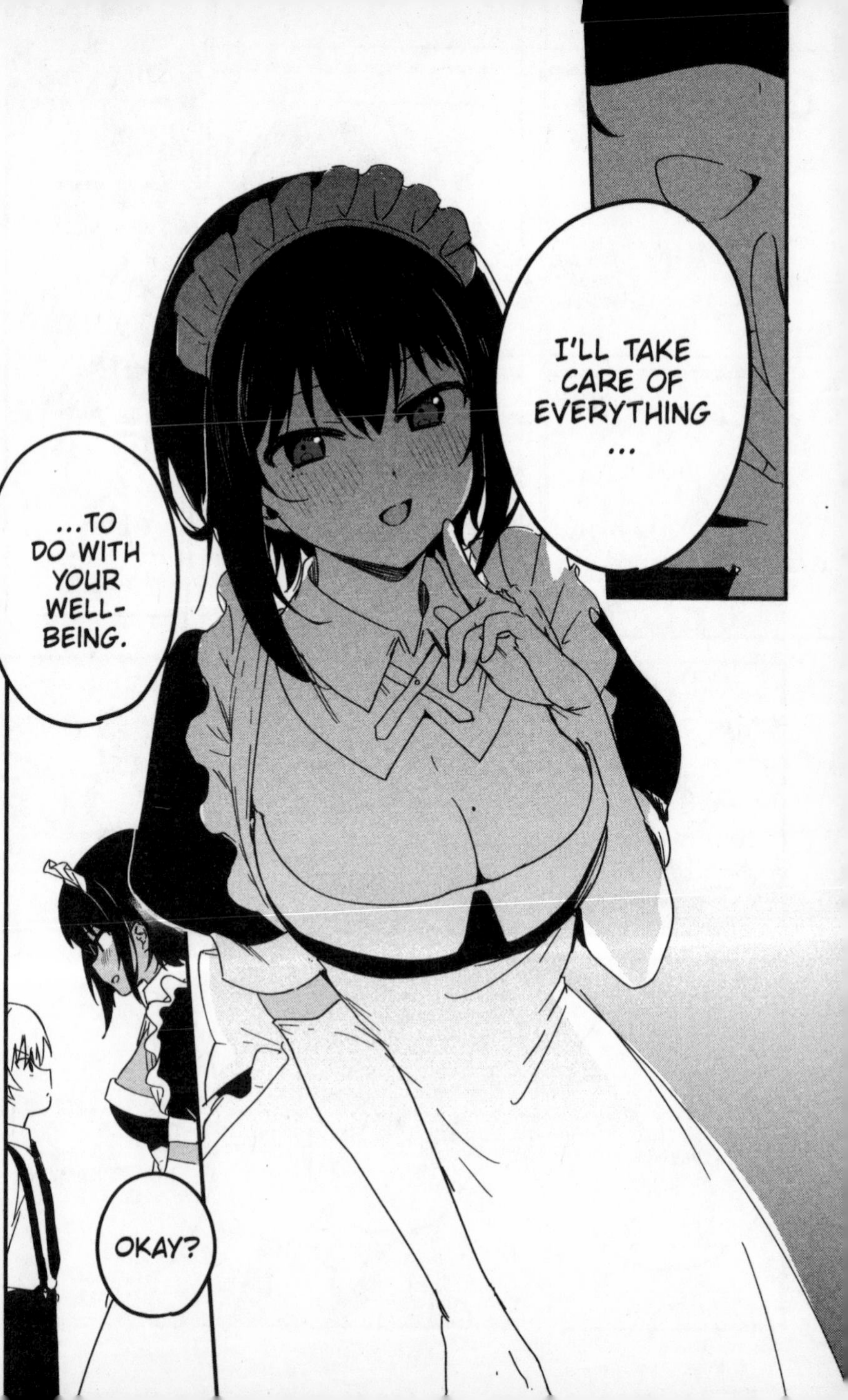
I'LL TAKE CARE OF EVERYTHING...
...TO DO WITH YOUR WELL-BEING.
OKAY?

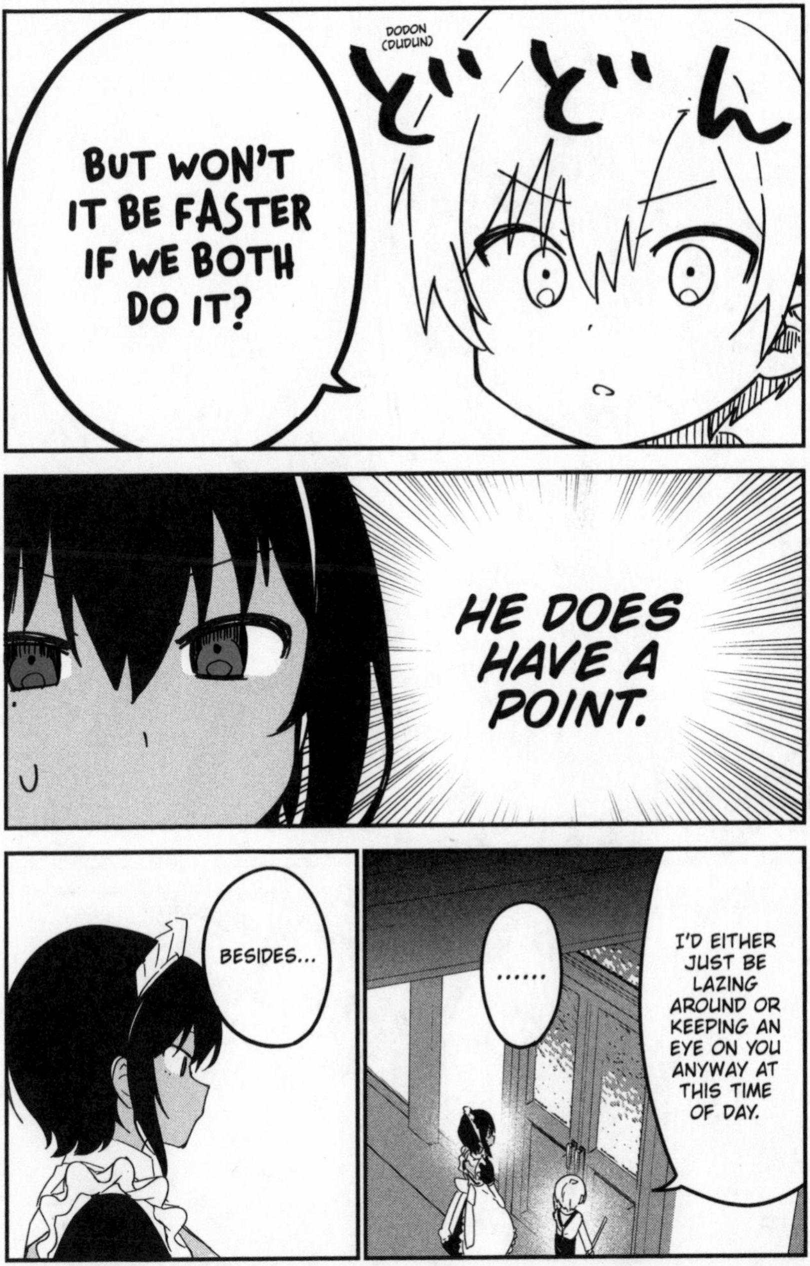
DODON (DUDUN)
どどん
BUT WON'T IT BE FASTER IF WE BOTH DO IT?
HE DOES HAVE A POINT.
I'D EITHER JUST BE LAZING AROUND OR KEEPING AN EYE ON YOU ANYWAY AT THIS TIME OF DAY.
......
BESIDES...

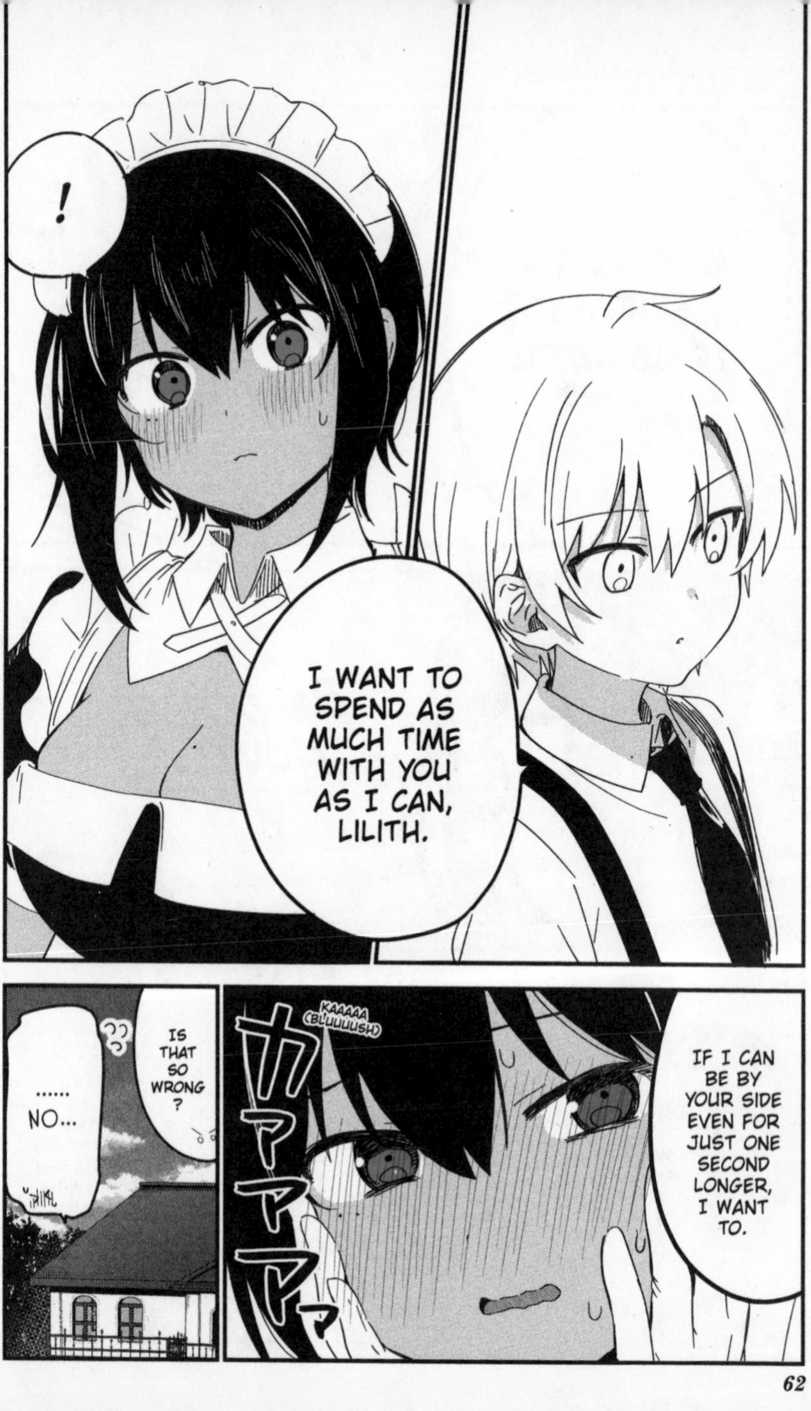
I WANT TO SPEND AS MUCH TIME WITH YOU AS I CAN, LILITH.
!
IF I CAN BE BY YOUR SIDE EVEN FOR JUST ONE SECOND LONGER, I WANT TO.
KAAAAA (BLUUUUSH)
IS THAT SO WRONG?
...... NO...

CHAPTER 31

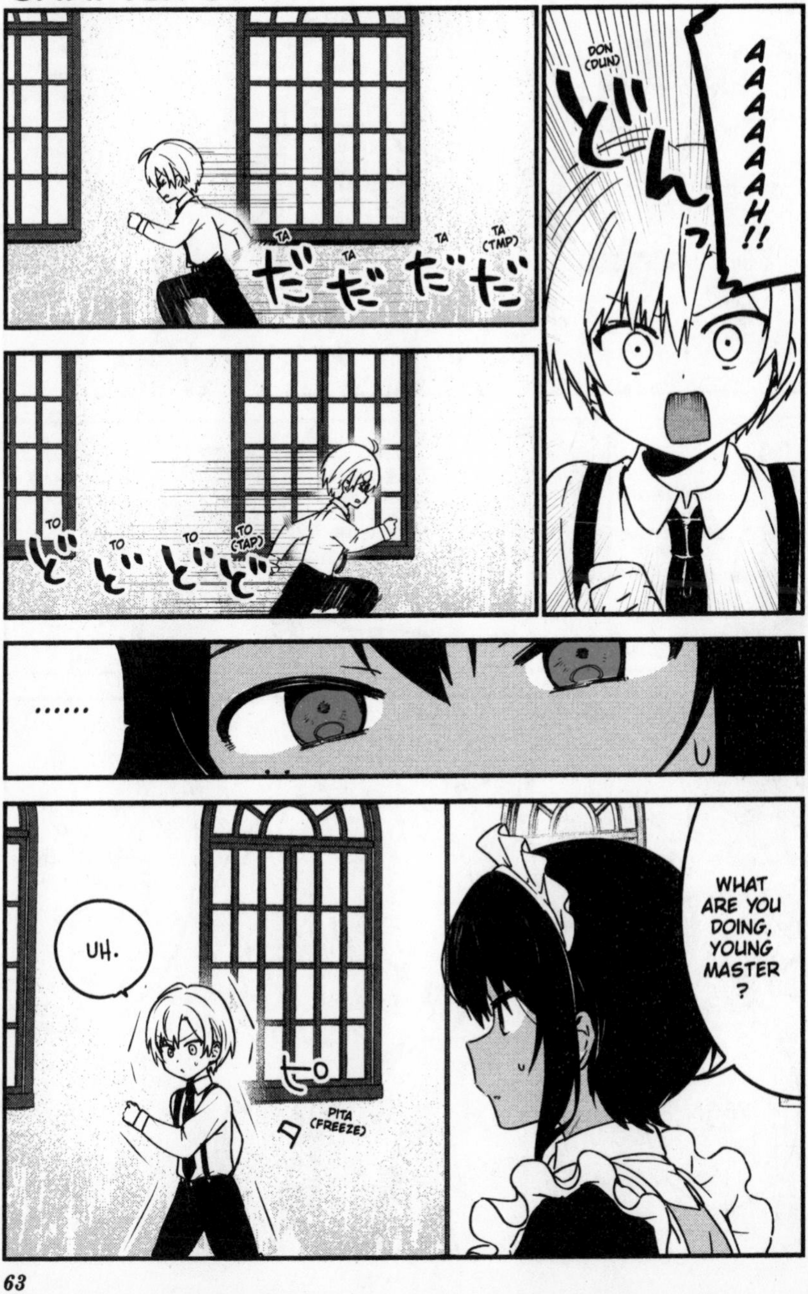
DON (DUN)
どんっ
AAAAAAAH!!
TA TA TA TA (TMP)
だだだだ
TO TO TO TO (TAP)
どどどど
......
WHAT ARE YOU DOING, YOUNG MASTER?
UH.
ピタ
PITA (FREEZE)

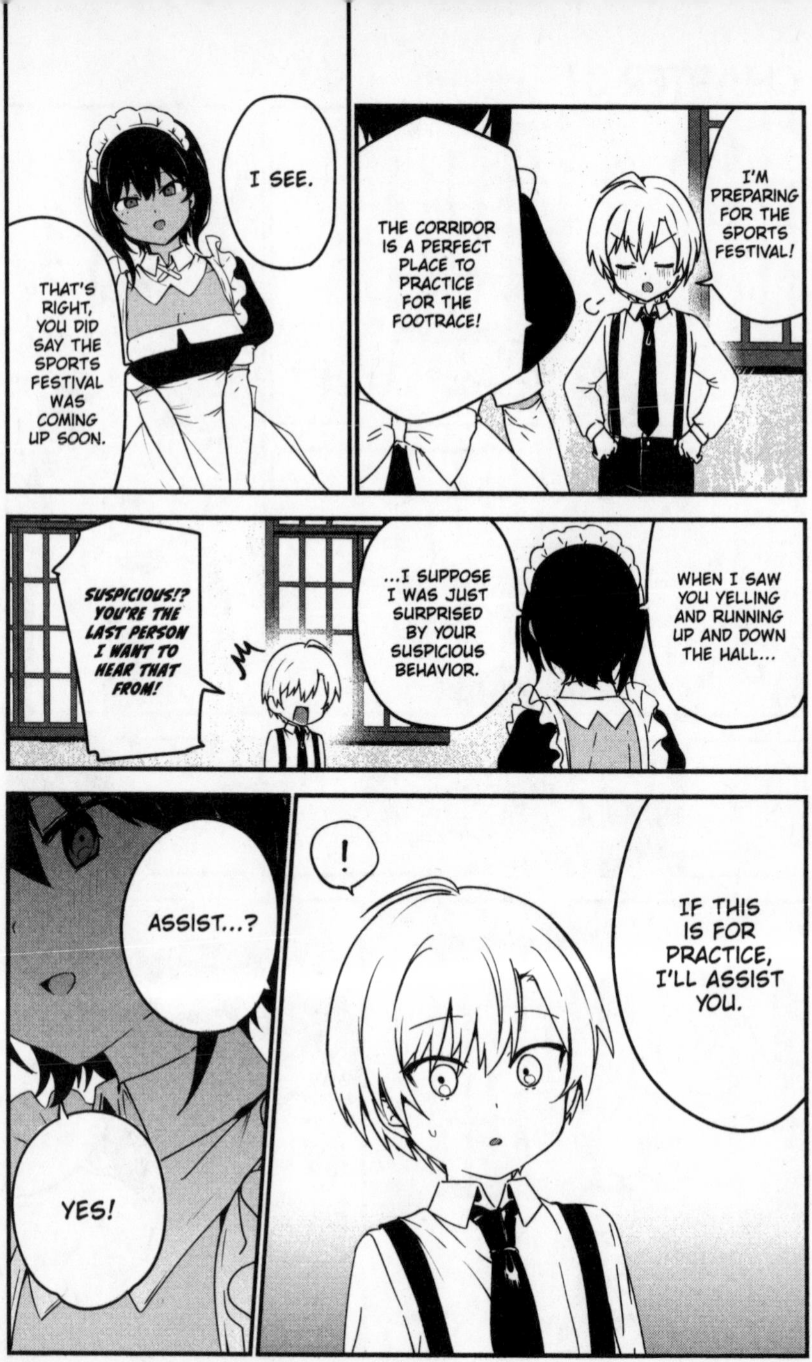
I'M PREPARING FOR THE SPORTS FESTIVAL!
THE CORRIDOR IS A PERFECT PLACE TO PRACTICE FOR THE FOOTRACE!
I SEE.
THAT'S RIGHT, YOU DID SAY THE SPORTS FESTIVAL WAS COMING UP SOON.
WHEN I SAW YOU YELLING AND RUNNING UP AND DOWN THE HALL...
...I SUPPOSE I WAS JUST SURPRISED BY YOUR SUSPICIOUS BEHAVIOR.
SUSPICIOUS!? YOU'RE THE LAST PERSON I WANT TO HEAR THAT FROM!
IF THIS IS FOR PRACTICE, I'LL ASSIST YOU.
!
ASSIST...?
YES!

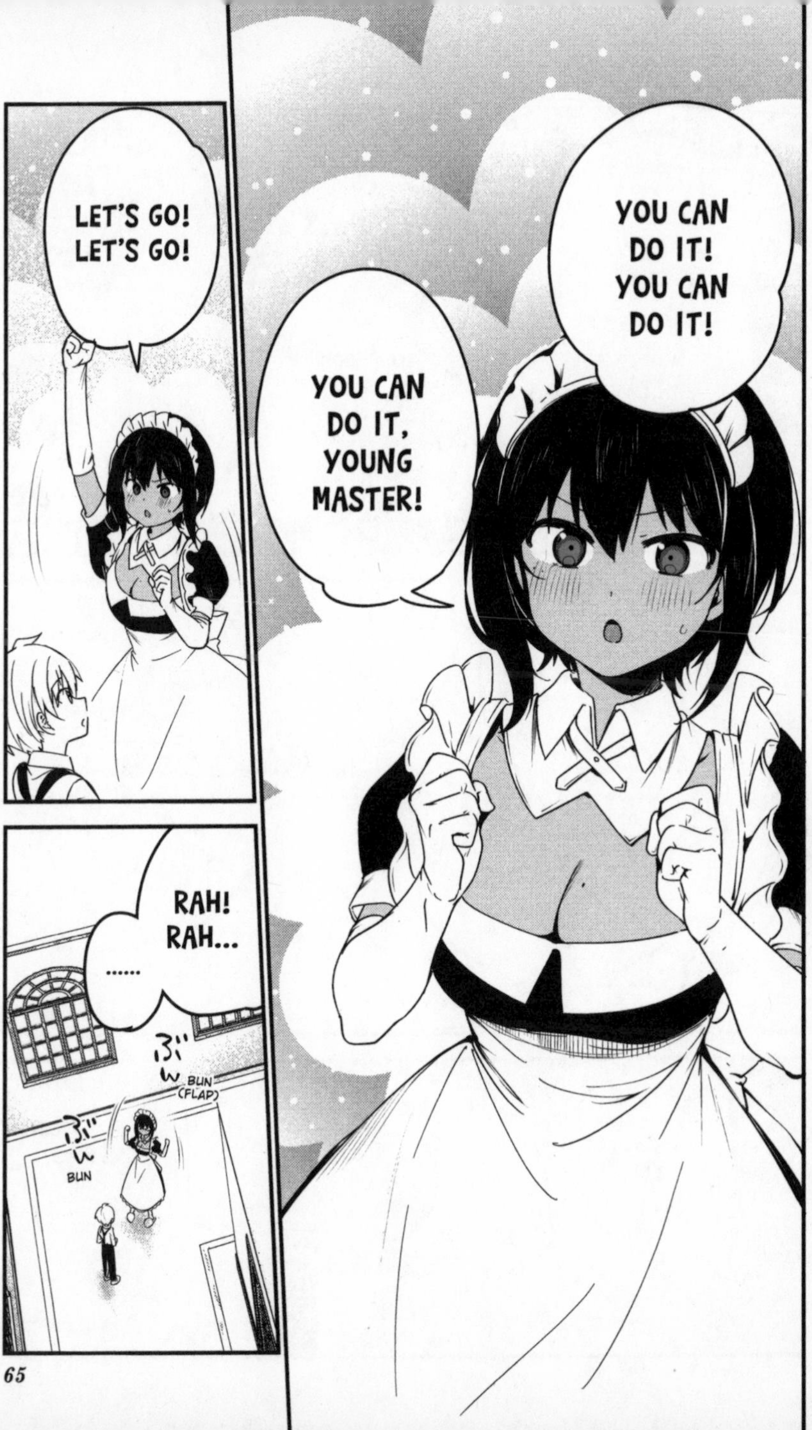
YOU CAN DO IT! YOU CAN DO IT!
YOU CAN DO IT, YOUNG MASTER!
LET'S GO! LET'S GO!
RAH! RAH... ......
ぶん
BUN (FLAP)
ぶん
BUN

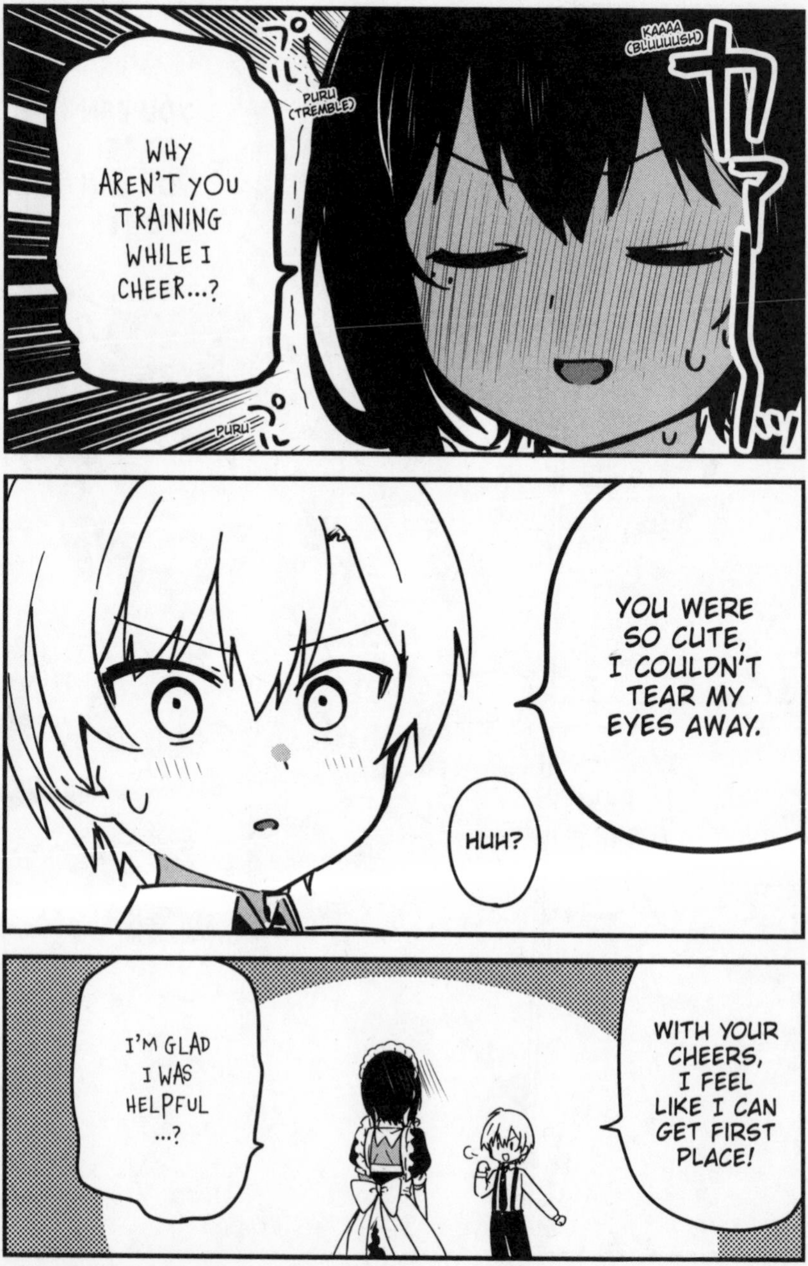
KAAAA (BLUUUUSH)
PURU (TREMBLE)
WHY AREN'T YOU TRAINING WHILE I CHEER...?
PURU
YOU WERE SO CUTE, I COULDN'T TEAR MY EYES AWAY.
HUH?
WITH YOUR CHEERS, I FEEL LIKE I CAN GET FIRST PLACE!
I'M GLAD I WAS HELPFUL ...?

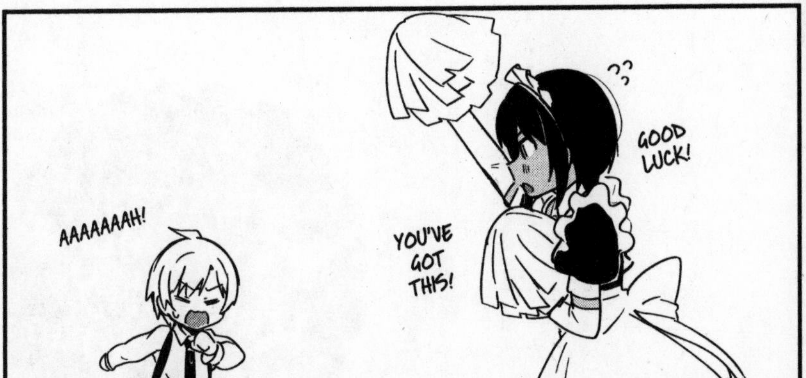
GOOD LUCK!
YOU'VE GOT THIS!
AAAAAAAH!

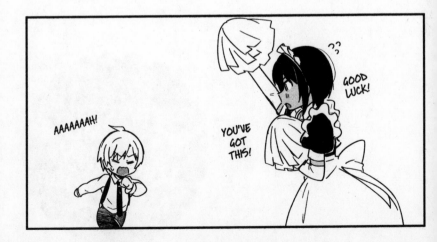

The Maid I Hired Recently Is Mysterious

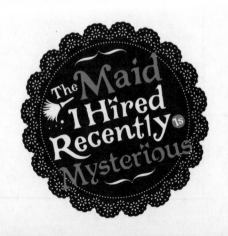

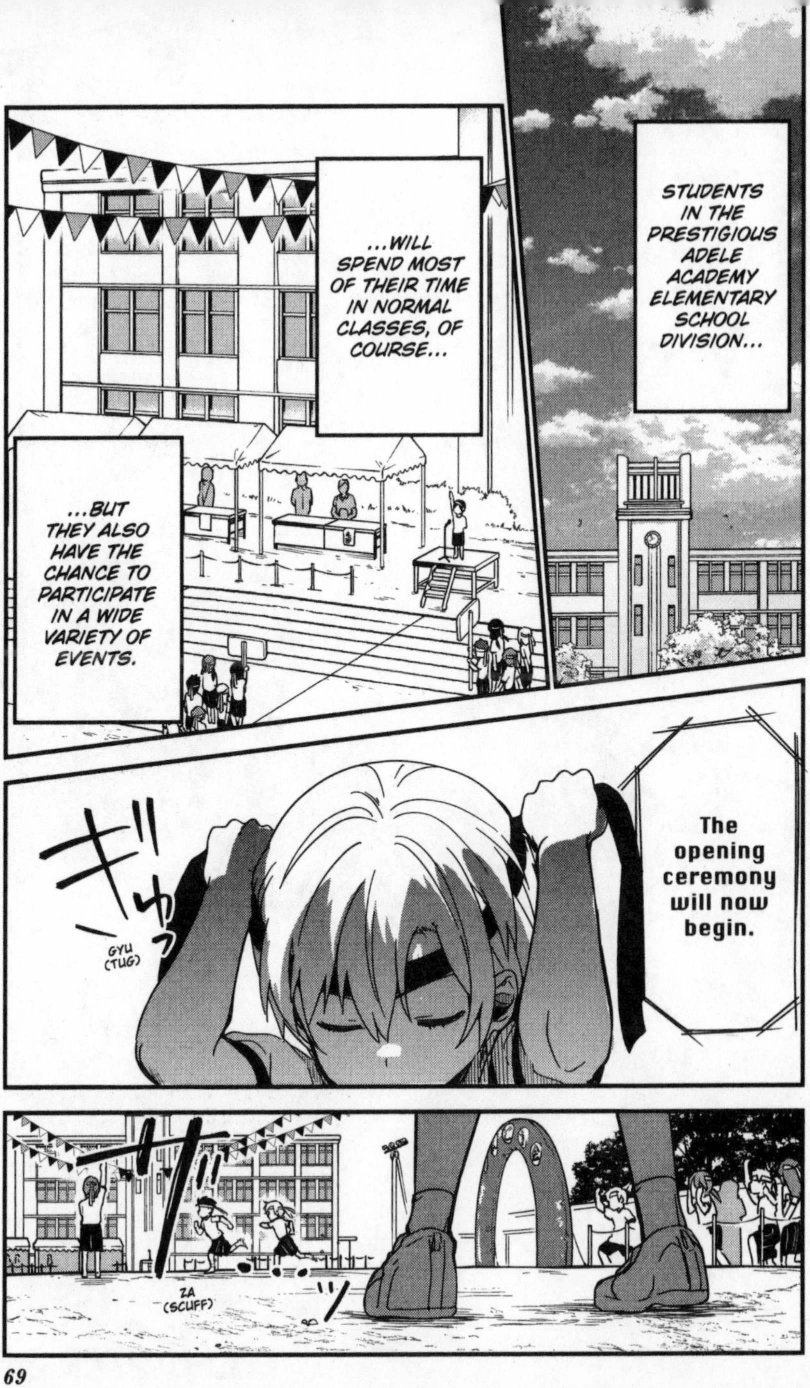
STUDENTS IN THE PRESTIGIOUS ADELE ACADEMY ELEMENTARY SCHOOL DIVISION...
...WILL SPEND MOST OF THEIR TIME IN NORMAL CLASSES, OF COURSE...
...BUT THEY ALSO HAVE THE CHANCE TO PARTICIPATE IN A WIDE VARIETY OF EVENTS.
The opening ceremony will now begin.
ギリゅっ
GYU (TUG)
ザッ
ZA (SCUFF)

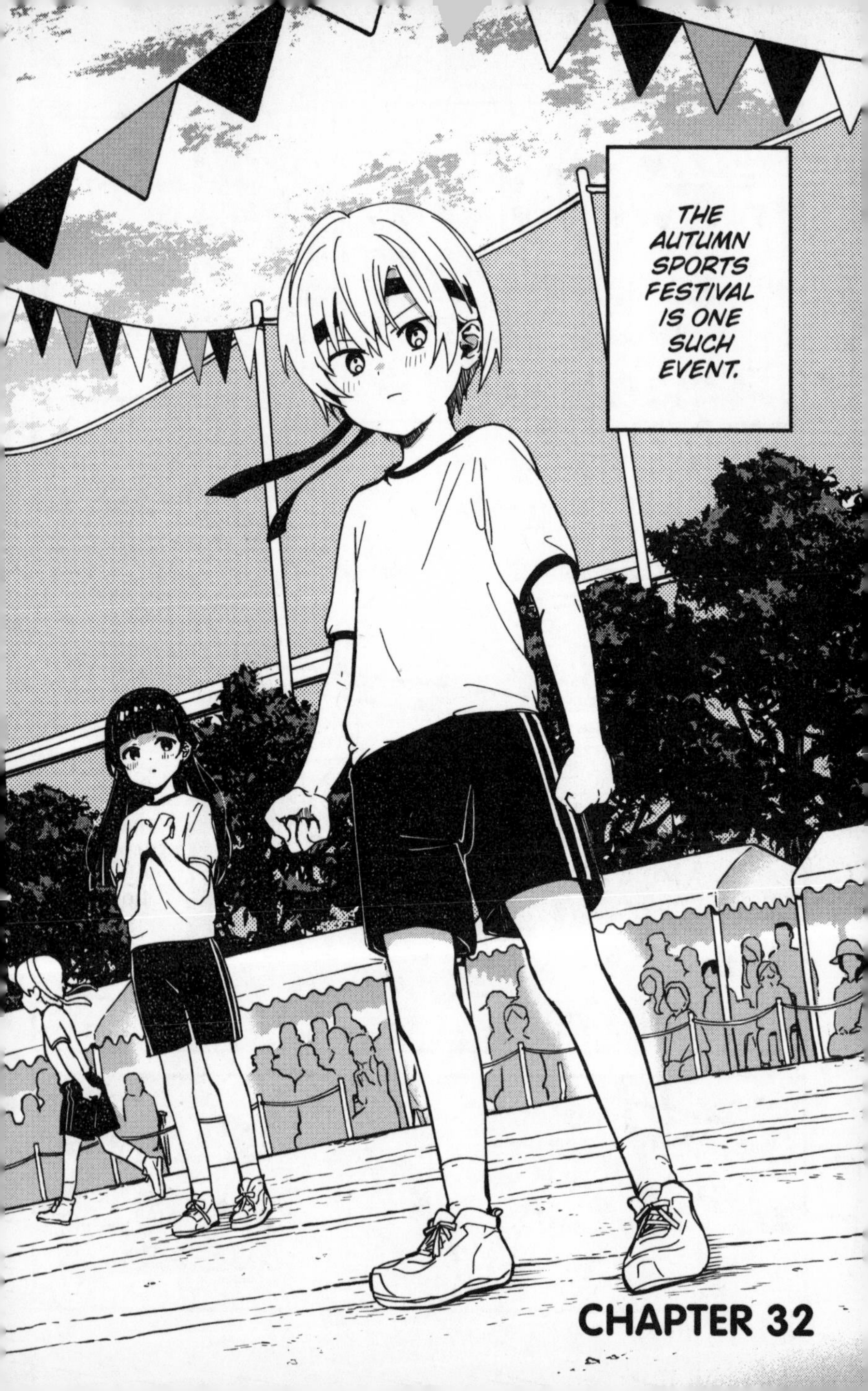
THE AUTUMN SPORTS FESTIVAL IS ONE SUCH EVENT.
CHAPTER 32

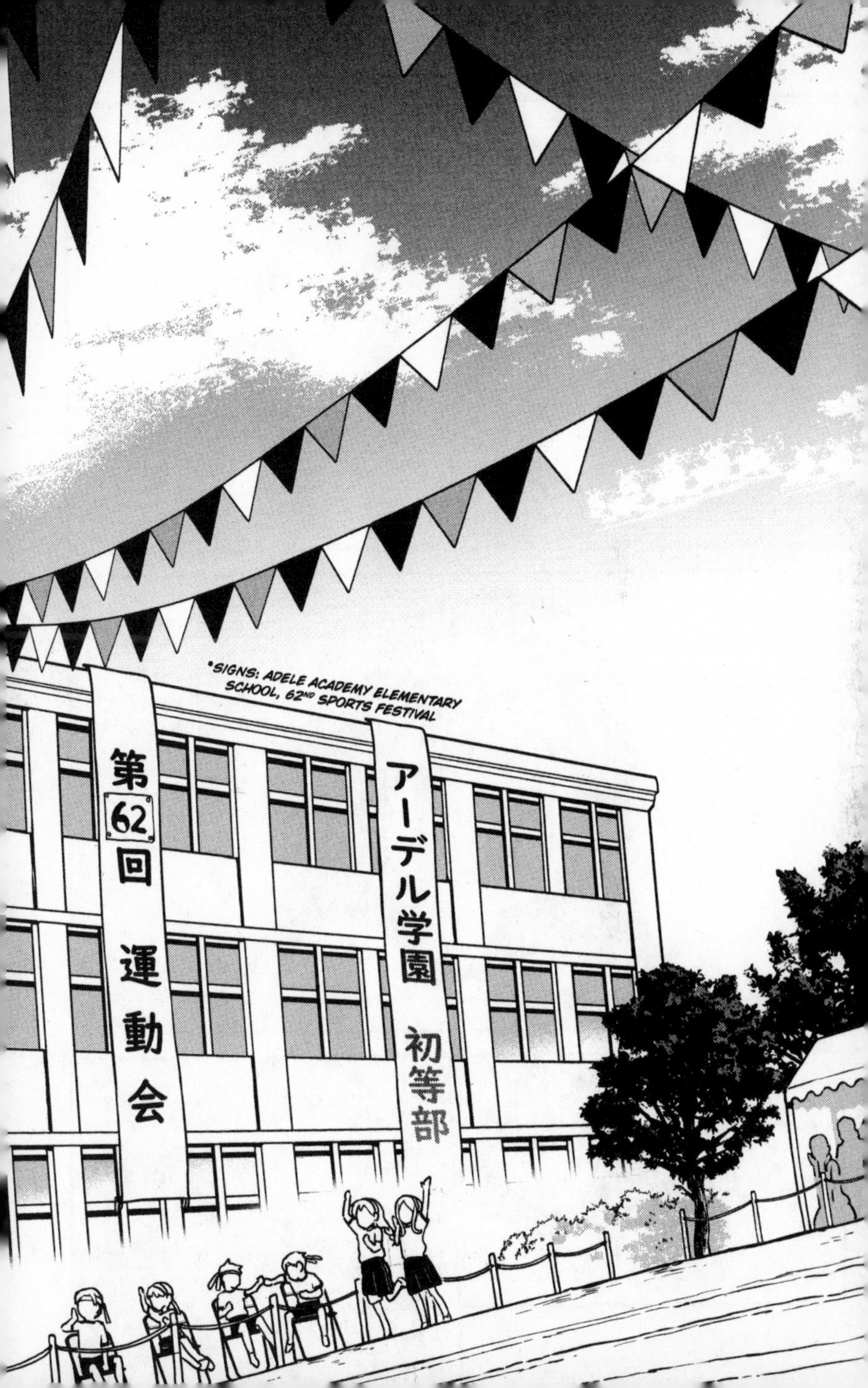
*SIGNS: ADELE ACADEMY ELEMENTARY SCHOOL, 62ND SPORTS FESTIVAL
アーデル学園 初等部
第62回 運動会

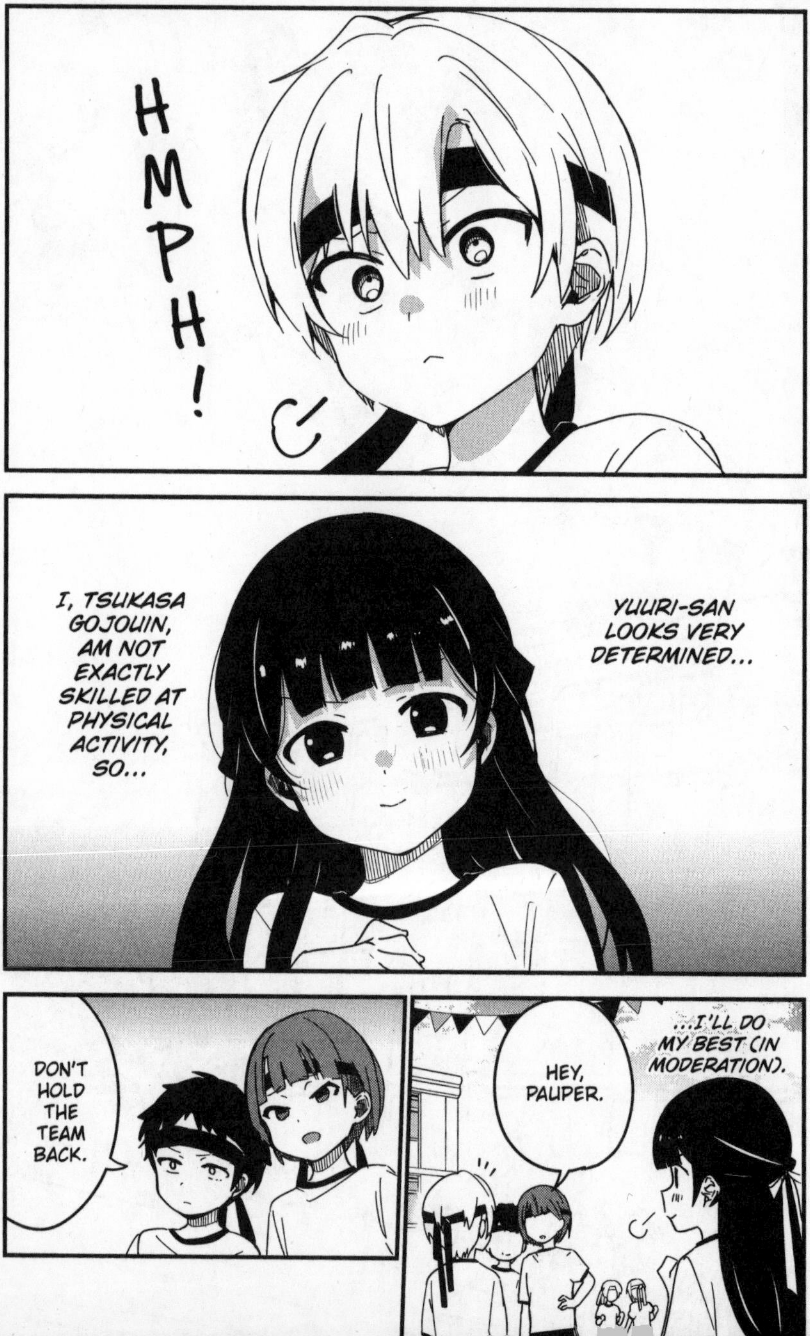
HMPH!
YUURI-SAN LOOKS VERY DETERMINED...
I, TSUKASA GOJOUIN, AM NOT EXACTLY SKILLED AT PHYSICAL ACTIVITY, SO...
...I'LL DO MY BEST (IN MODERATION).
HEY, PAUPER.
DON'T HOLD THE TEAM BACK.

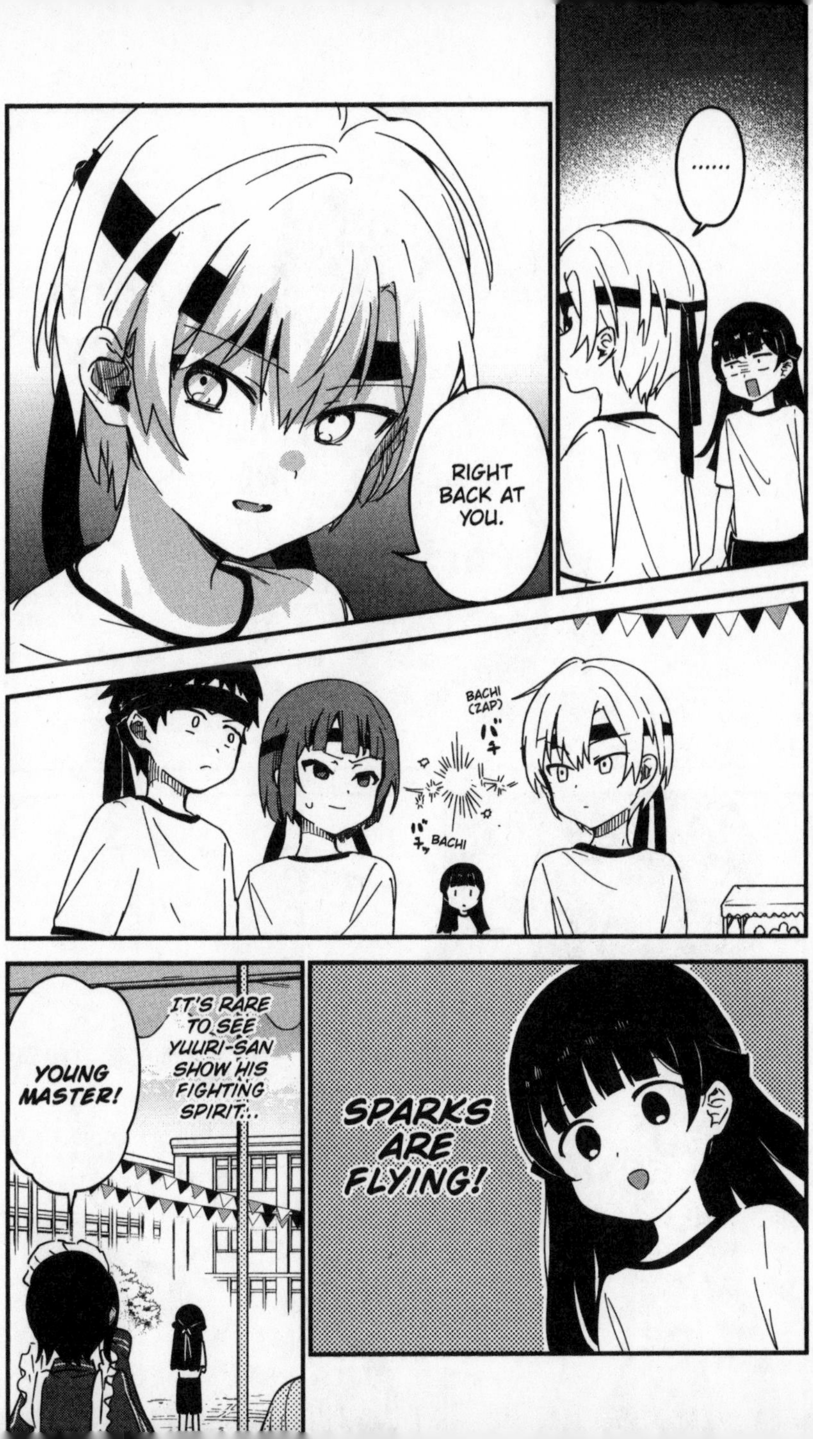
......
RIGHT BACK AT YOU.
BACHI (ZAP) バチ
バチッ BACHI
SPARKS ARE FLYING!
IT'S RARE TO SEE YUURI-SAN SHOW HIS FIGHTING SPIRIT...
YOUNG MASTER!

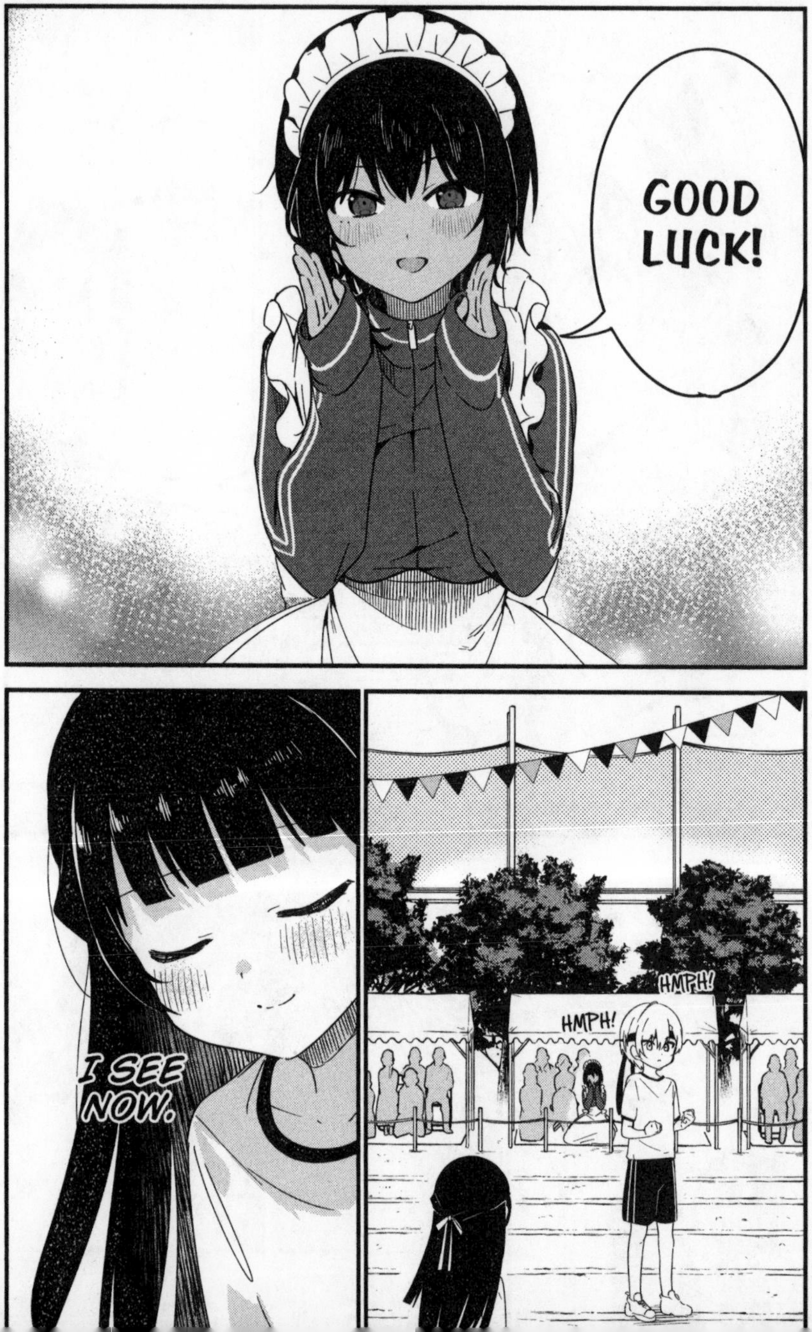
GOOD LUCK!
HMPH!
HMPH!
I SEE NOW.

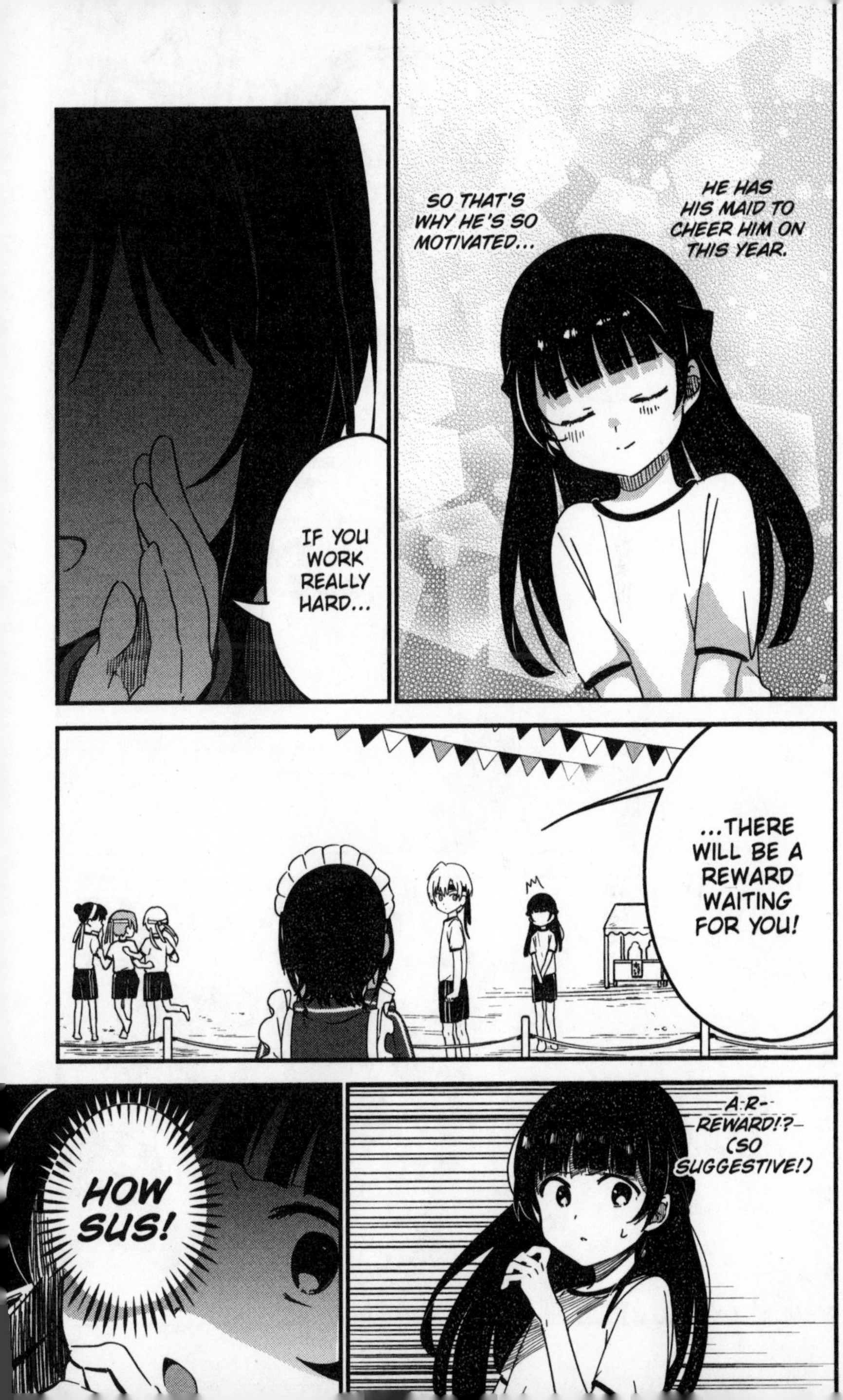
HE HAS HIS MAID TO CHEER HIM ON THIS YEAR.
SO THAT'S WHY HE'S SO MOTIVATED...
IF YOU WORK REALLY HARD...
...THERE WILL BE A REWARD WAITING FOR YOU!
A-R-REWARD!? (SO SUGGESTIVE!)
HOW SUS!

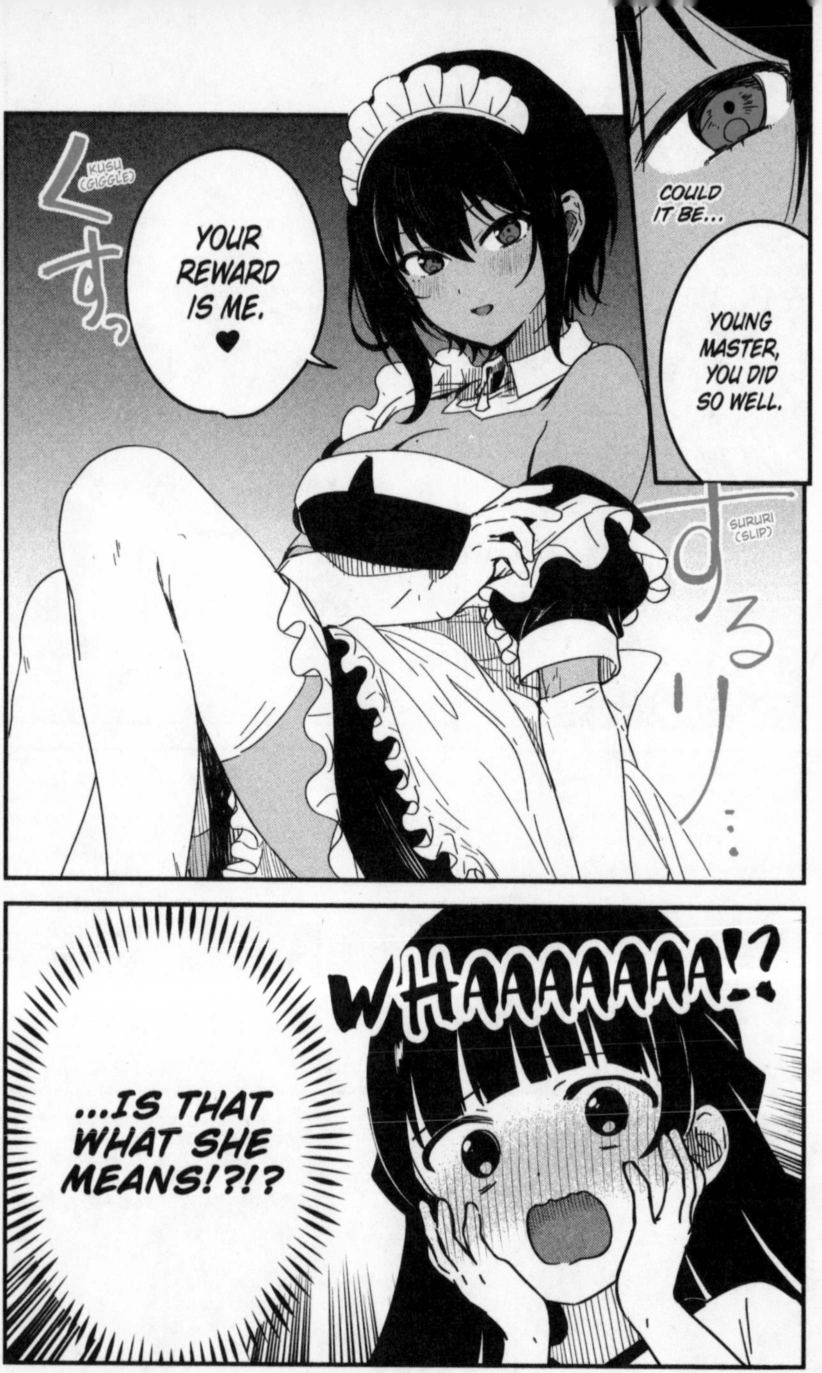
COULD IT BE...
YOUNG MASTER, YOU DID SO WELL.
するり…
SURURI (SLIP)
くすっ
KUSU (GIGGLE)
YOUR REWARD IS ME. ♥
WHAAAAAAA!?
...IS THAT WHAT SHE MEANS!?!?

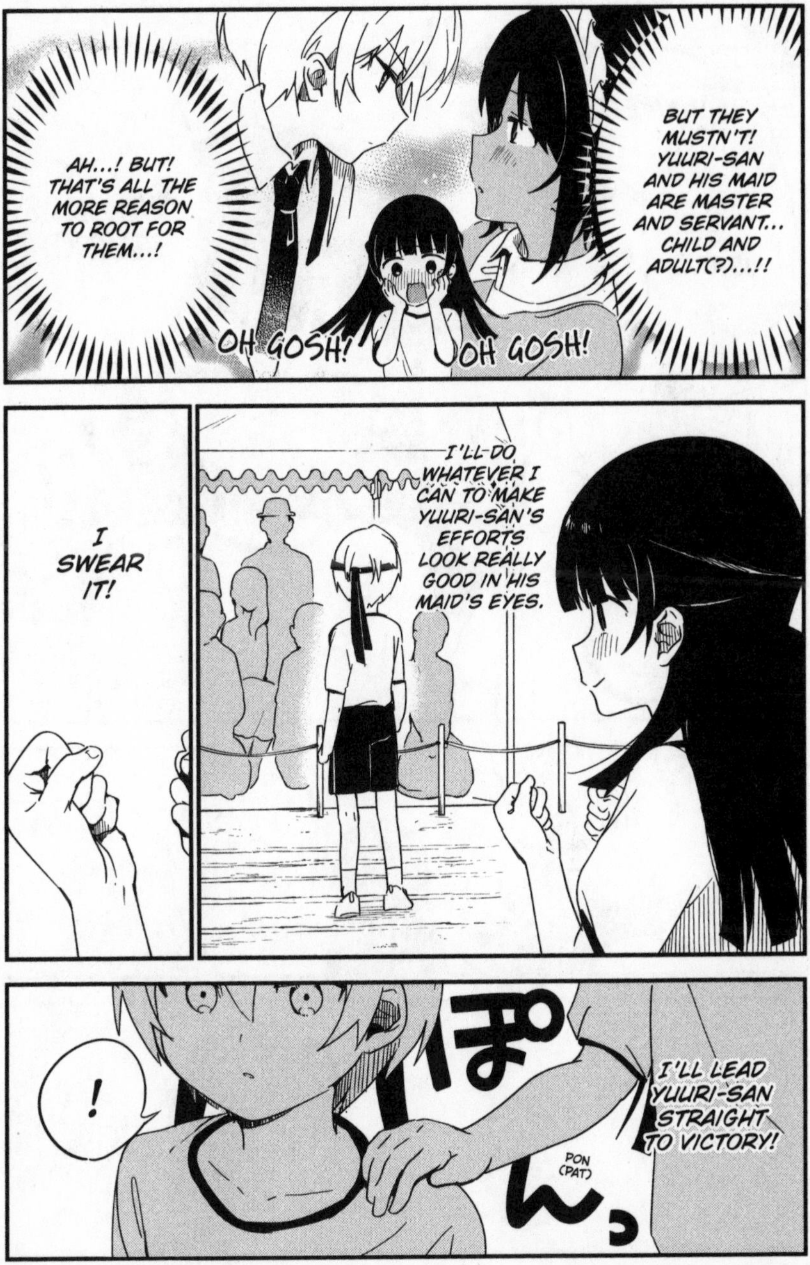
BUT THEY MUSTN'T! YUURI-SAN AND HIS MAID ARE MASTER AND SERVANT... CHILD AND ADULT(?)...!!
AH...! BUT! THAT'S ALL THE MORE REASON TO ROOT FOR THEM...!
OH GOSH!
OH GOSH!
I'LL DO WHATEVER I CAN TO MAKE YUURI-SAN'S EFFORTS LOOK REALLY GOOD IN HIS MAID'S EYES.
I SWEAR IT!
I'LL LEAD YUURI-SAN STRAIGHT TO VICTORY!
ぽんっ
PON (PAT)
!

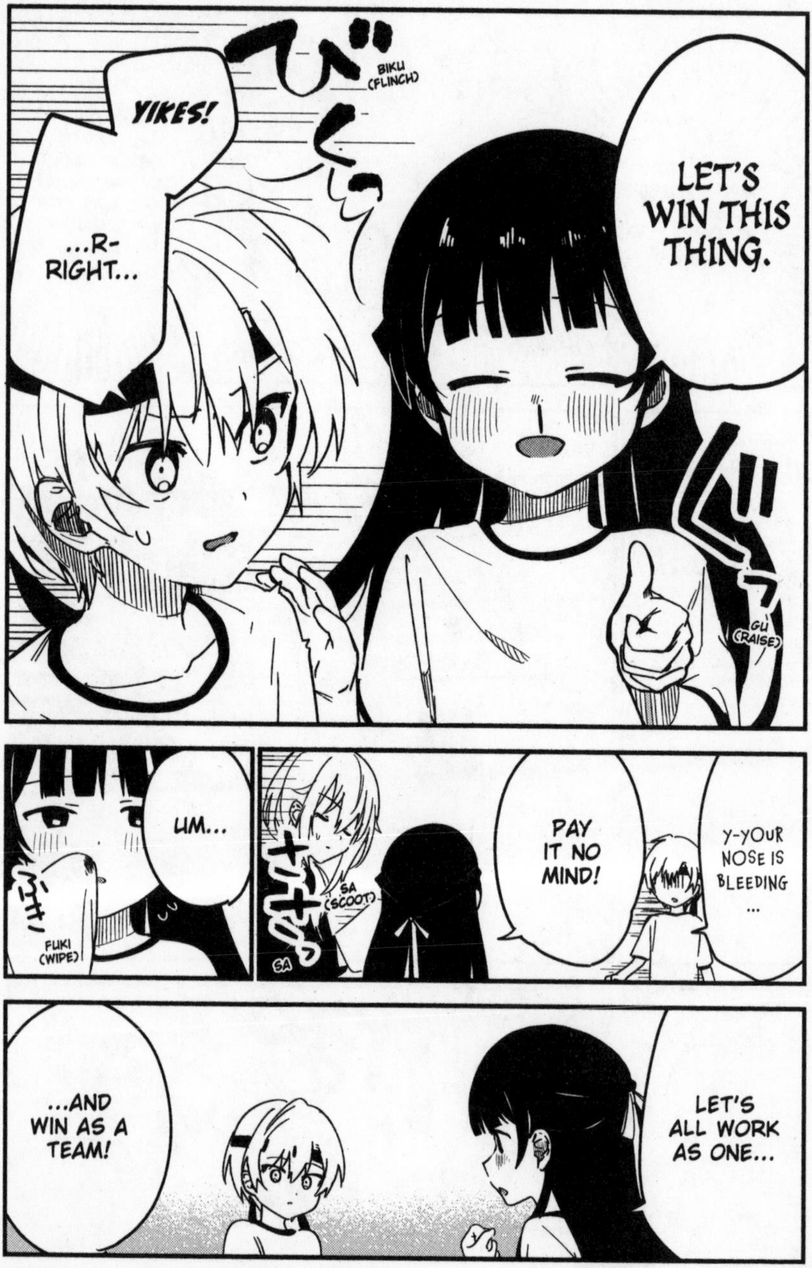

LET'S WIN THIS THING.
GU (RAISE)
BIKU (FLINCH)
YIKES!
...R- RIGHT...
Y-YOUR NOSE IS BLEEDING ...
PAY IT NO MIND!
SA (SCOOT)
SA
UM...
FUKI (WIPE)
LET'S ALL WORK AS ONE...
...AND WIN AS A TEAM!

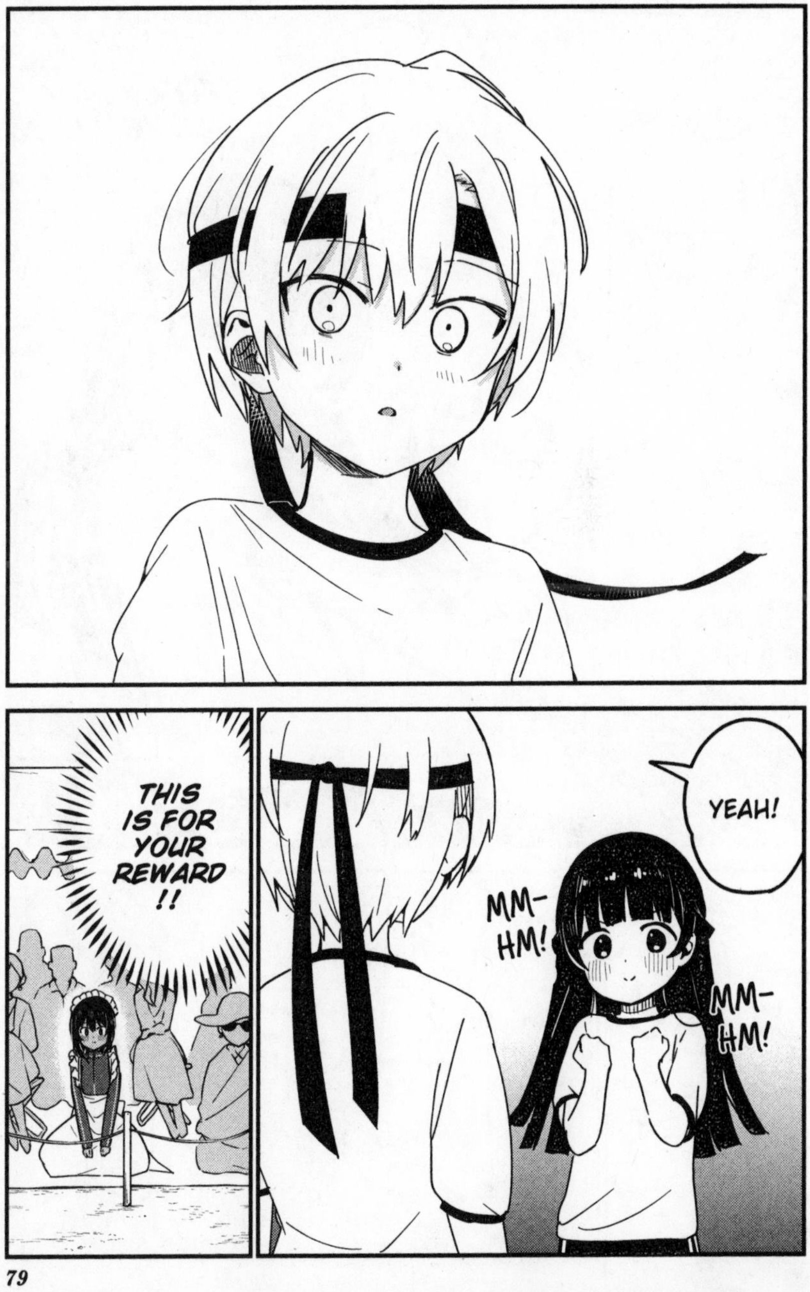
YEAH!
MM-HM!
MM-HM!
THIS IS FOR YOUR REWARD!!

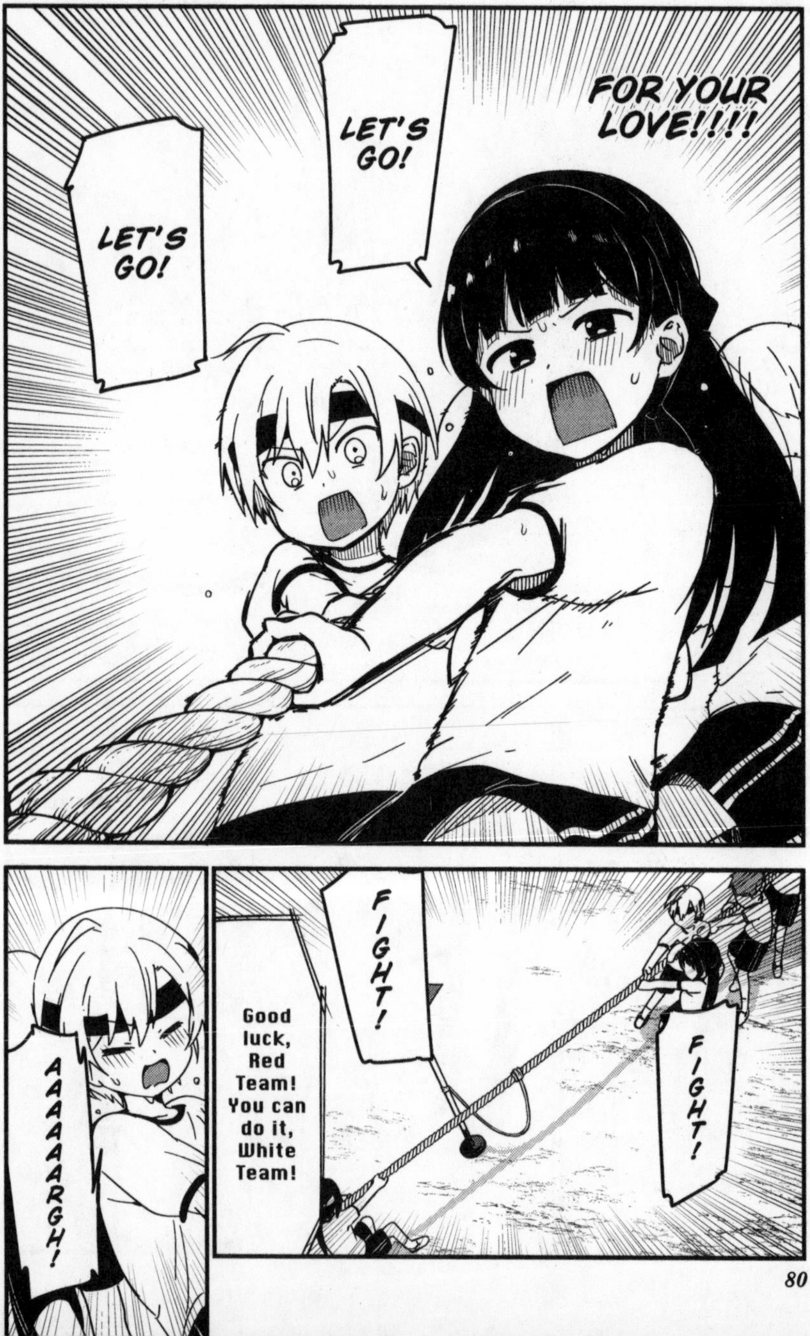
FOR YOUR LOVE!!!!
LET'S GO!
LET'S GO!
FIGHT!
FIGHT!
Good luck, Red Team! You can do it, White Team!
AAAAAARGH!

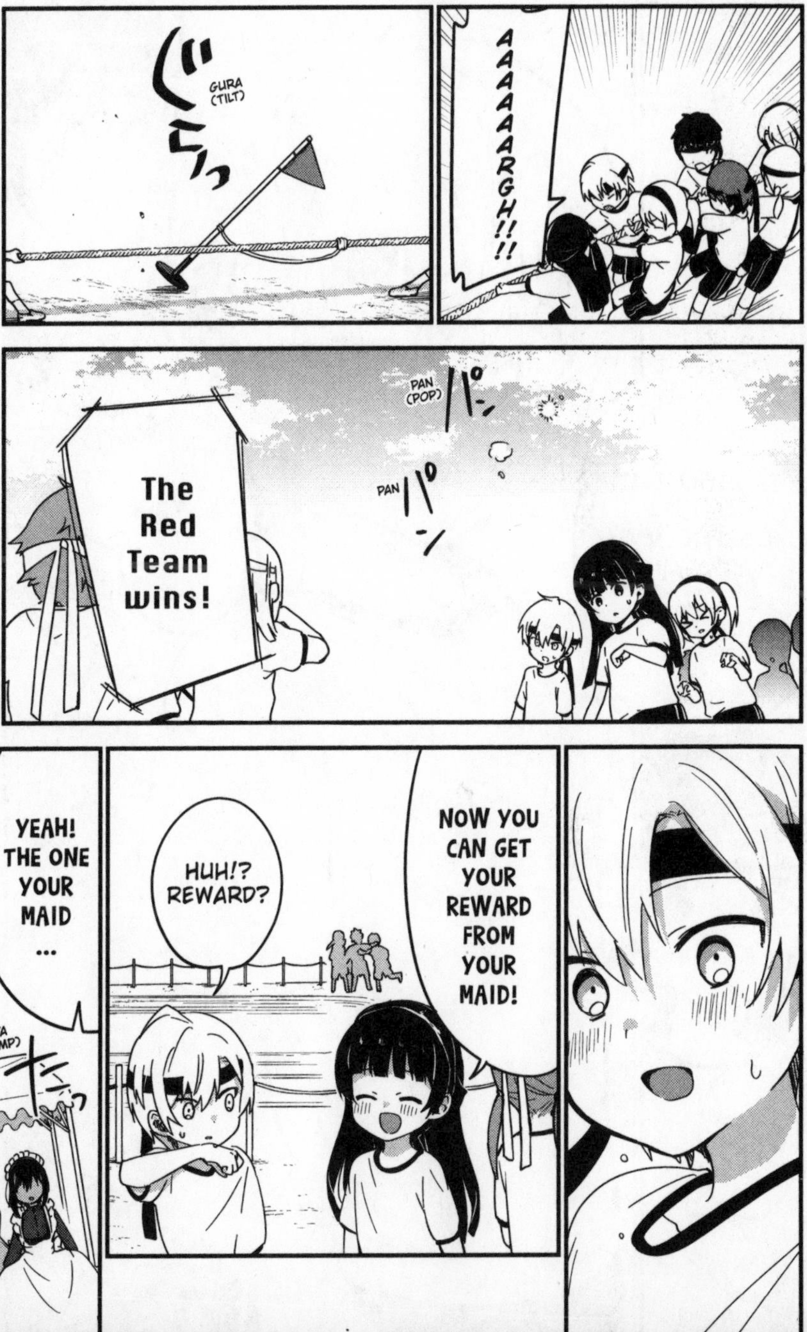
AAAAAAARGH!!!
GURA (TILT)
PAN (POP)
PAN
The Red Team wins!
NOW YOU CAN GET YOUR REWARD FROM YOUR MAID!
HUH!? REWARD?
YEAH! THE ONE YOUR MAID ...
TA (TMP)

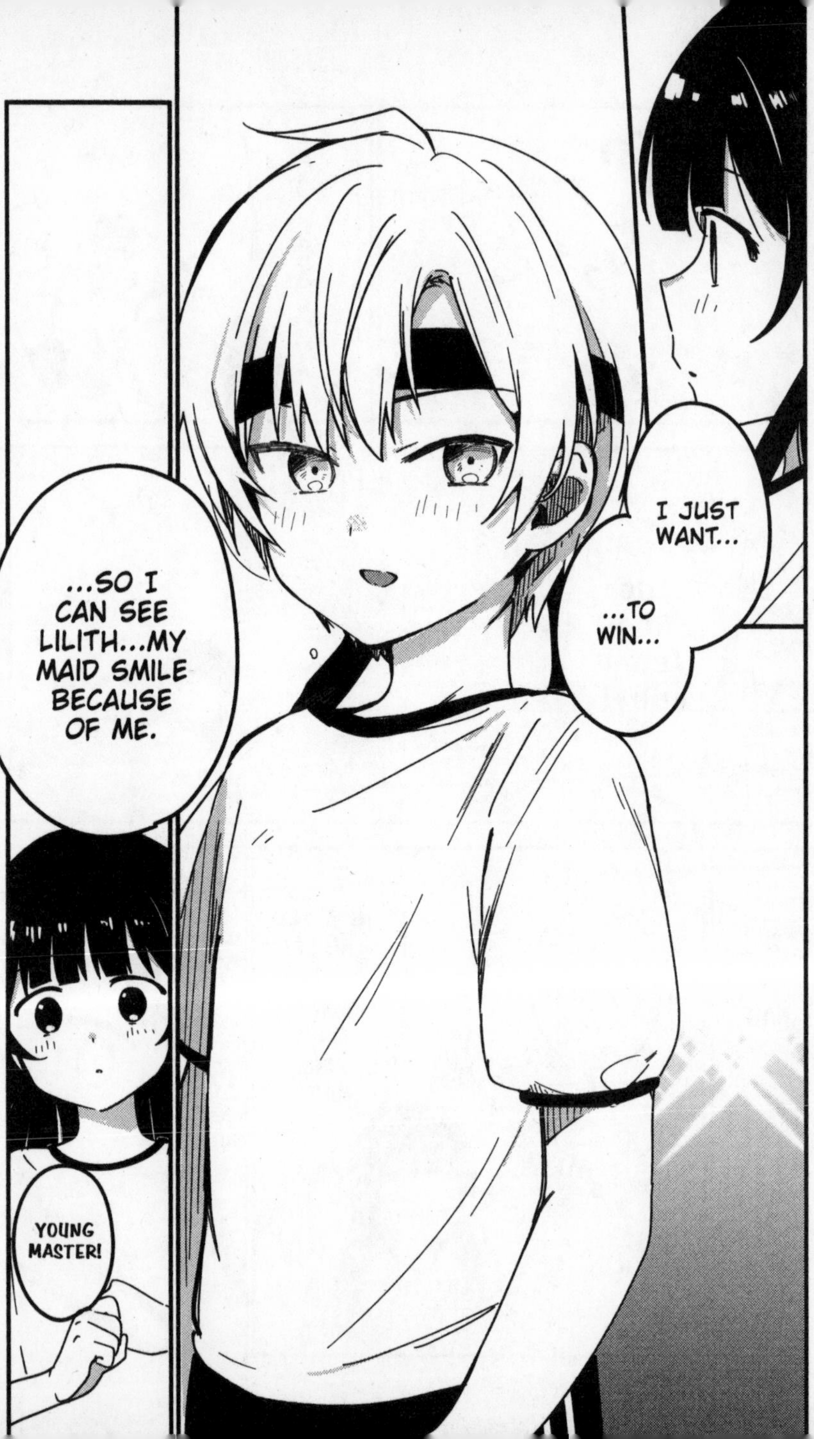
I JUST WANT...
...TO WIN...
...SO I CAN SEE LILITH...MY MAID SMILE BECAUSE OF ME.
YOUNG MASTER!

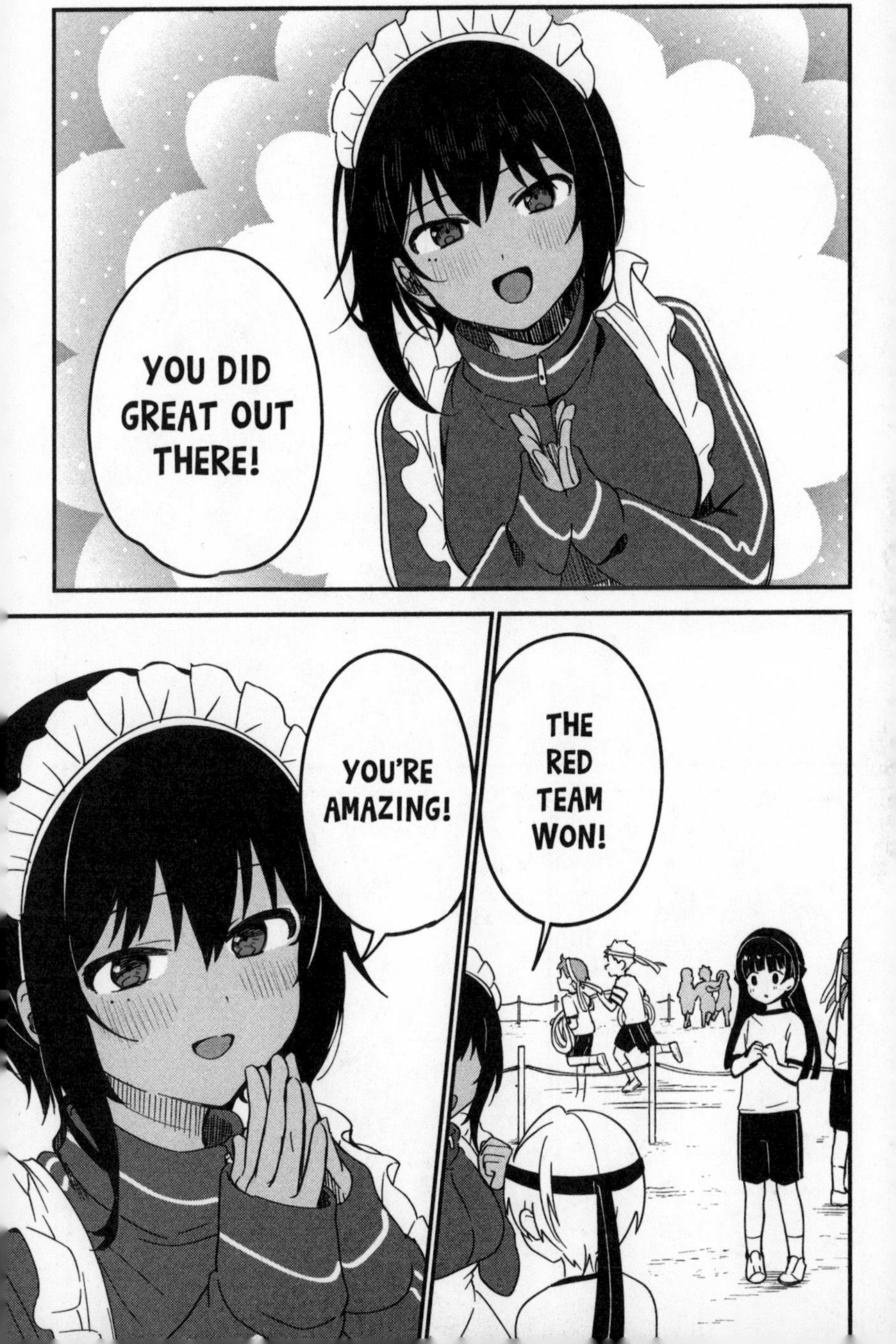
YOU DID GREAT OUT THERE!
THE RED TEAM WON!
YOU'RE AMAZING!

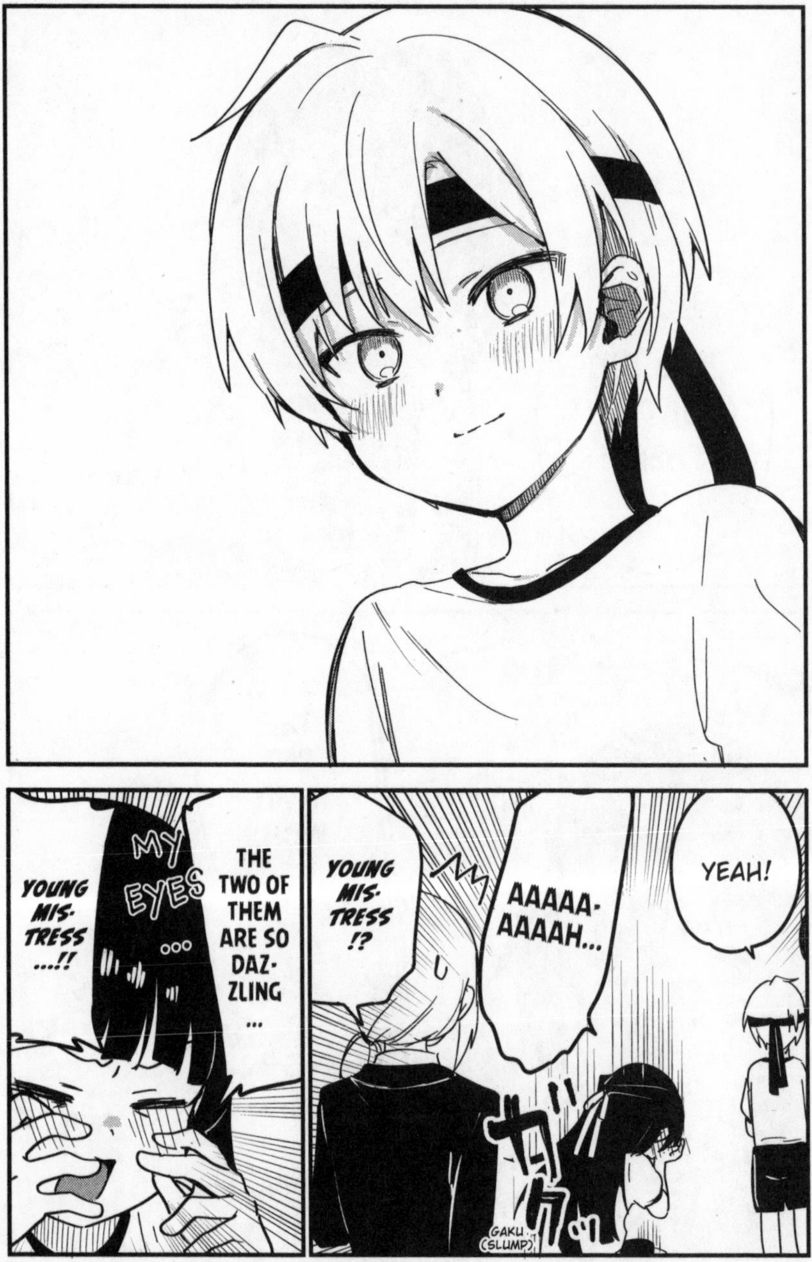

YEAH!
AAAAA-AAAAH...
YOUNG MIS-TRESS !?
GAKU (SLUMP)
THE TWO OF THEM ARE SO DAZ-ZLING ...
MY EYES ...
YOUNG MIS-TRESS ...!!

The Maid I Hired Recently Is Mysterious

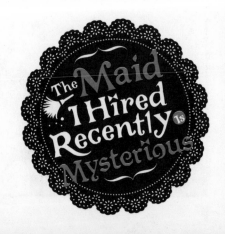

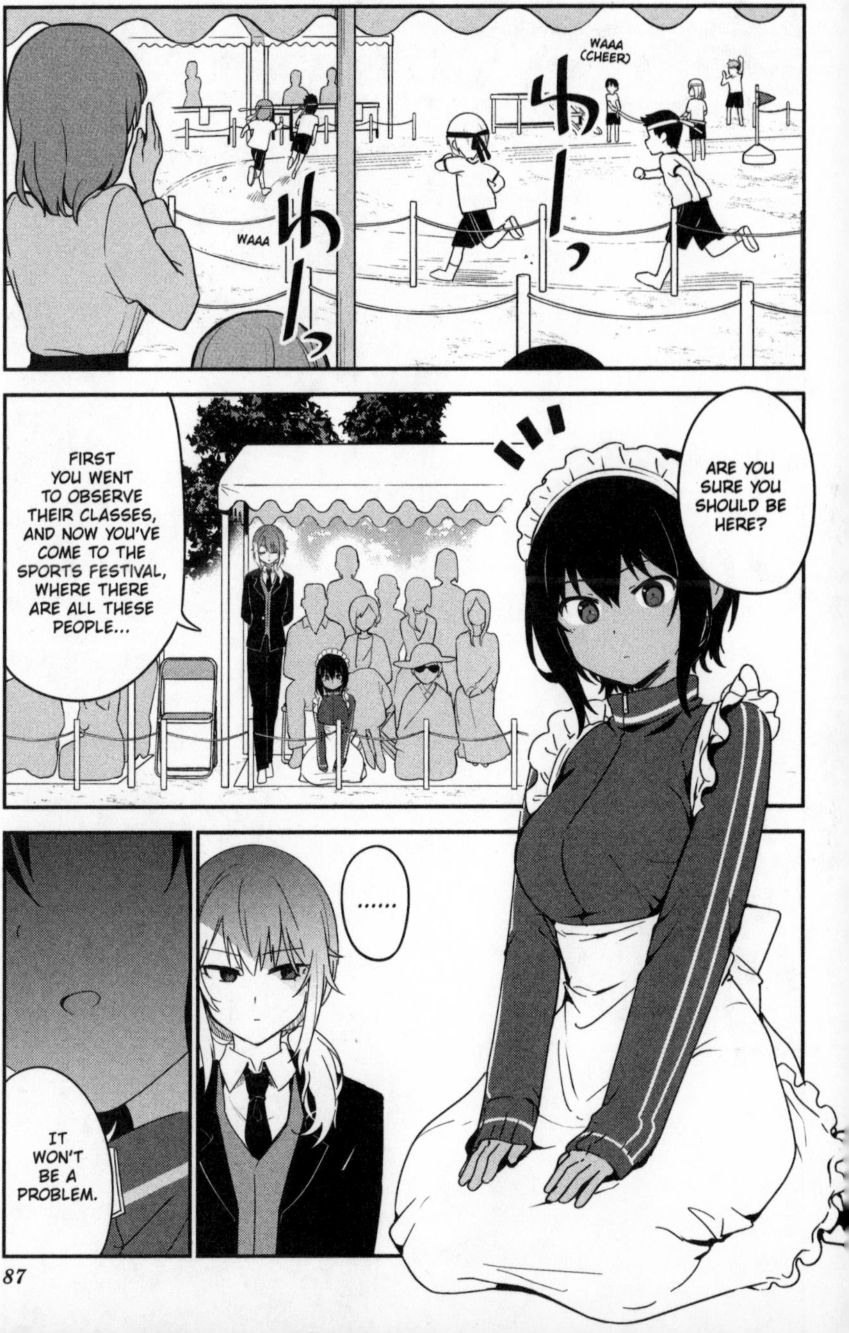

WAAA (CHEER)
WAAA
ARE YOU SURE YOU SHOULD BE HERE?
FIRST YOU WENT TO OBSERVE THEIR CLASSES, AND NOW YOU'VE COME TO THE SPORTS FESTIVAL, WHERE THERE ARE ALL THESE PEOPLE...
....
IT WON'T BE A PROBLEM.

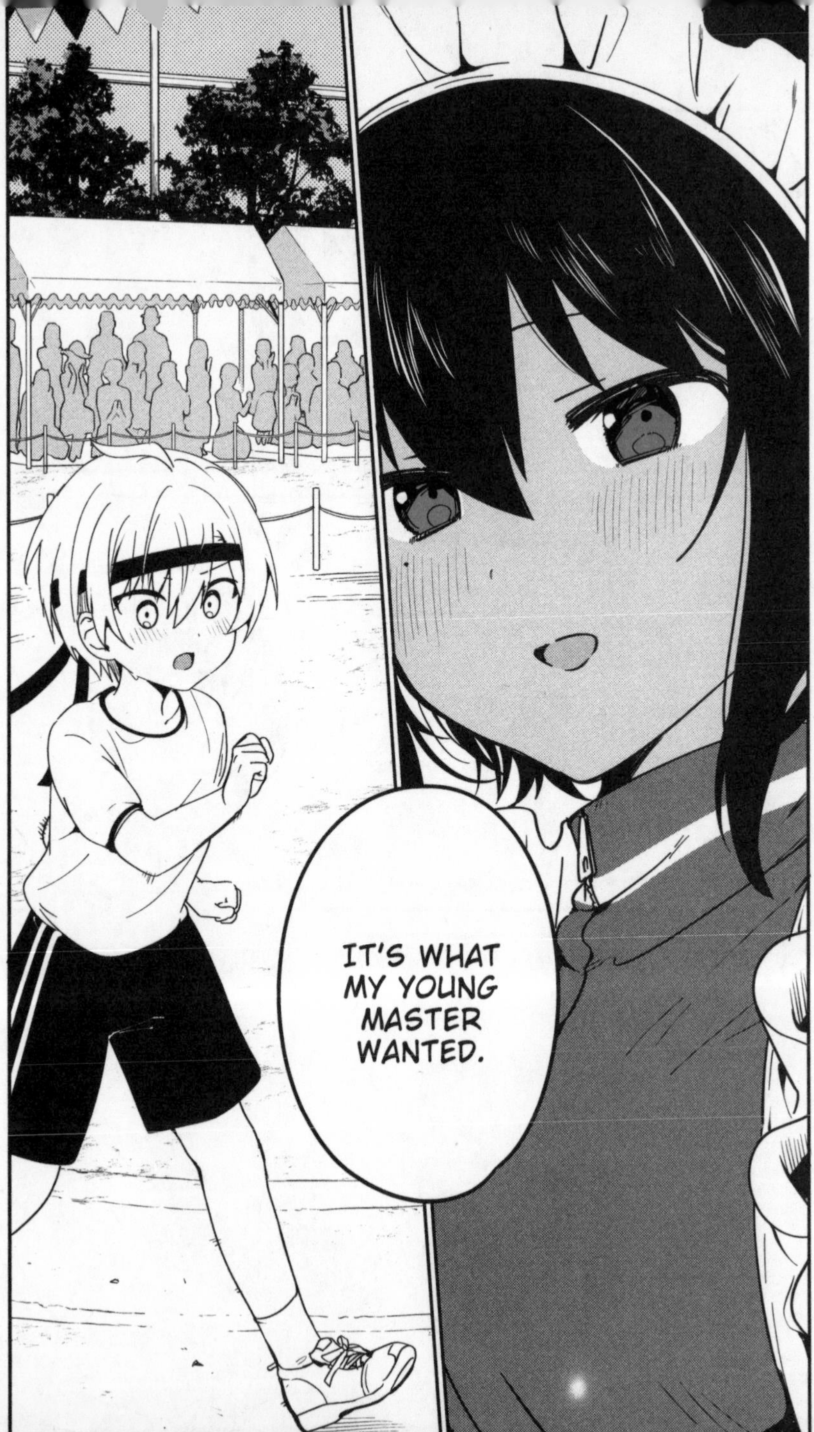
IT'S WHAT MY YOUNG MASTER WANTED.

CHAPTER 33

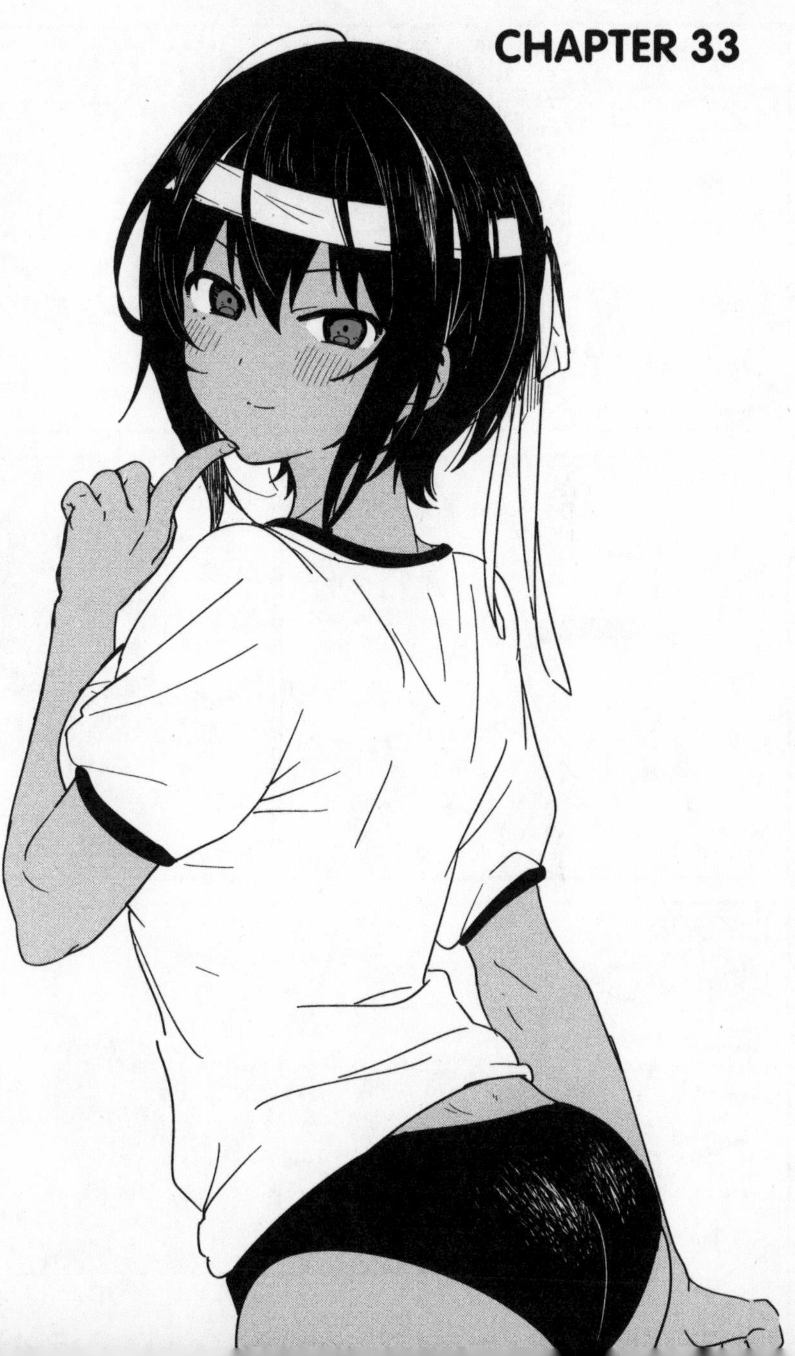

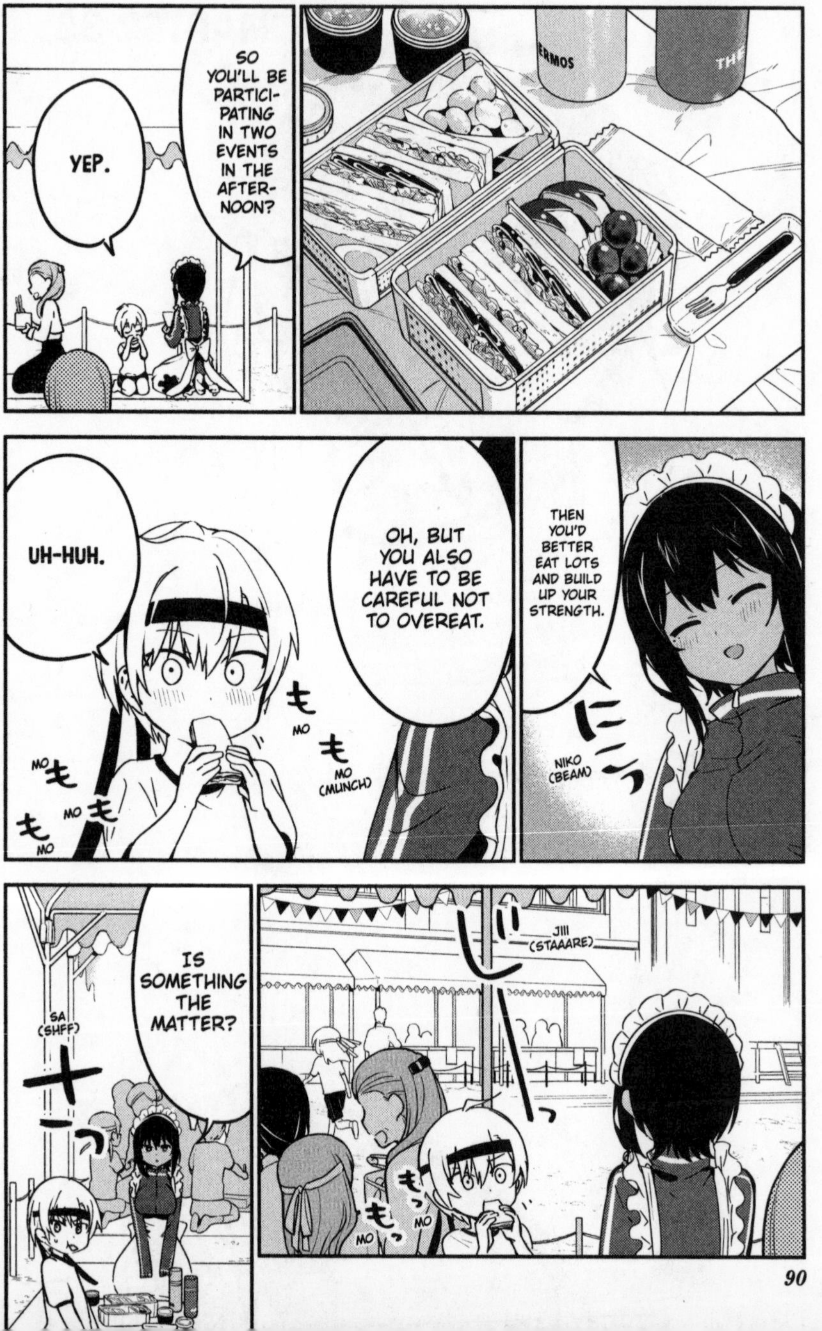
ERMOS
THE
SO YOU'LL BE PARTICI-PATING IN TWO EVENTS IN THE AFTER-NOON?
YEP.
THEN YOU'D BETTER EAT LOTS AND BUILD UP YOUR STRENGTH.
NIKO (BEAM)
OH, BUT YOU ALSO HAVE TO BE CAREFUL NOT TO OVEREAT.
MO
MO (MUNCH)
UH-HUH.
MO
MO
MO
JIII (STAAARE)
MO
MO
IS SOMETHING THE MATTER?
SA (SHFF)

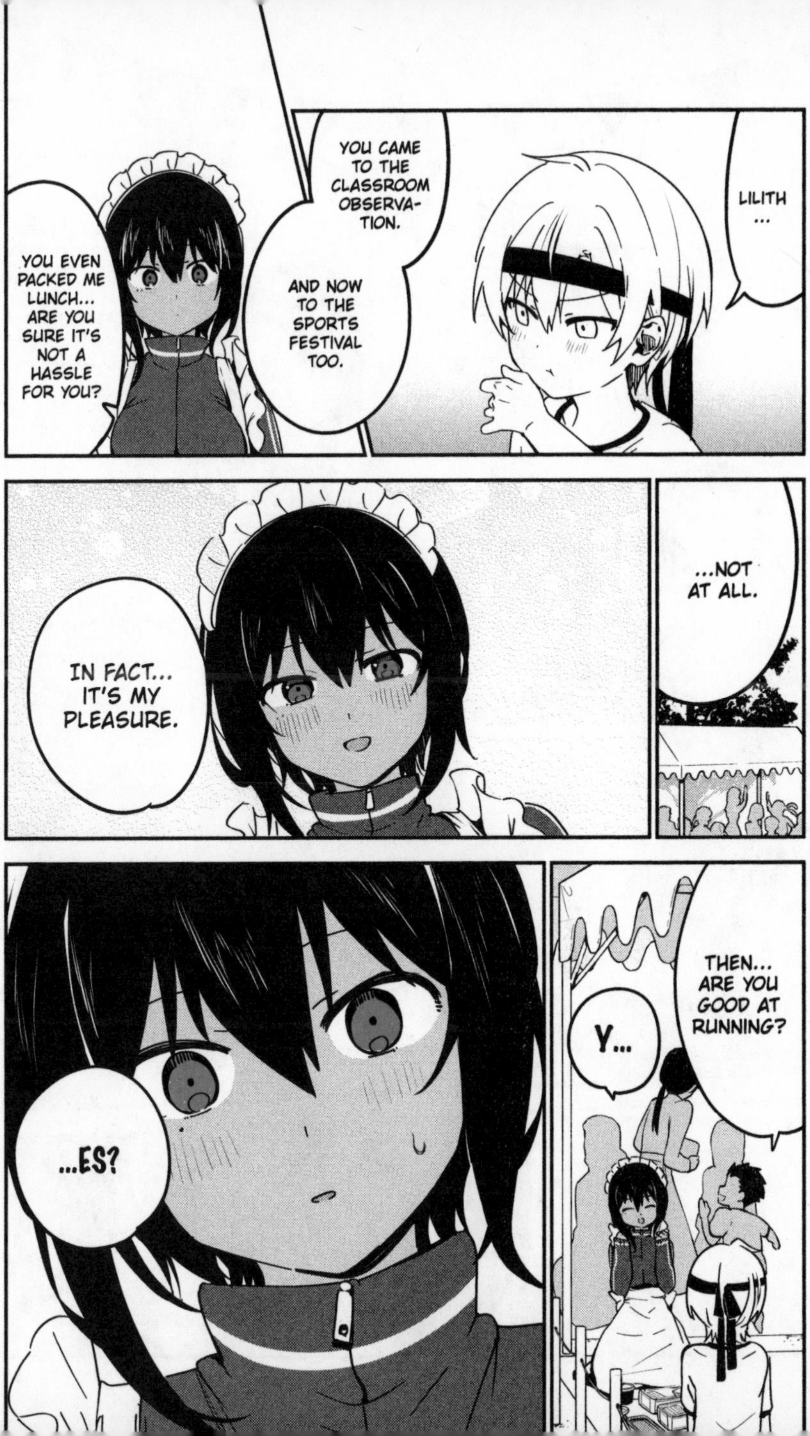
LILITH ...
YOU CAME TO THE CLASSROOM OBSERVA- TION.
AND NOW TO THE SPORTS FESTIVAL TOO.
YOU EVEN PACKED ME LUNCH... ARE YOU SURE IT'S NOT A HASSLE FOR YOU?
...NOT AT ALL.
IN FACT... IT'S MY PLEASURE.
THEN... ARE YOU GOOD AT RUNNING?
Y...
...ES?

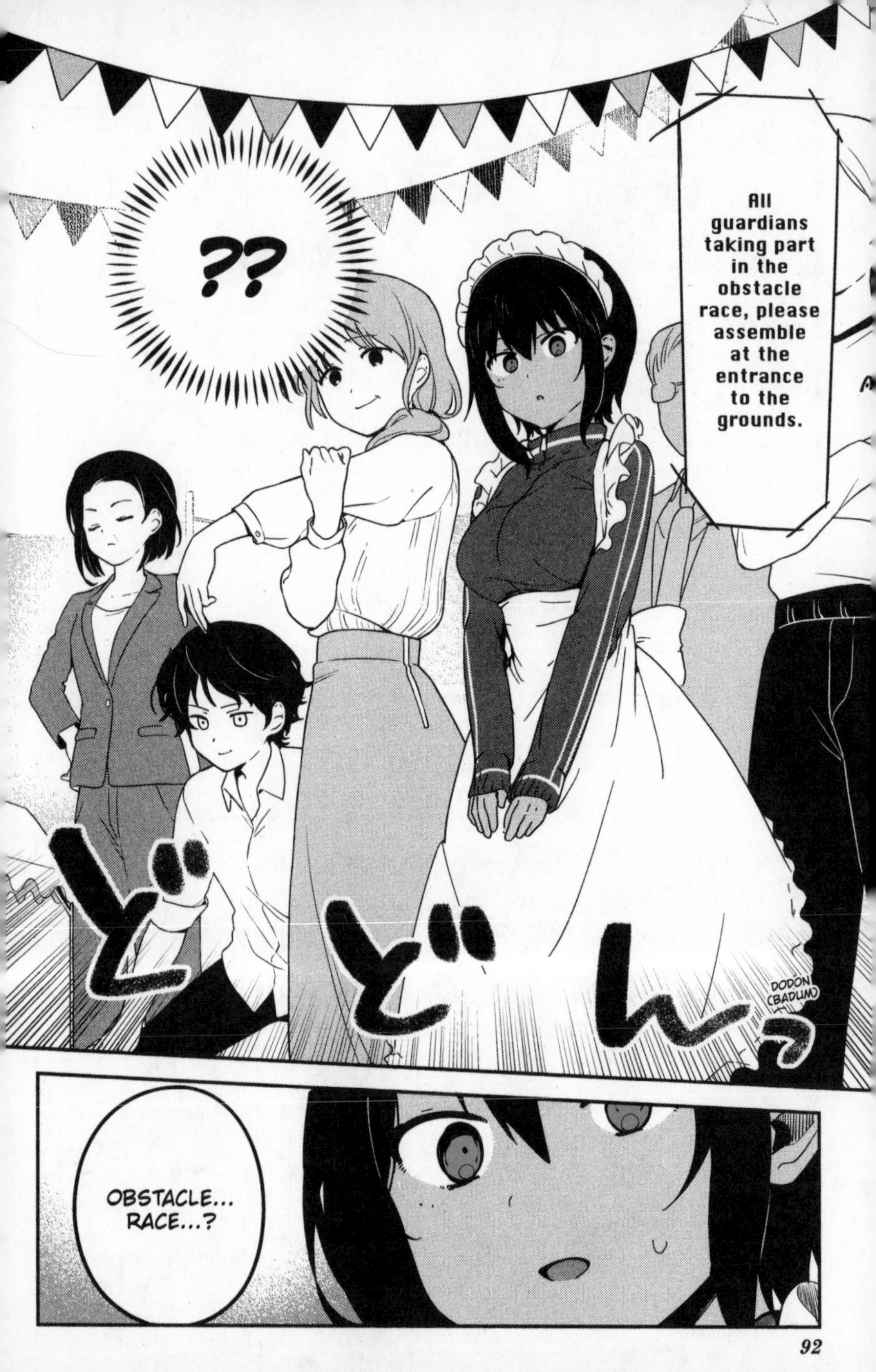
All guardians taking part in the obstacle race, please assemble at the entrance to the grounds.
??
どどんっ
DODON (BADUM)
OBSTACLE... RACE...?

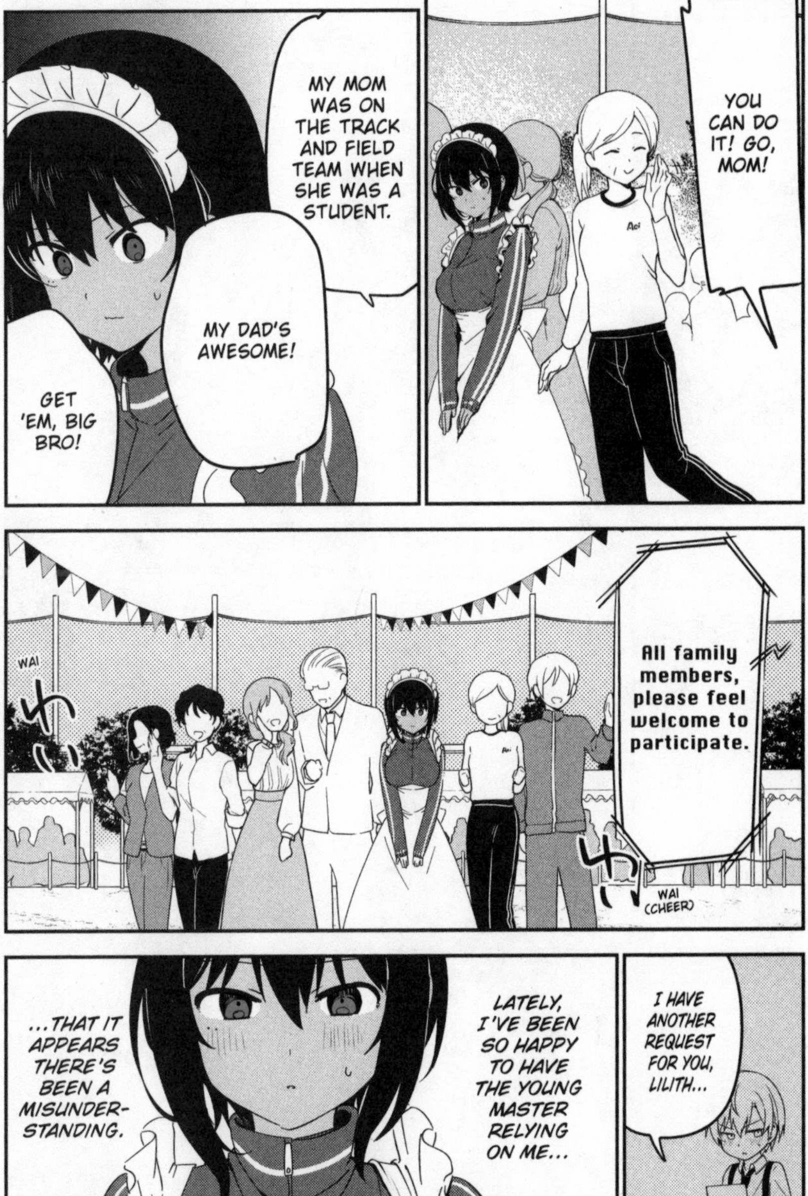
YOU CAN DO IT! GO, MOM!
MY MOM WAS ON THE TRACK AND FIELD TEAM WHEN SHE WAS A STUDENT.
MY DAD'S AWESOME!
GET 'EM, BIG BRO!
All family members, please feel welcome to participate.
WAI
WAI (CHEER)
I HAVE ANOTHER REQUEST FOR YOU, LILITH...
LATELY, I'VE BEEN SO HAPPY TO HAVE THE YOUNG MASTER RELYING ON ME...
...THAT IT APPEARS THERE'S BEEN A MISUNDERSTANDING.

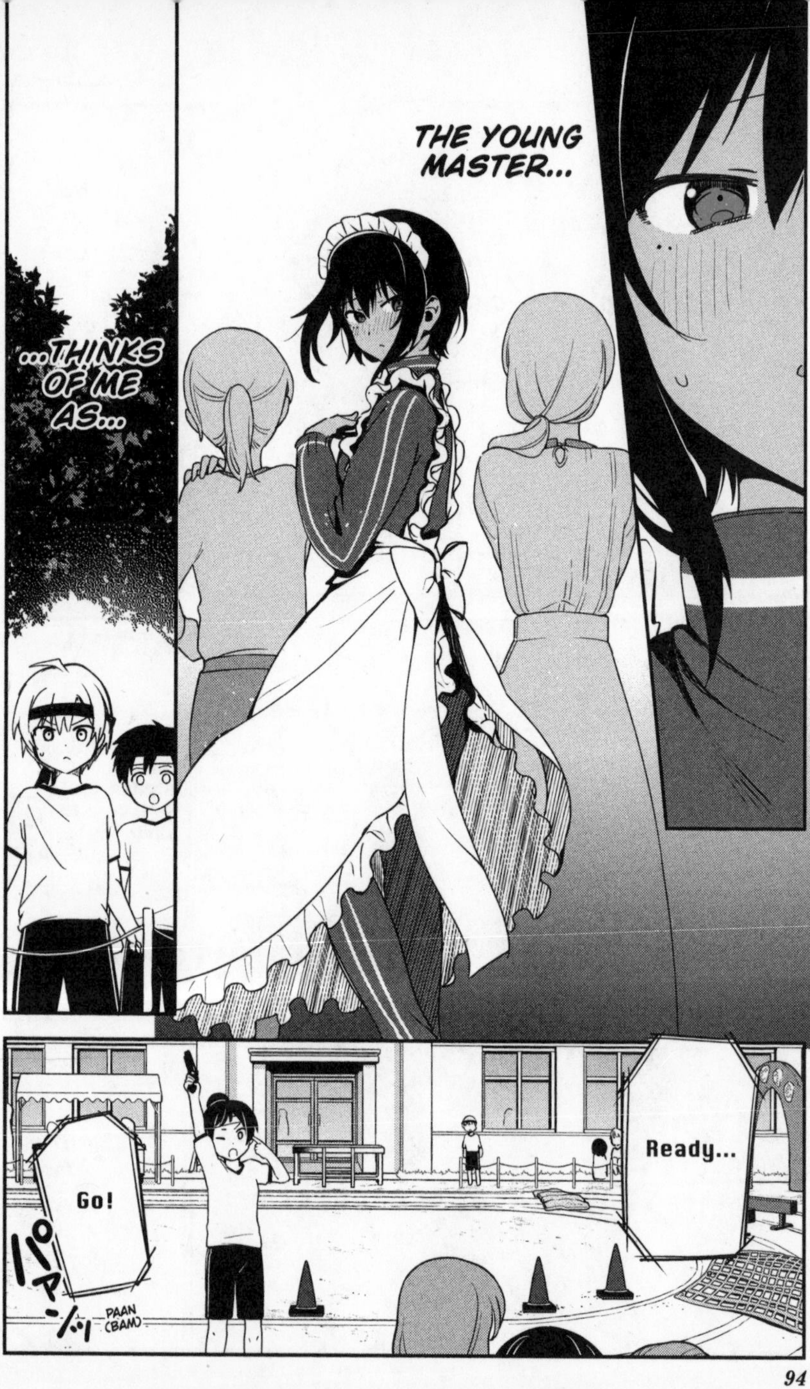
THE YOUNG MASTER...
...THINKS OF ME AS...
Ready...
Go!
パァンッ
PAAN (BAM)

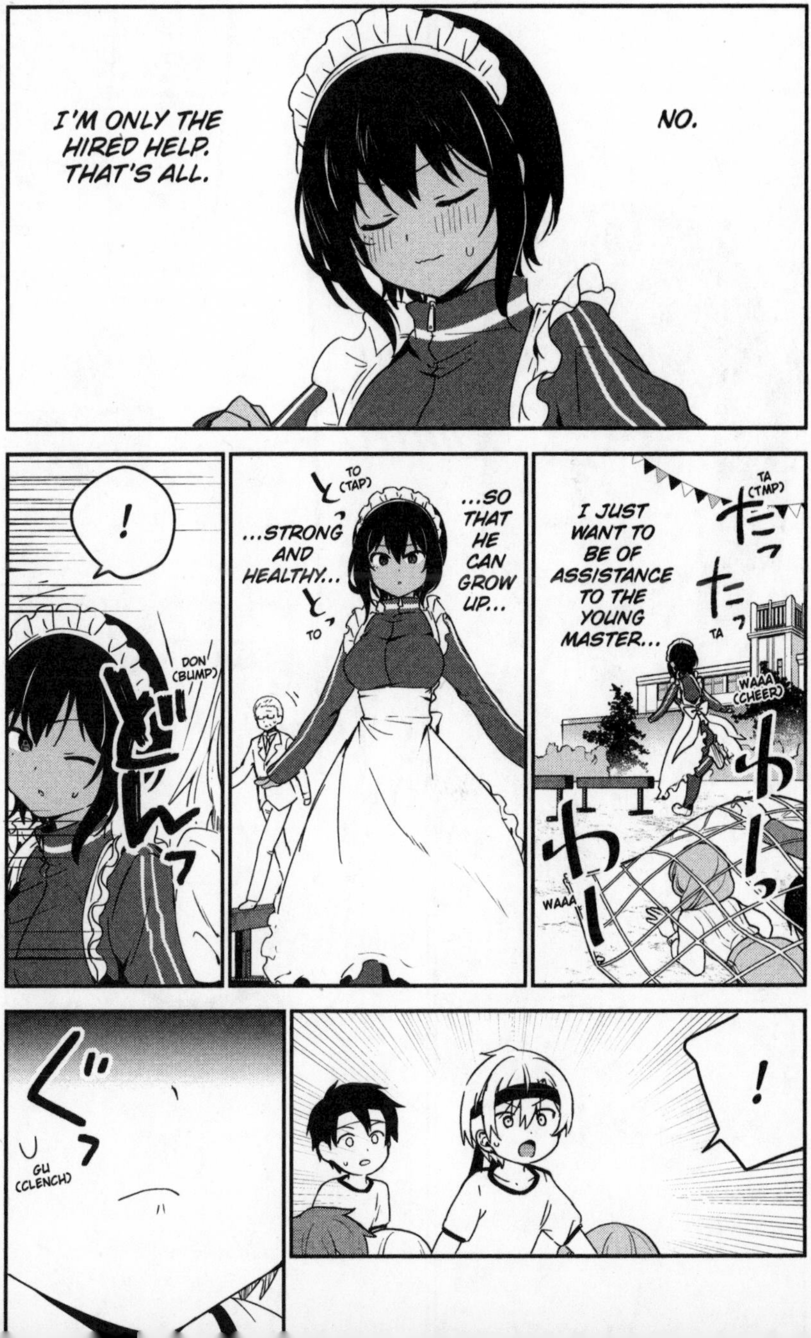
NO.
I'M ONLY THE HIRED HELP. THAT'S ALL.
TA (TMP)
I JUST WANT TO BE OF ASSISTANCE TO THE YOUNG MASTER...
TA
WAAA (CHEER)
WAAA
...SO THAT HE CAN GROW UP...
TO (TAP)
...STRONG AND HEALTHY...
TO
!
DON (BUMP)
!
GU (CLENCH)

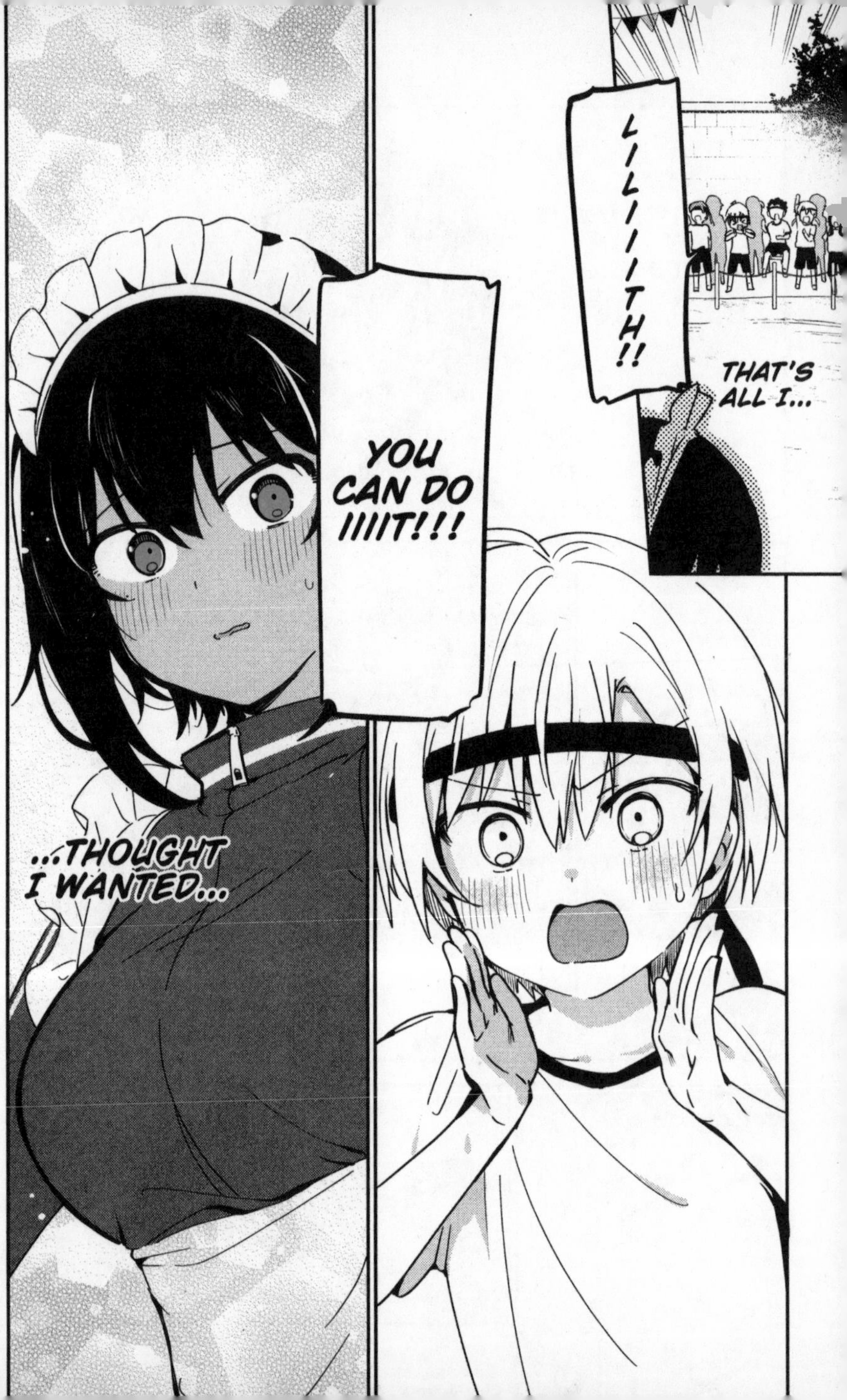
LILIIIITH!!
THAT'S ALL I...
YOU CAN DO IIIIT!!!
...THOUGHT I WANTED...

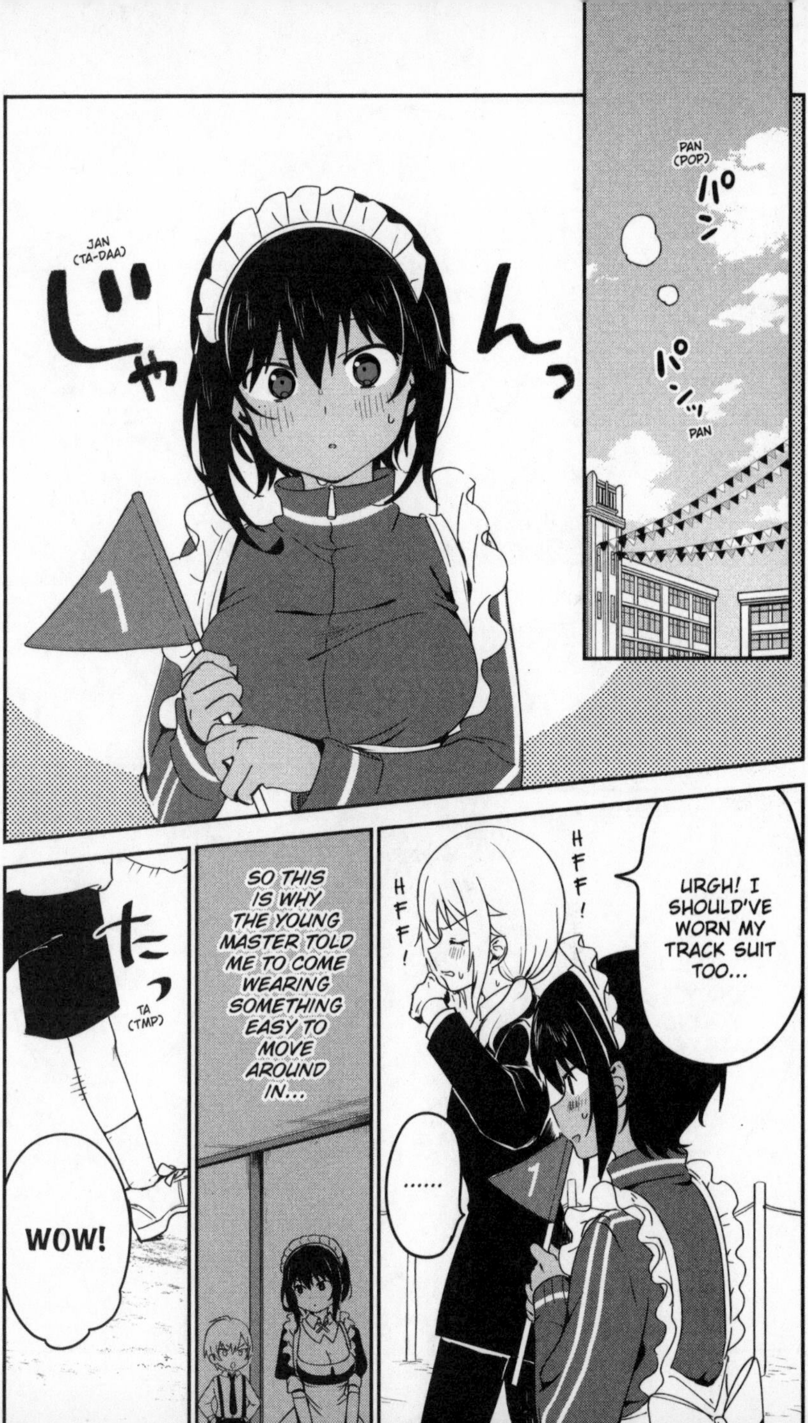
PAN (POP)
パン
パンッ
PAN
JAN (TA-DAA)
じゃんっ
HFF! HFF!
URGH! I SHOULD'VE WORN MY TRACK SUIT TOO...
......
SO THIS IS WHY THE YOUNG MASTER TOLD ME TO COME WEARING SOMETHING EASY TO MOVE AROUND IN...
たっ
TA (TMP)
WOW!

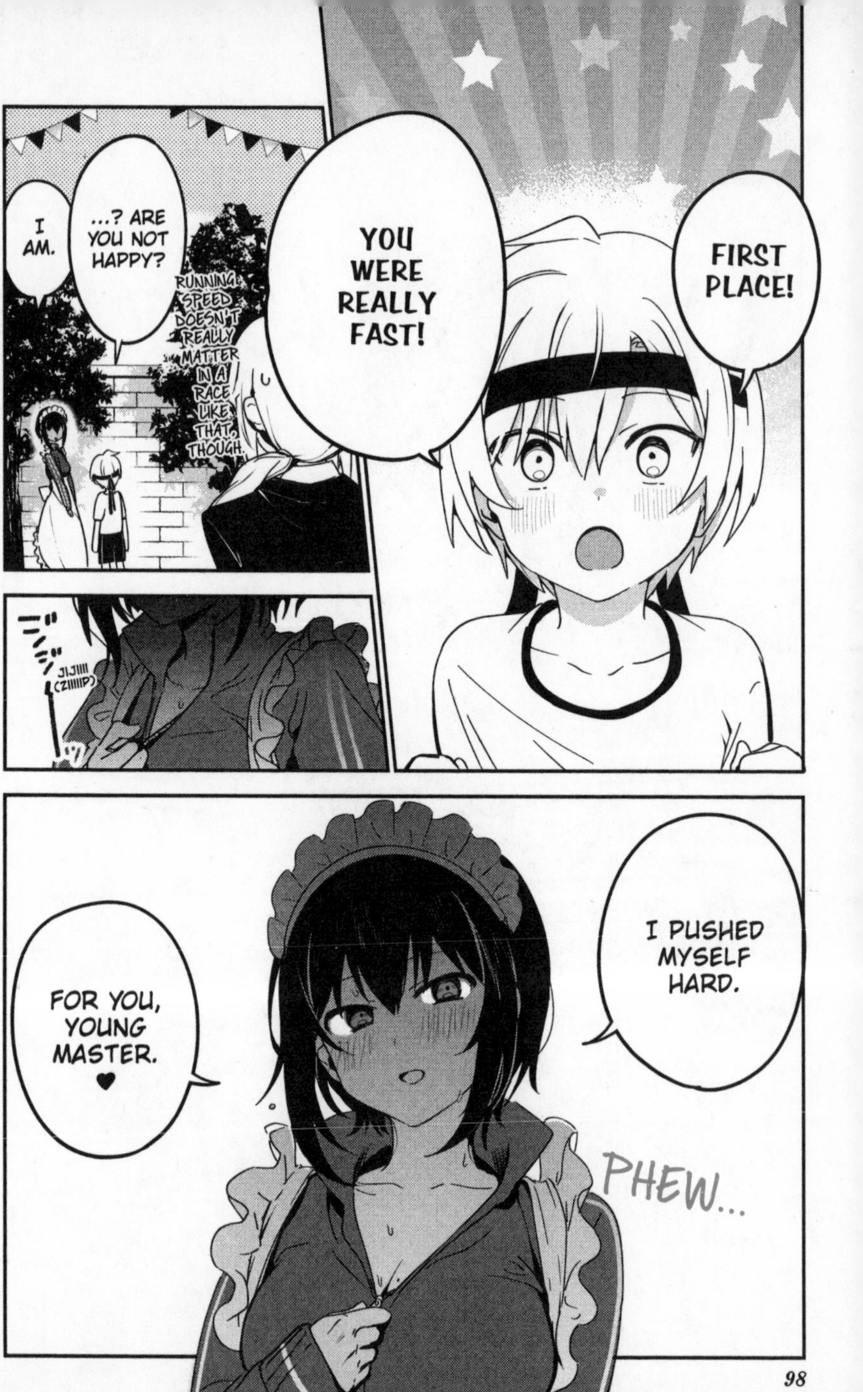
FIRST PLACE!
YOU WERE REALLY FAST!
...? ARE YOU NOT HAPPY?
I AM.
RUNNING SPEED DOESN'T REALLY MATTER IN A RACE LIKE THAT, THOUGH.
JIJIIII (ZIIIIIP)
I PUSHED MYSELF HARD.
FOR YOU, YOUNG MASTER. ♥
PHEW...

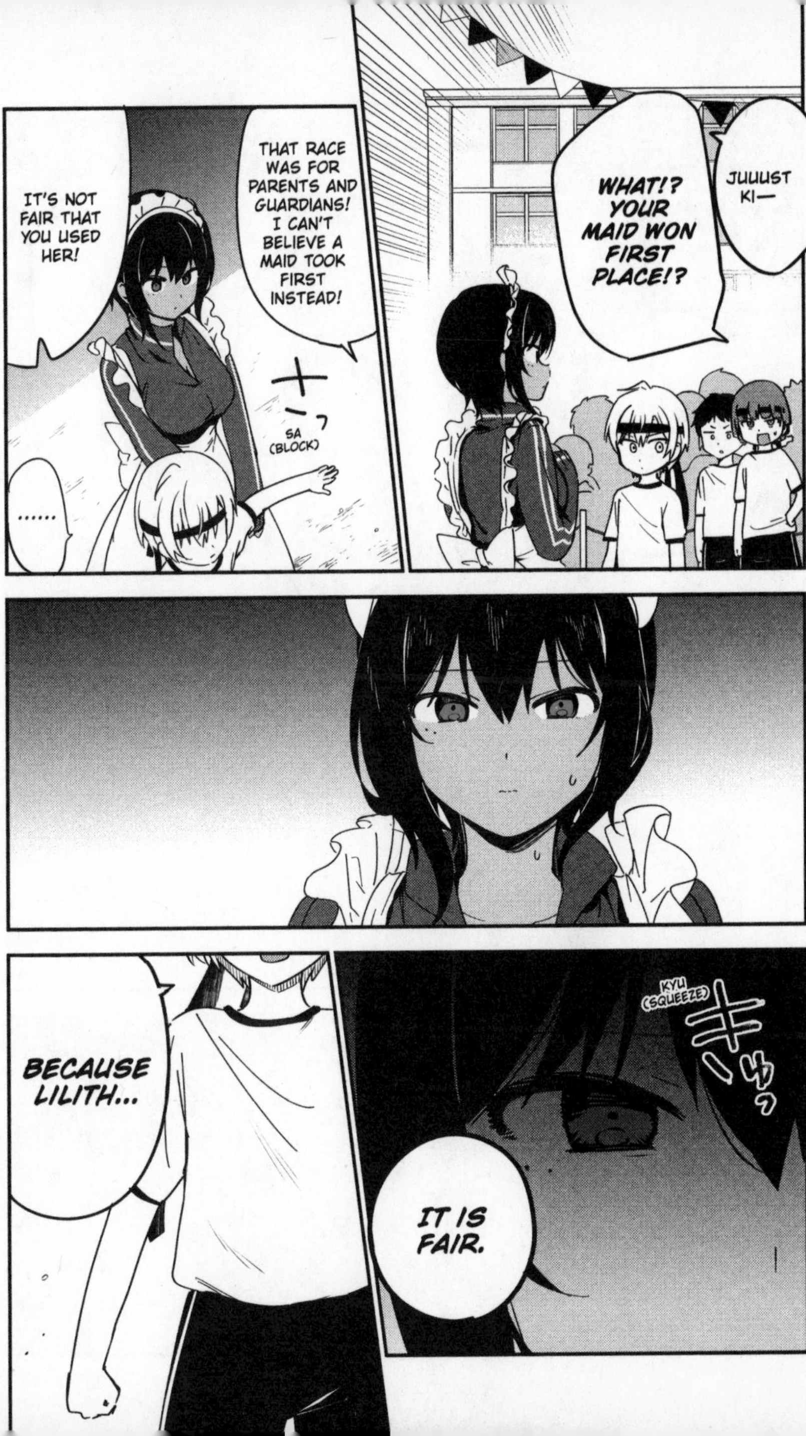
JUUUST KI—
WHAT!? YOUR MAID WON FIRST PLACE!?
THAT RACE WAS FOR PARENTS AND GUARDIANS! I CAN'T BELIEVE A MAID TOOK FIRST INSTEAD!
IT'S NOT FAIR THAT YOU USED HER!
SA (BLOCK)
......
KYU (SQUEEZE)
IT IS FAIR.
BECAUSE LILITH...

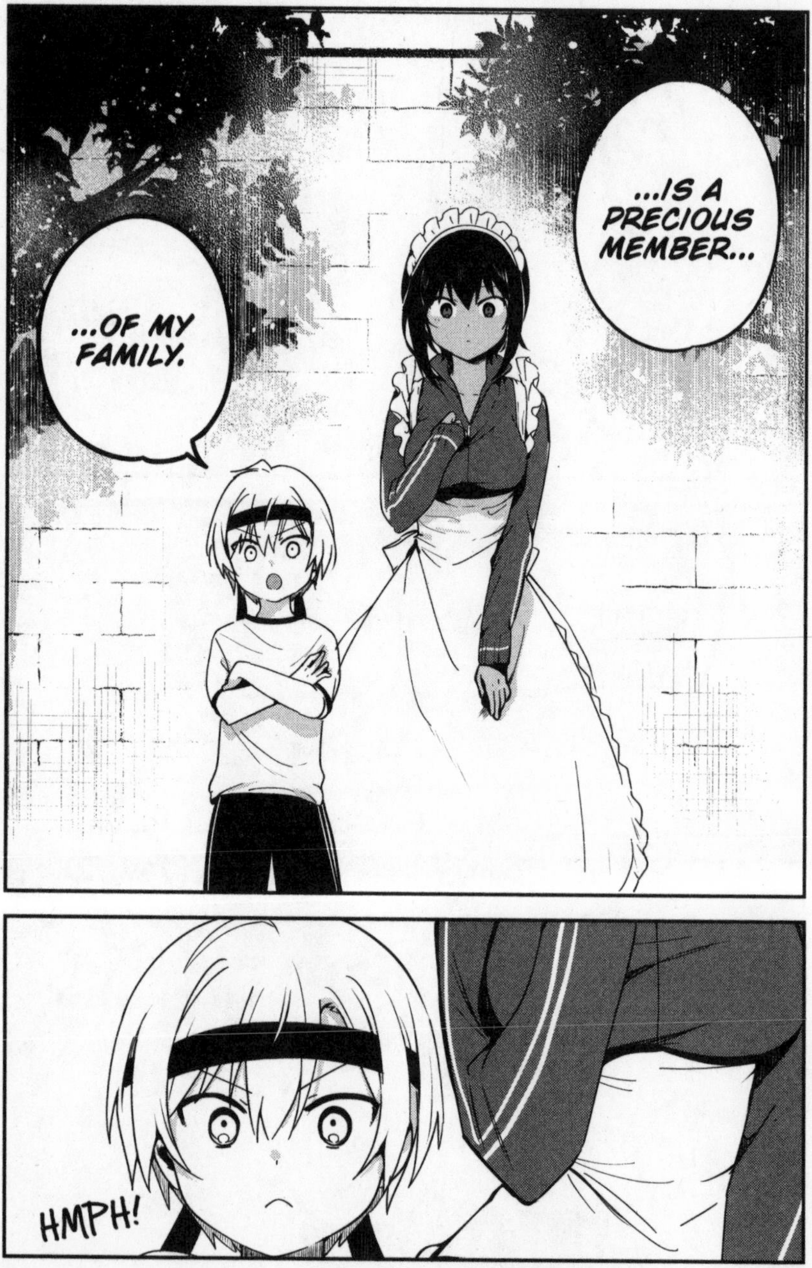
...IS A PRECIOUS MEMBER...
...OF MY FAMILY.
HMPH!

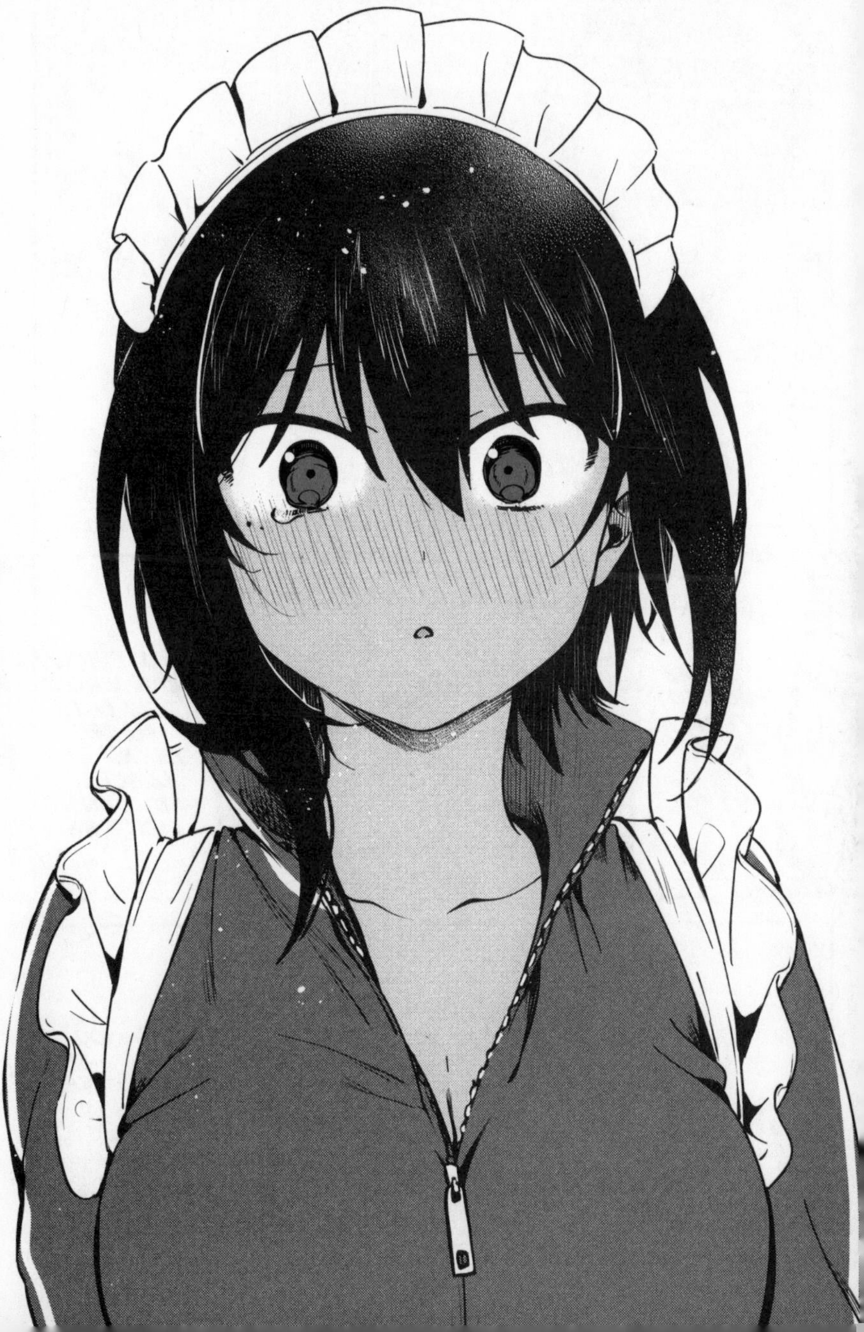

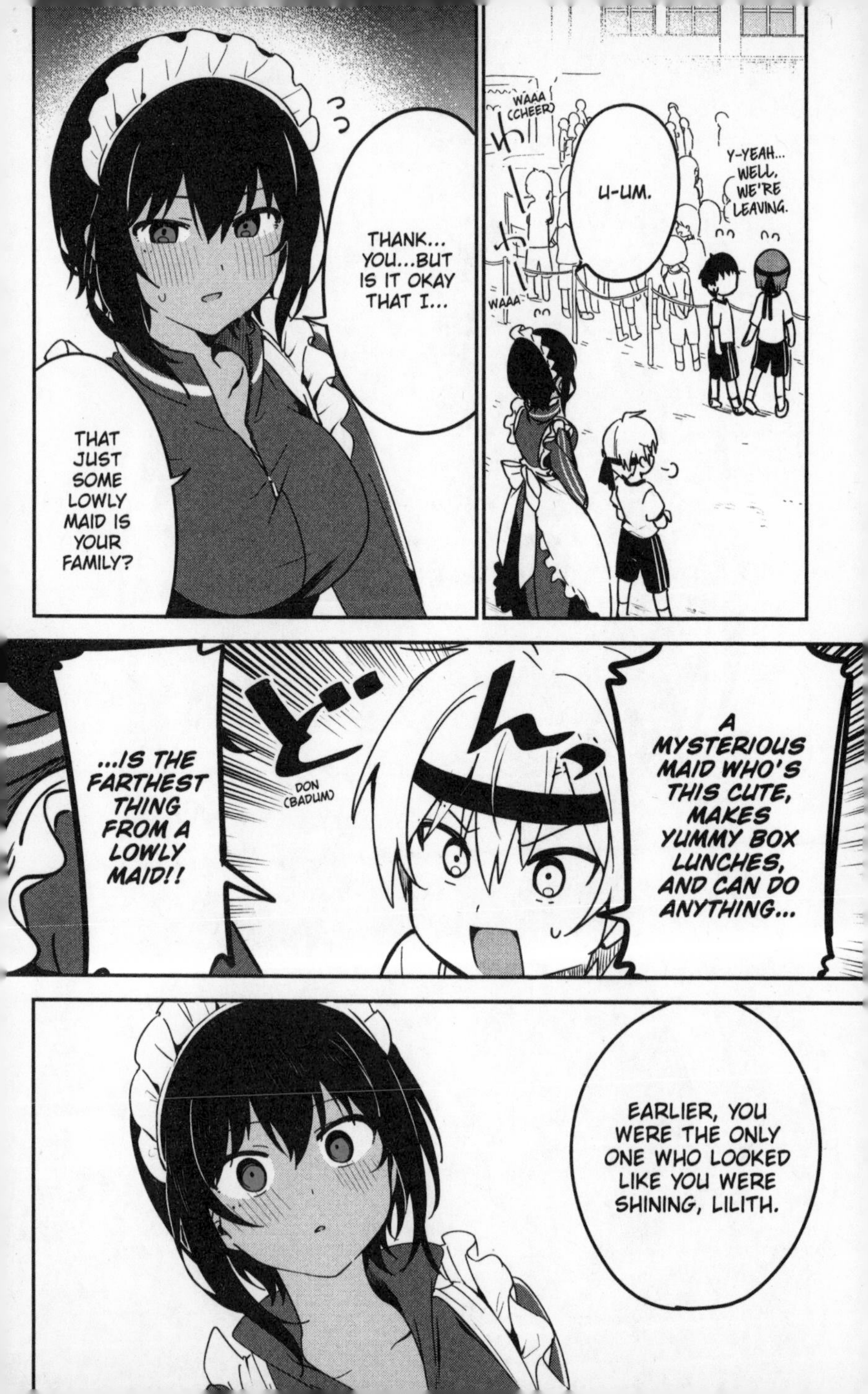

Y-YEAH... WELL, WE'RE LEAVING.
WAAA (CHEER)
U-UM.
WAAA
THANK... YOU...BUT IS IT OKAY THAT I...
THAT JUST SOME LOWLY MAID IS YOUR FAMILY?
A MYSTERIOUS MAID WHO'S THIS CUTE, MAKES YUMMY BOX LUNCHES, AND CAN DO ANYTHING...
DON (BADUM)
...IS THE FARTHEST THING FROM A LOWLY MAID!!
EARLIER, YOU WERE THE ONLY ONE WHO LOOKED LIKE YOU WERE SHINING, LILITH.

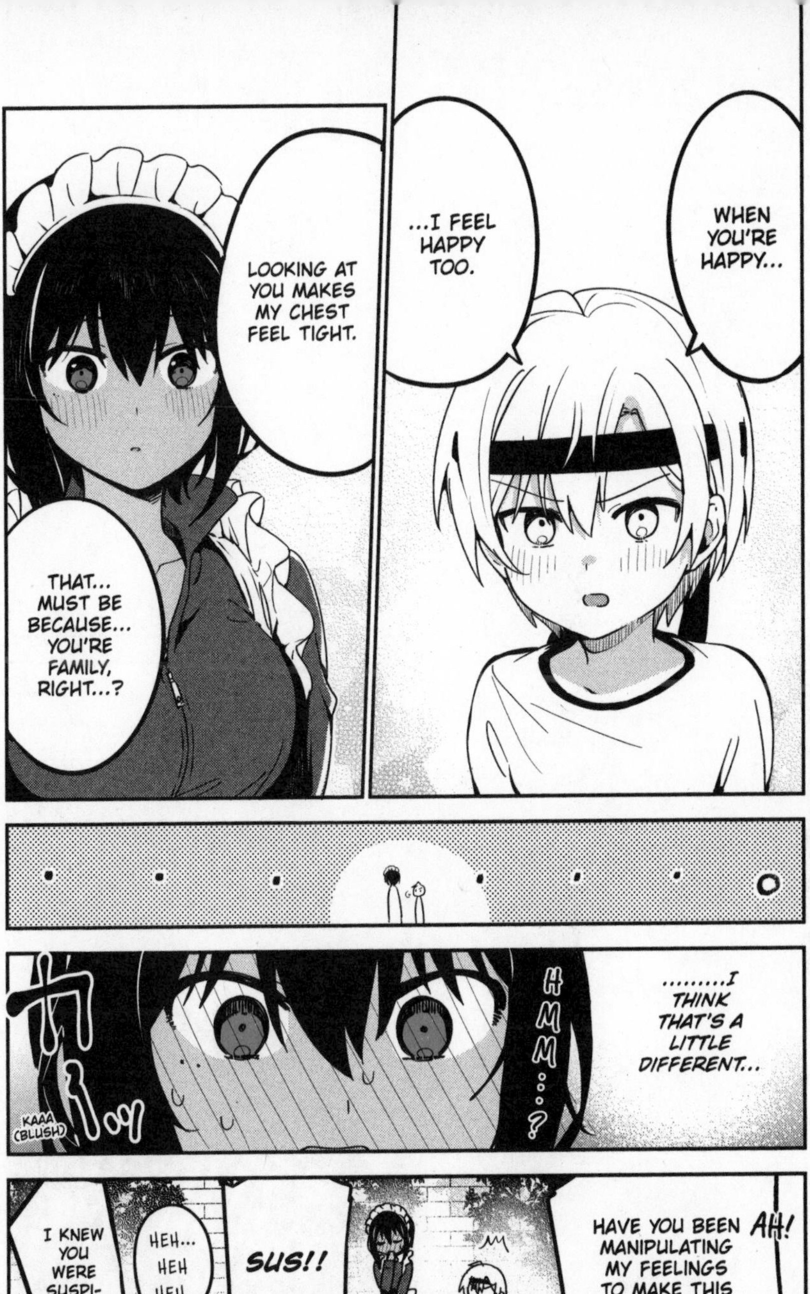
WHEN YOU'RE HAPPY...
...I FEEL HAPPY TOO.
LOOKING AT YOU MAKES MY CHEST FEEL TIGHT.
THAT... MUST BE BECAUSE... YOU'RE FAMILY, RIGHT...?
.........I THINK THAT'S A LITTLE DIFFERENT...
HMM...?
KAAA (BLUSH)
AH!
HAVE YOU BEEN MANIPULATING MY FEELINGS TO MAKE THIS HAPPEN?
SUS!!
HEH... HEH HEH.
I KNEW YOU WERE SUSPI-CIOUS!

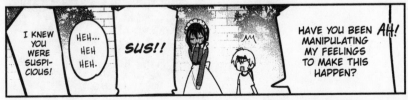

The Maid I Hired Recently Is Mysterious

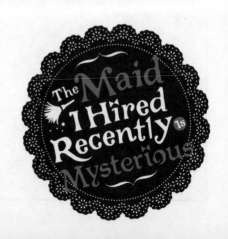

CHAPTER 34

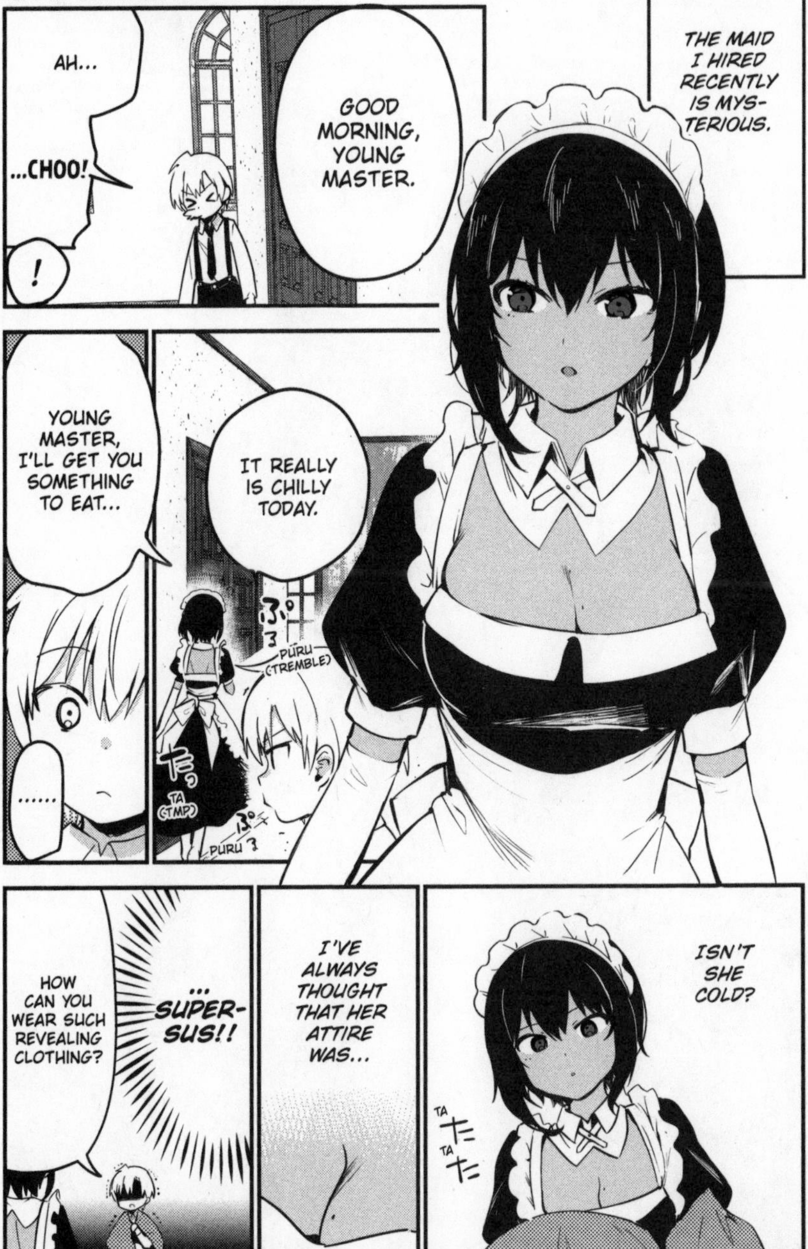
THE MAID I HIRED RECENTLY IS MYSTERIOUS.
GOOD MORNING, YOUNG MASTER.
AH...
...CHOO!
!
IT REALLY IS CHILLY TODAY.
PURU (TREMBLE)
TA (TMP)
PURU
YOUNG MASTER, I'LL GET YOU SOMETHING TO EAT...
......
ISN'T SHE COLD?
TA
TA
I'VE ALWAYS THOUGHT THAT HER ATTIRE WAS...
...SUPER-SUS!!
HOW CAN YOU WEAR SUCH REVEALING CLOTHING?

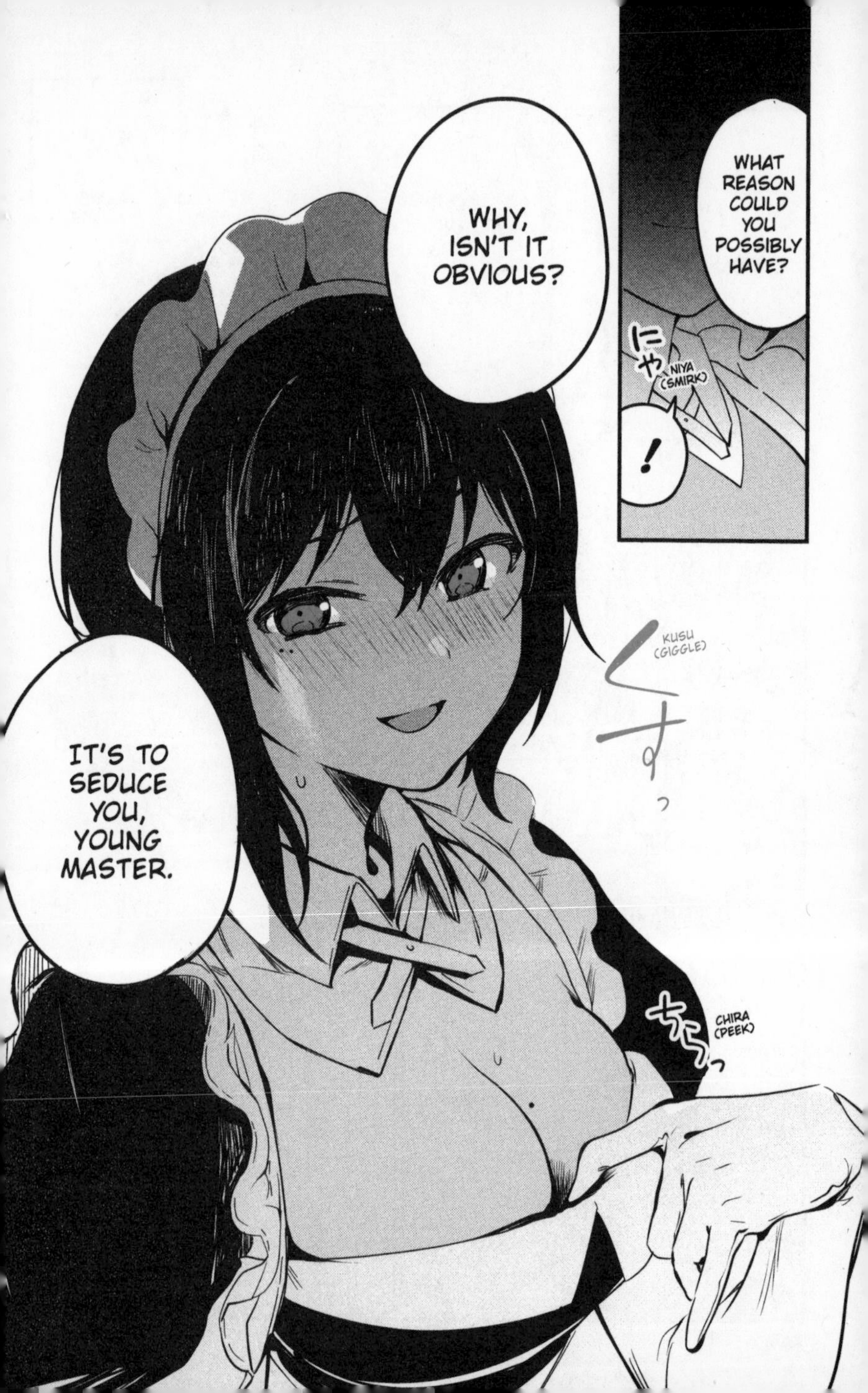
WHAT REASON COULD YOU POSSIBLY HAVE?
にや
NIYA (SMIRK)
!
WHY, ISN'T IT OBVIOUS?
くすっ
KUSU (GIGGLE)
IT'S TO SEDUCE YOU, YOUNG MASTER.
ちらっ
CHIRA (PEEK)

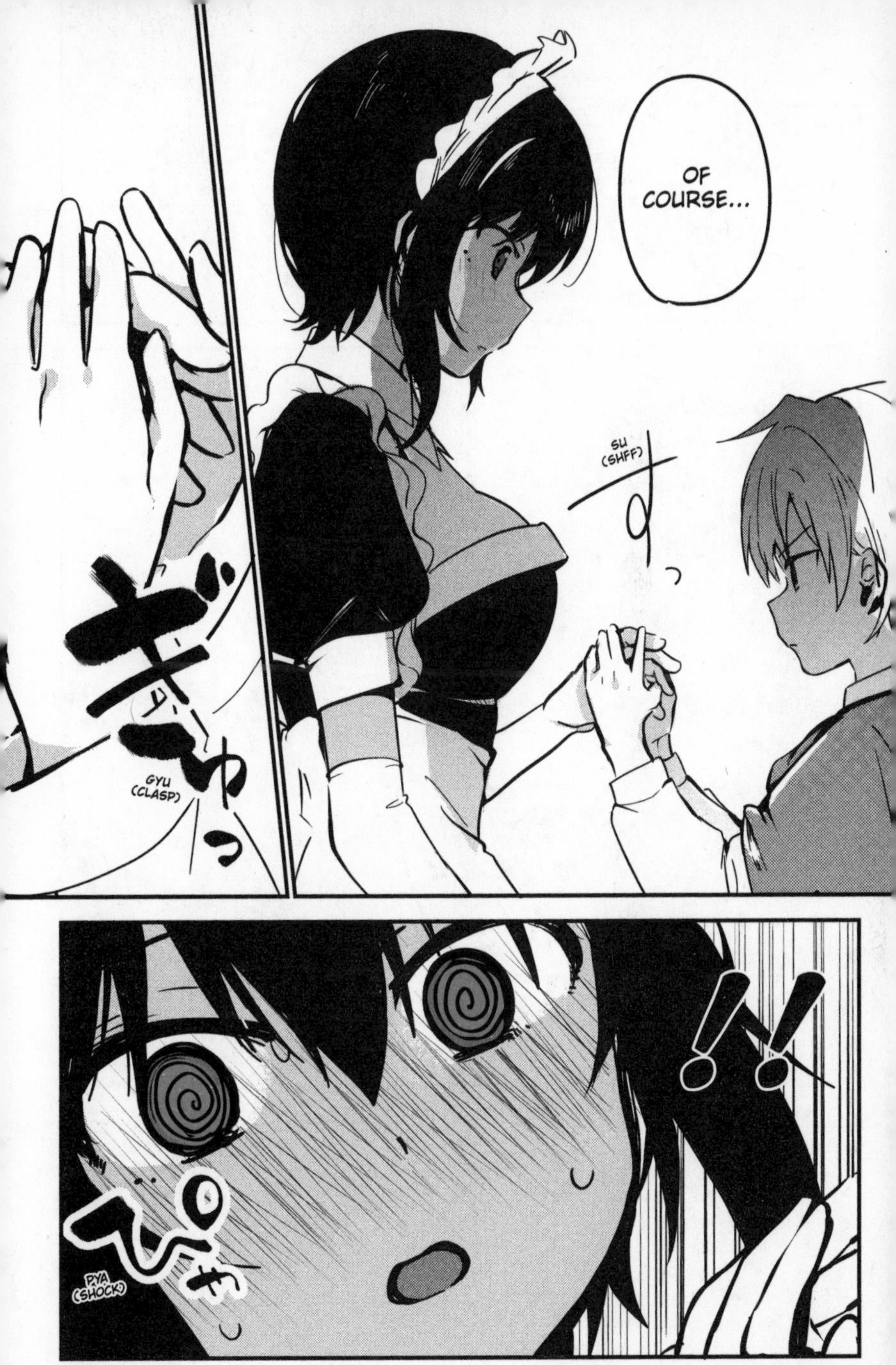
OF COURSE...
SU (SHFF)
GYU (CLASP)
PYA (SHOCK)

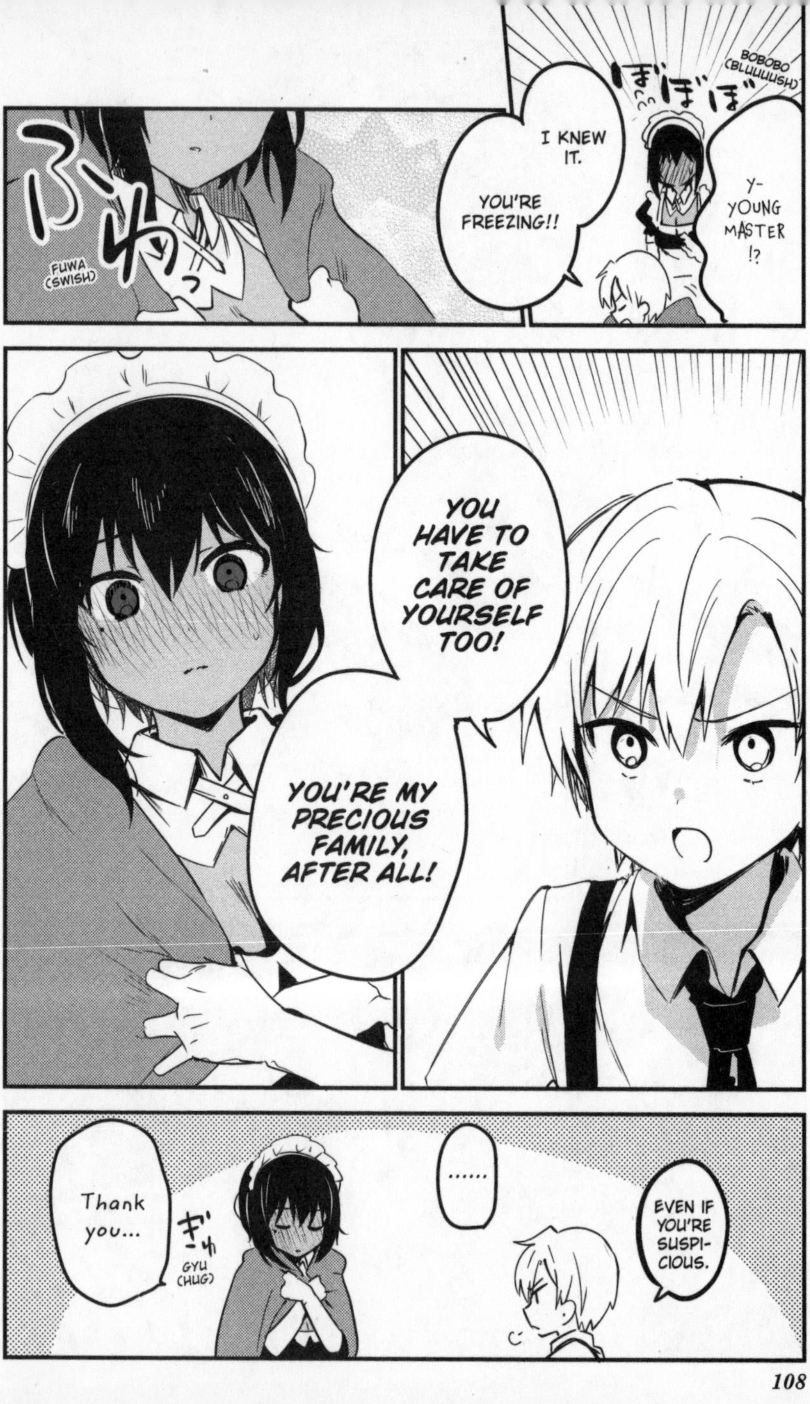
ぼぼぼ
BOBOBO (BLUUUUSH)
Y-YOUNG MASTER!?
I KNEW IT. YOU'RE FREEZING!!
ふぁっ
FUWA (SWISH)
YOU HAVE TO TAKE CARE OF YOURSELF TOO!
YOU'RE MY PRECIOUS FAMILY, AFTER ALL!
EVEN IF YOU'RE SUSPICIOUS.
......
ぎゅ
GYU (HUG)
Thank you...

The Maid I Hired Recently Is Mysterious

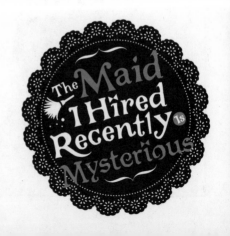

CHAPTER 35

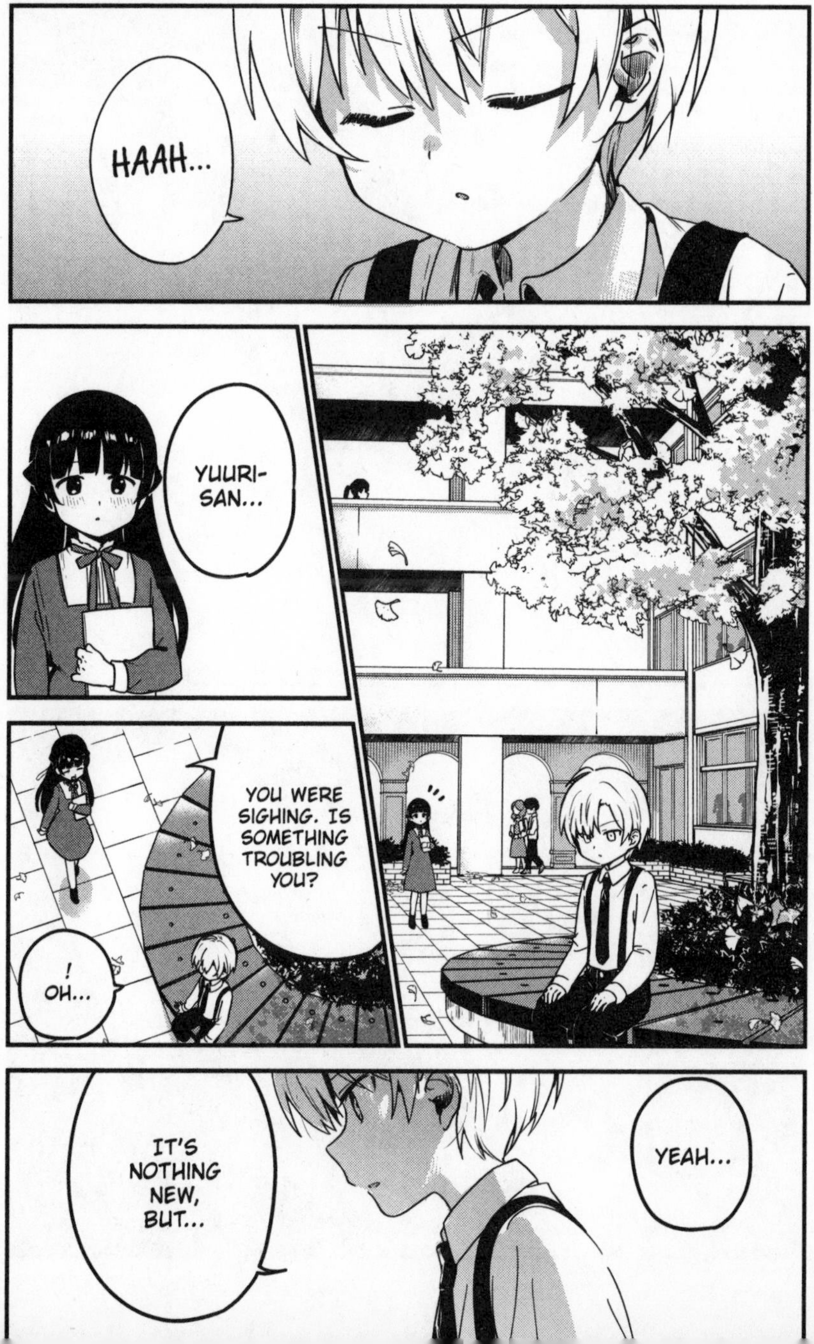
HAAH...
YUURI-SAN...
YOU WERE SIGHING. IS SOMETHING TROUBLING YOU?
! OH...
YEAH...
IT'S NOTHING NEW, BUT...

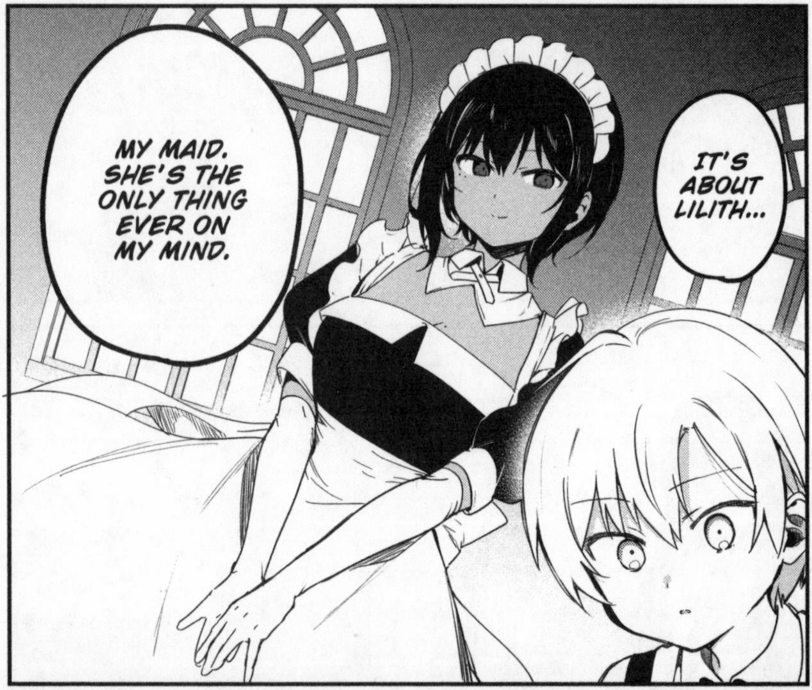
IT'S ABOUT LILITH...
MY MAID. SHE'S THE ONLY THING EVER ON MY MIND.
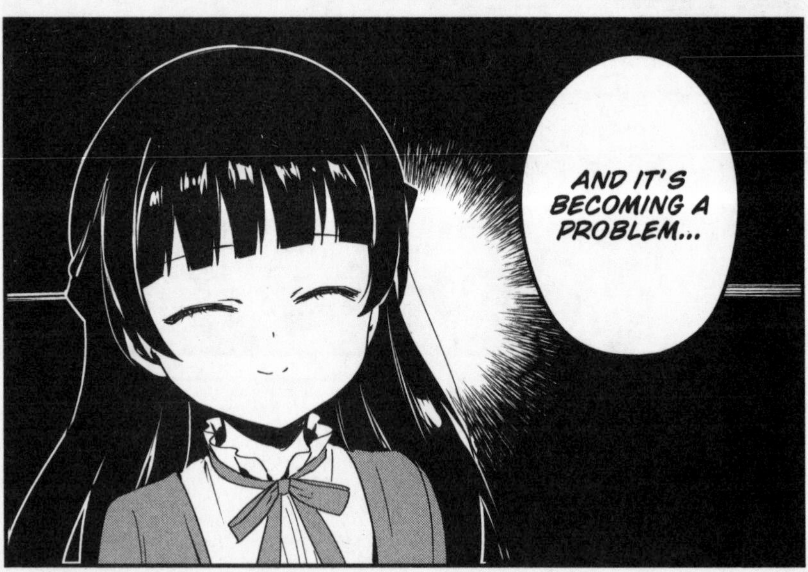
AND IT'S BECOMING A PROBLEM...

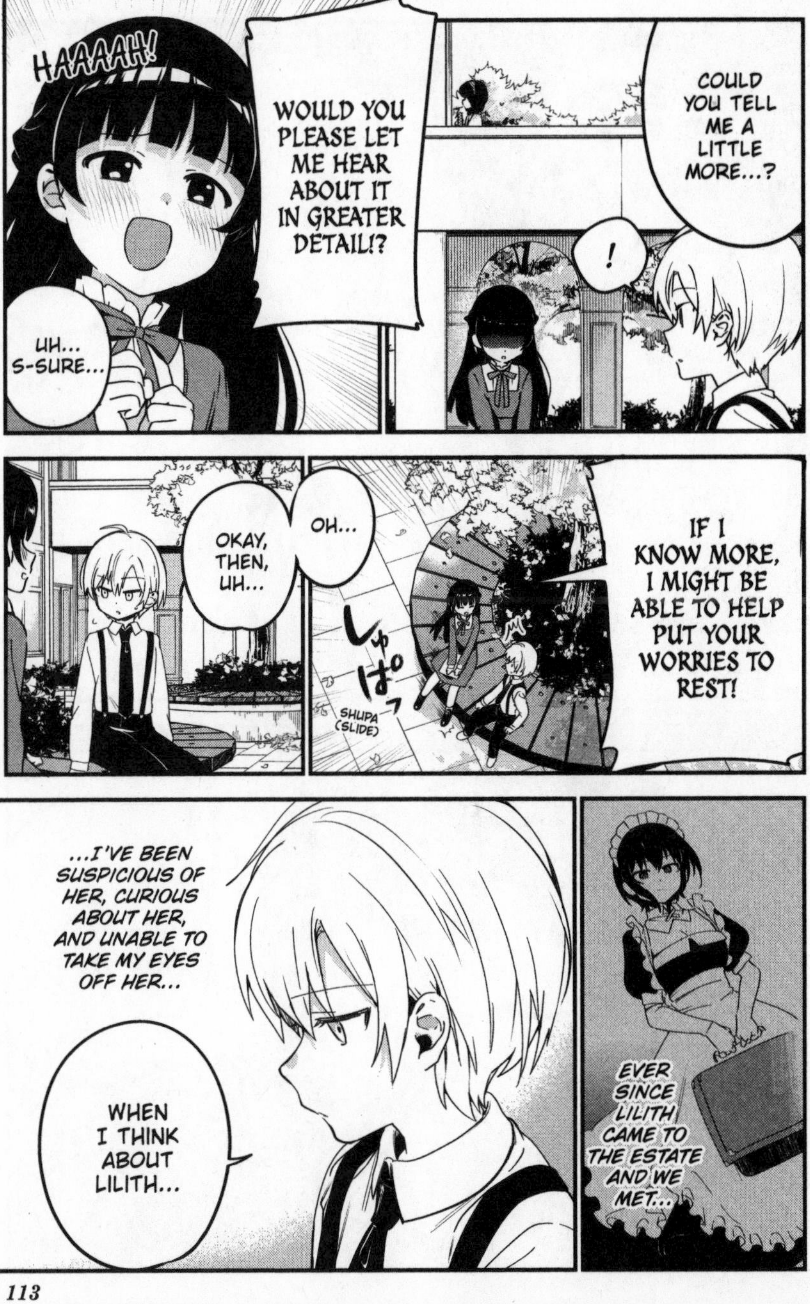
COULD YOU TELL ME A LITTLE MORE...?
!
HAAAAH!
WOULD YOU PLEASE LET ME HEAR ABOUT IT IN GREATER DETAIL!?
UH... S-SURE...
IF I KNOW MORE, I MIGHT BE ABLE TO HELP PUT YOUR WORRIES TO REST!
しゅぱっ
SHUPA (SLIDE)
OH...
OKAY, THEN, UH...
EVER SINCE LILITH CAME TO THE ESTATE AND WE MET...
...I'VE BEEN SUSPICIOUS OF HER, CURIOUS ABOUT HER, AND UNABLE TO TAKE MY EYES OFF HER...
WHEN I THINK ABOUT LILITH...

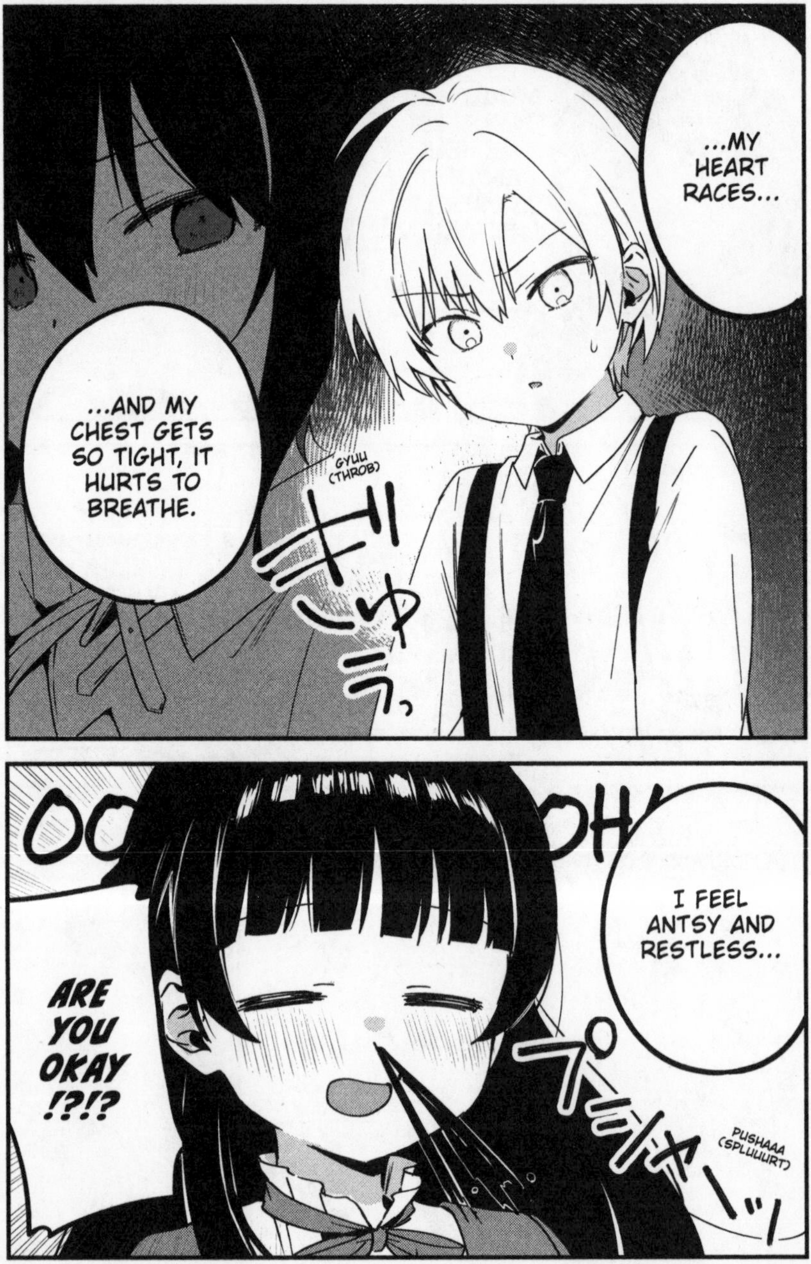
...MY HEART RACES...
...AND MY CHEST GETS SO TIGHT, IT HURTS TO BREATHE.
GYUU (THROB)
I FEEL ANTSY AND RESTLESS...
PUSHAAA (SPLUUURT)
ARE YOU OKAY !?!?

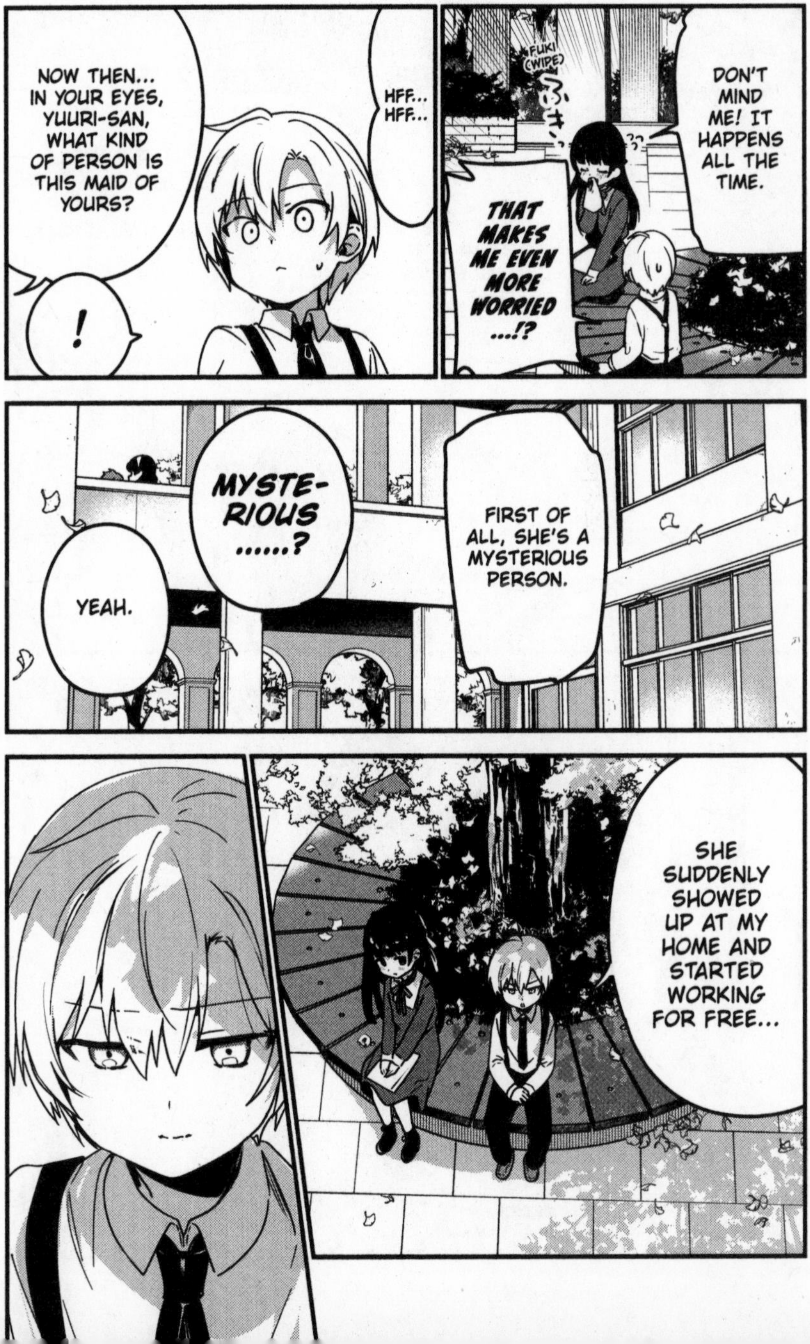
DON'T MIND ME! IT HAPPENS ALL THE TIME.
FUKI (WIPE)
ふき
THAT MAKES ME EVEN MORE WORRIED ...!?
HFF... HFF...
NOW THEN... IN YOUR EYES, YUURI-SAN, WHAT KIND OF PERSON IS THIS MAID OF YOURS?
!
FIRST OF ALL, SHE'S A MYSTERIOUS PERSON.
MYSTE-RIOUS ......?
YEAH.
SHE SUDDENLY SHOWED UP AT MY HOME AND STARTED WORKING FOR FREE...

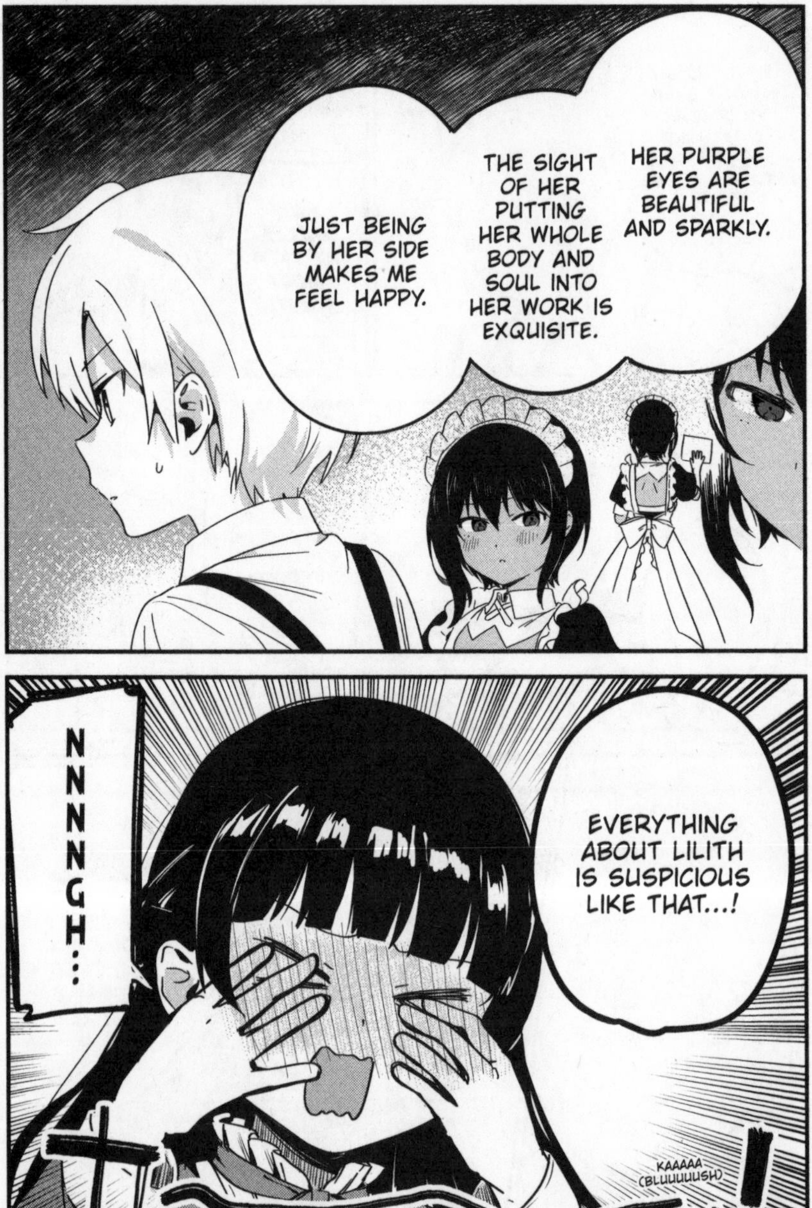
HER PURPLE EYES ARE BEAUTIFUL AND SPARKLY.
THE SIGHT OF HER PUTTING HER WHOLE BODY AND SOUL INTO HER WORK IS EXQUISITE.
JUST BEING BY HER SIDE MAKES ME FEEL HAPPY.
EVERYTHING ABOUT LILITH IS SUSPICIOUS LIKE THAT...!
KAAAAA (BLUUUUUSH)
NNNNGH...

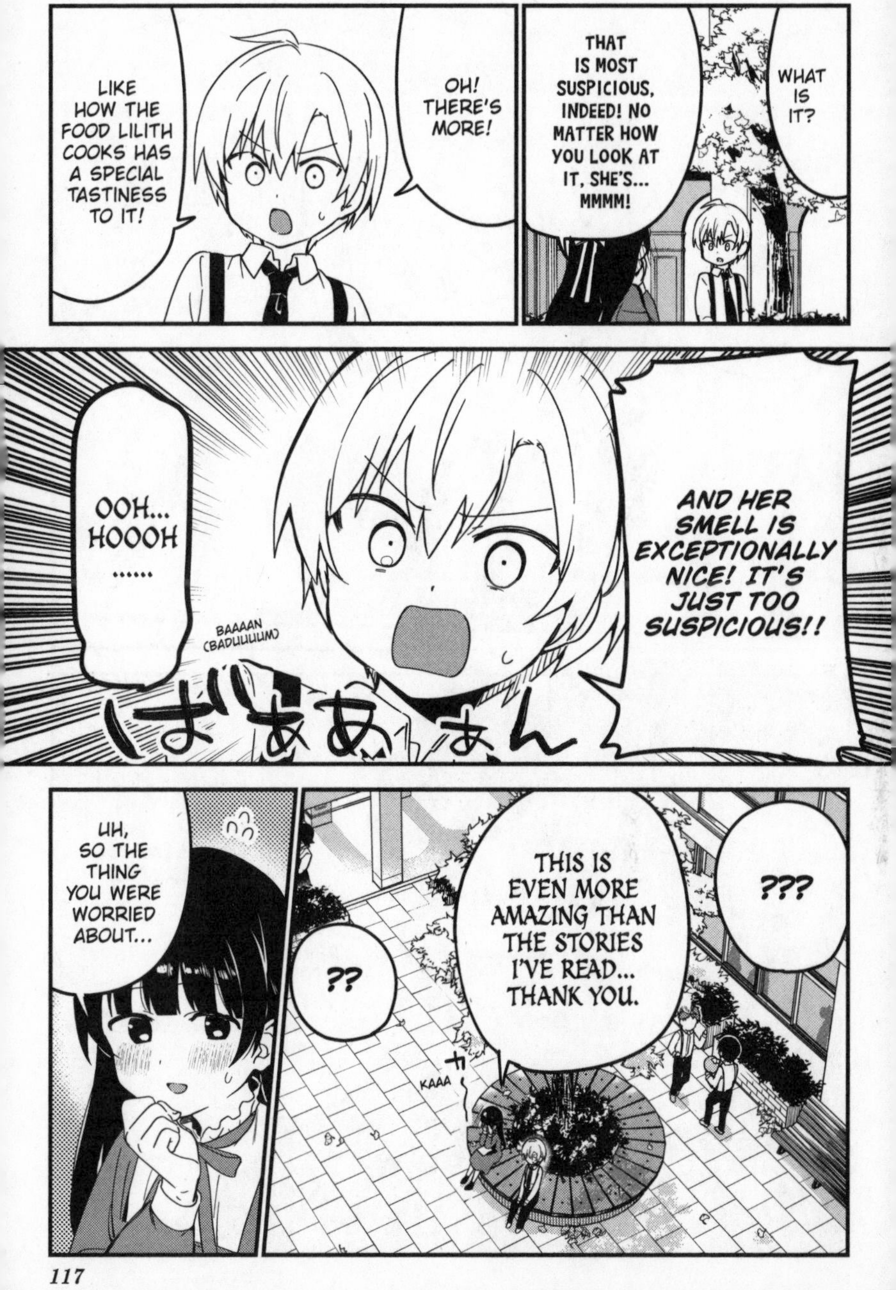
WHAT IS IT?
THAT IS MOST SUSPICIOUS, INDEED! NO MATTER HOW YOU LOOK AT IT, SHE'S... MMMM!
OH! THERE'S MORE!
LIKE HOW THE FOOD LILITH COOKS HAS A SPECIAL TASTINESS TO IT!
AND HER SMELL IS EXCEPTIONALLY NICE! IT'S JUST TOO SUSPICIOUS!!
ばあああん
BAAAAN (BADUUUUM)
OOH... HOOOH ......
???
THIS IS EVEN MORE AMAZING THAN THE STORIES I'VE READ... THANK YOU.
??
KAAA
UH, SO THE THING YOU WERE WORRIED ABOUT...

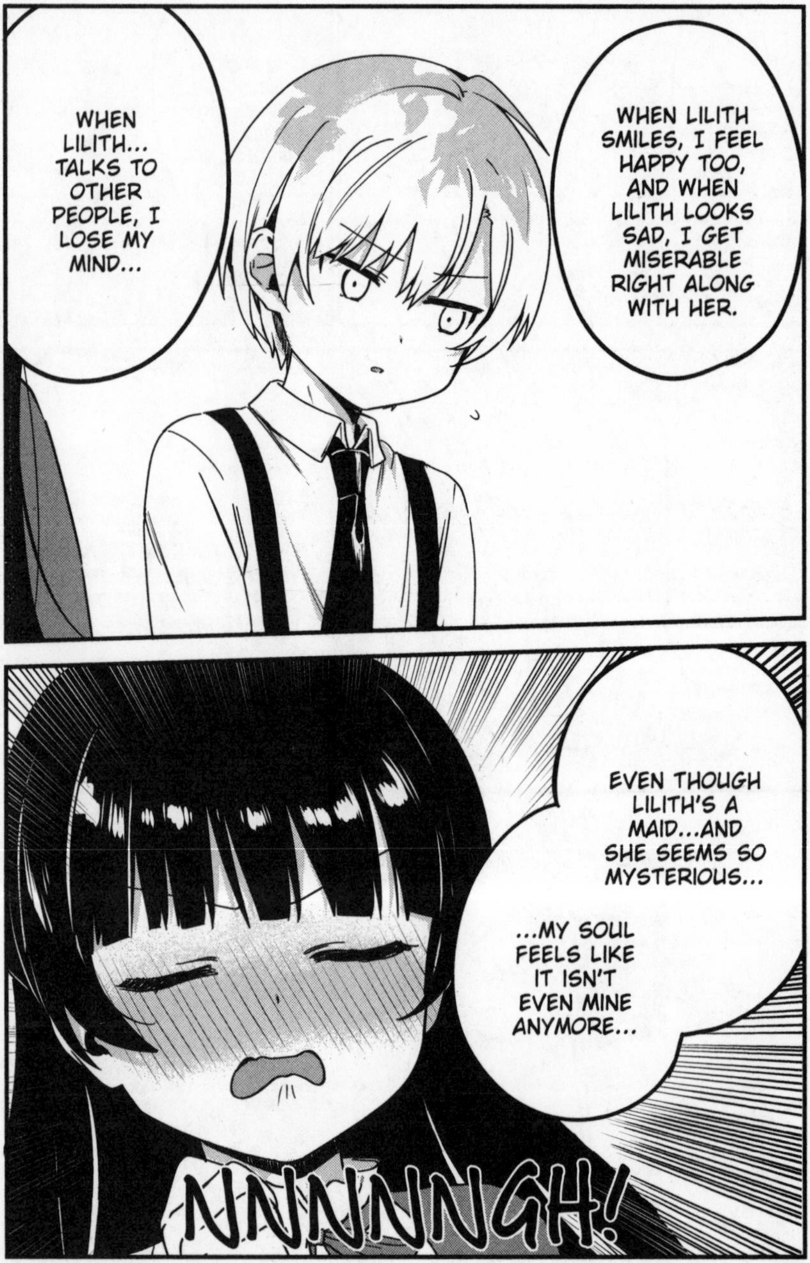
WHEN LILITH SMILES, I FEEL HAPPY TOO, AND WHEN LILITH LOOKS SAD, I GET MISERABLE RIGHT ALONG WITH HER.
WHEN LILITH... TALKS TO OTHER PEOPLE, I LOSE MY MIND...
EVEN THOUGH LILITH'S A MAID...AND SHE SEEMS SO MYSTERIOUS...
...MY SOUL FEELS LIKE IT ISN'T EVEN MINE ANYMORE...
NNNNNNGH!

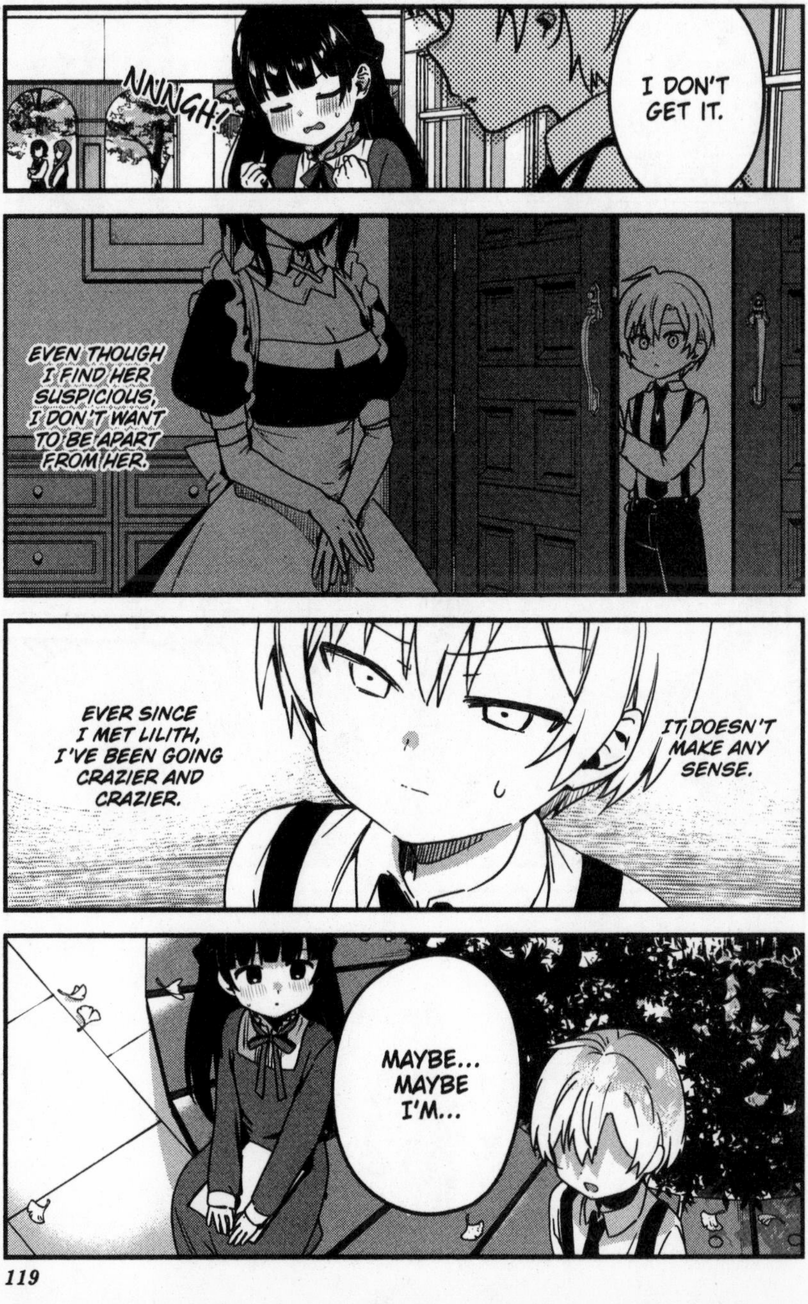
I DON'T GET IT.
NNNGH!
EVEN THOUGH I FIND HER SUSPICIOUS, I DON'T WANT TO BE APART FROM HER.
IT DOESN'T MAKE ANY SENSE.
EVER SINCE I MET LILITH, I'VE BEEN GOING CRAZIER AND CRAZIER.
MAYBE... MAYBE I'M...

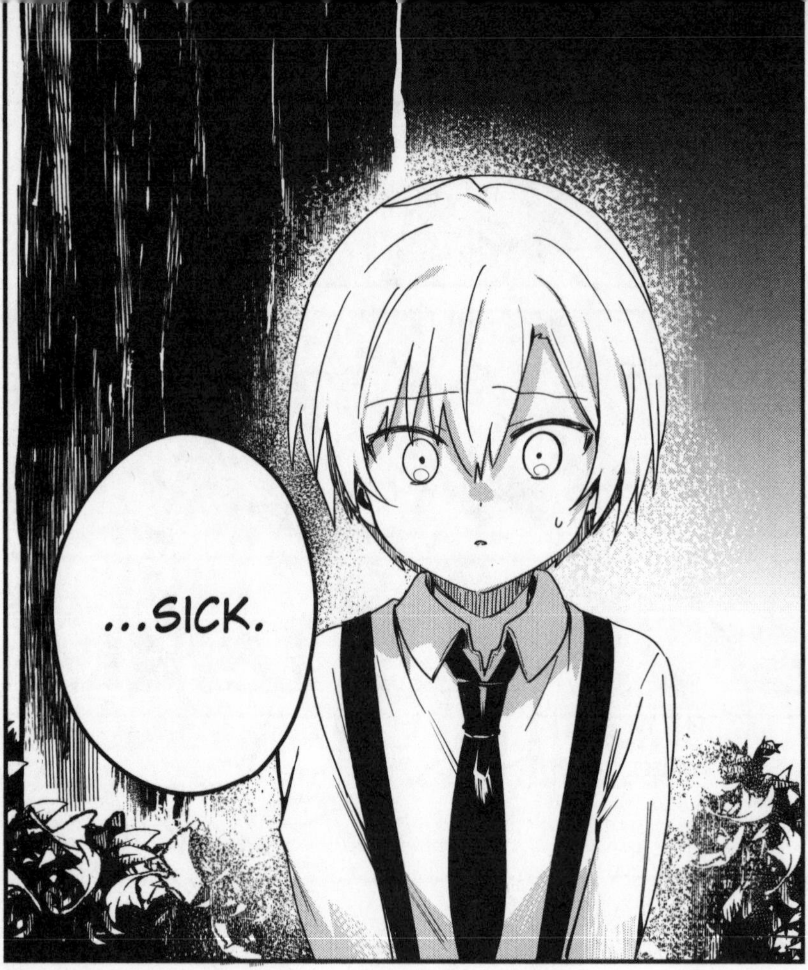
...SICK.
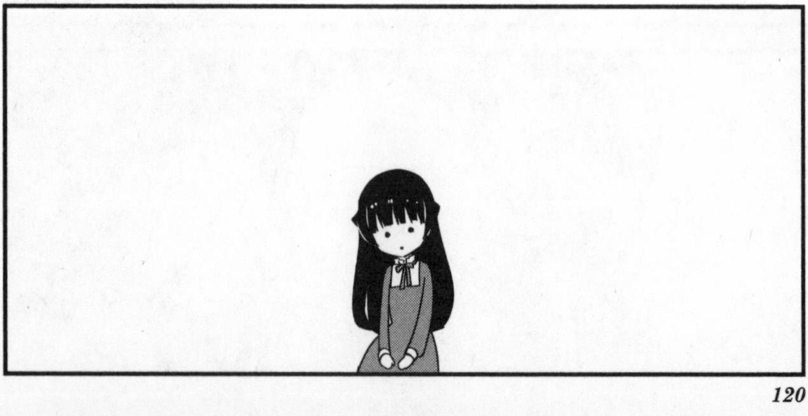

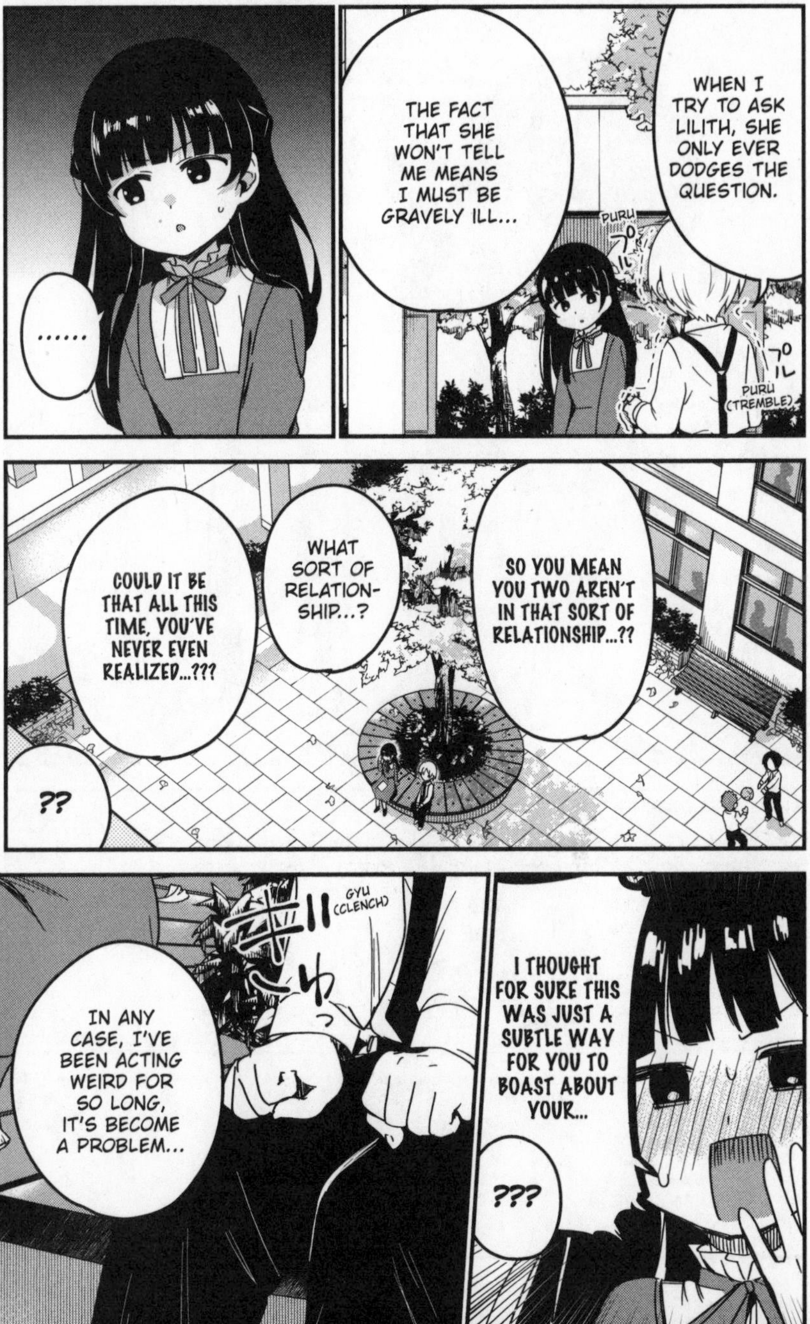
WHEN I TRY TO ASK LILITH, SHE ONLY EVER DODGES THE QUESTION.
THE FACT THAT SHE WON'T TELL ME MEANS I MUST BE GRAVELY ILL...
PURU
PURU (TREMBLE)
......
SO YOU MEAN YOU TWO AREN'T IN THAT SORT OF RELATIONSHIP...??
WHAT SORT OF RELATION-SHIP...?
COULD IT BE THAT ALL THIS TIME, YOU'VE NEVER EVEN REALIZED...???
??
I THOUGHT FOR SURE THIS WAS JUST A SUBTLE WAY FOR YOU TO BOAST ABOUT YOUR...
???
GYU (CLENCH)
IN ANY CASE, I'VE BEEN ACTING WEIRD FOR SO LONG, IT'S BECOME A PROBLEM...

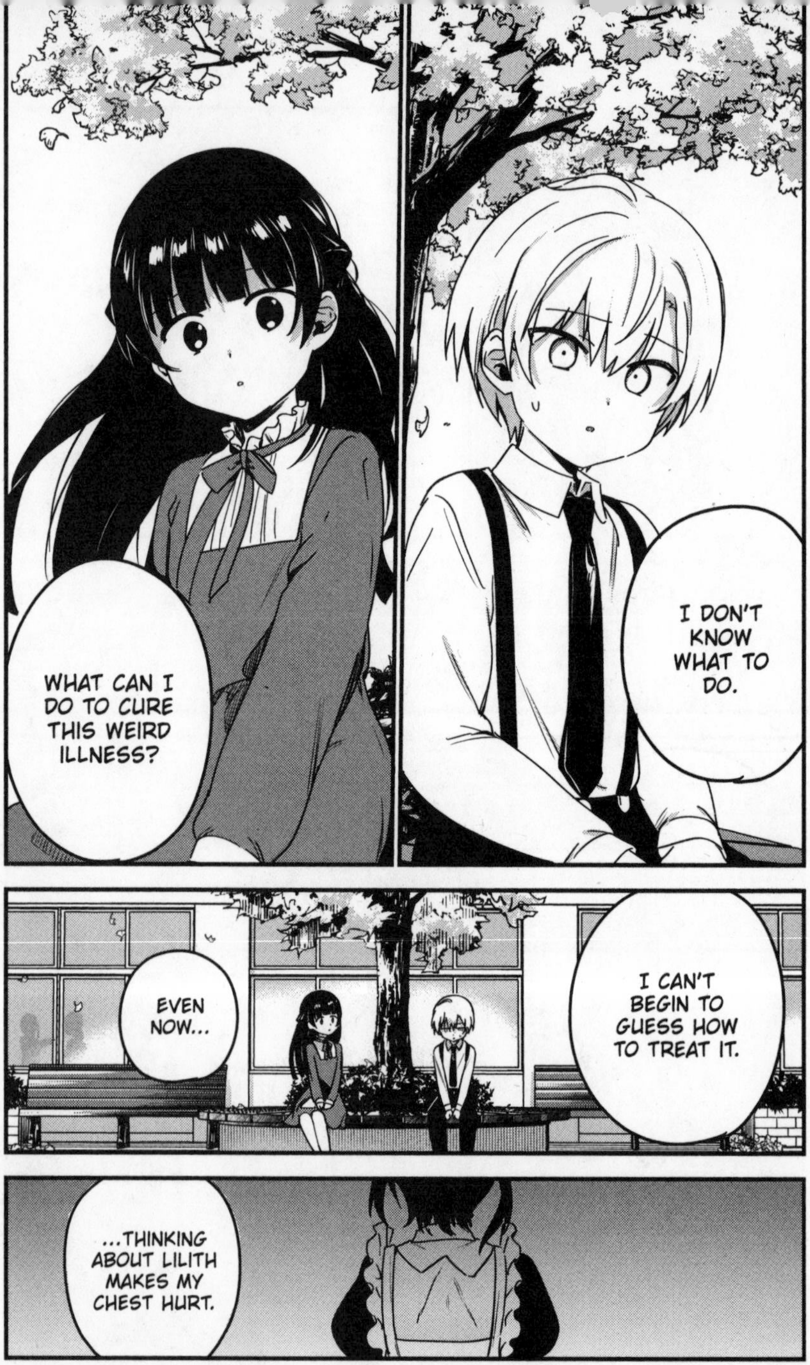
I DON'T KNOW WHAT TO DO.
WHAT CAN I DO TO CURE THIS WEIRD ILLNESS?
I CAN'T BEGIN TO GUESS HOW TO TREAT IT.
EVEN NOW...
...THINKING ABOUT LILITH MAKES MY CHEST HURT.

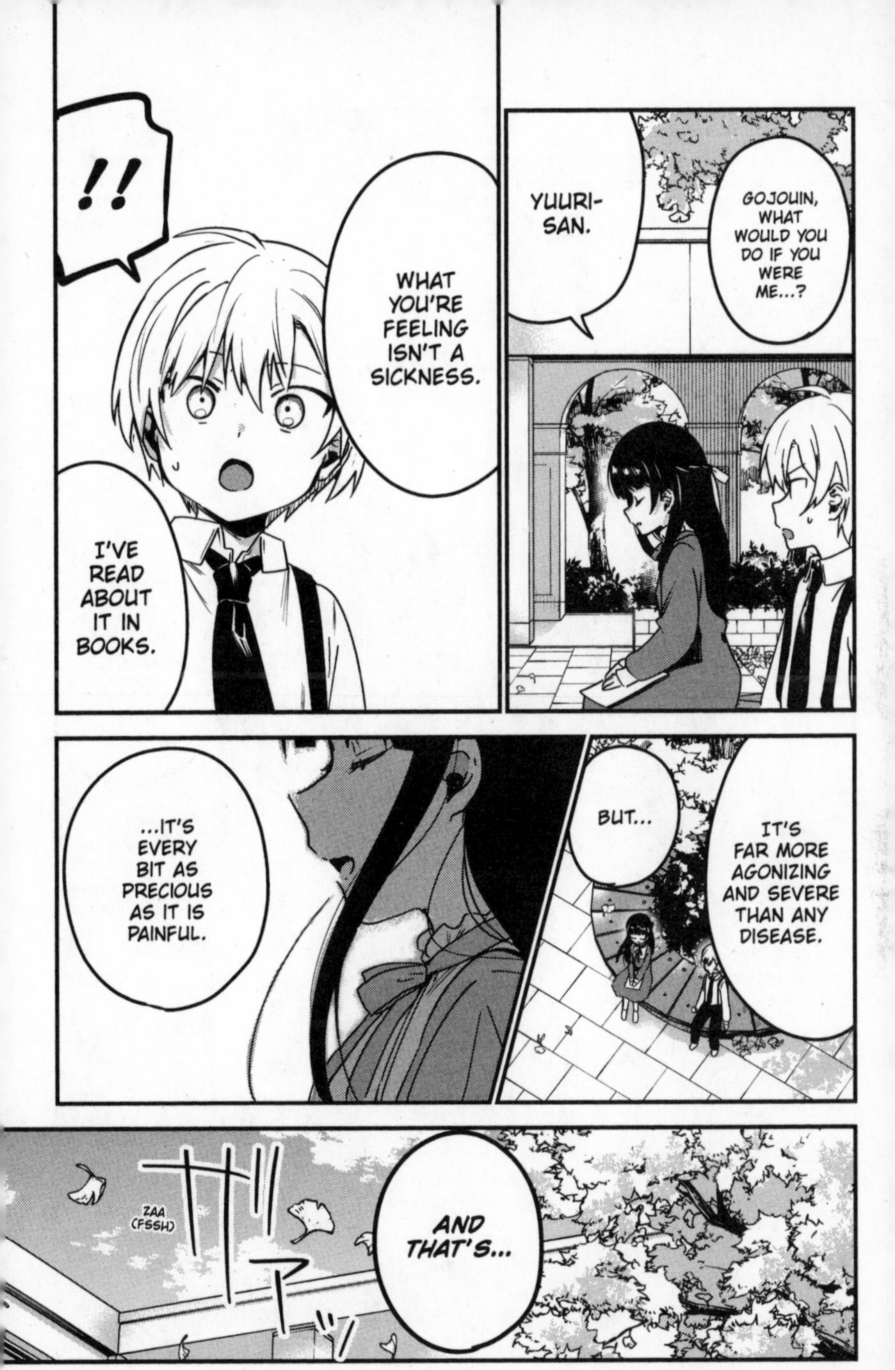
GOJOUIN, WHAT WOULD YOU DO IF YOU WERE ME...?
YUURI-SAN.
WHAT YOU'RE FEELING ISN'T A SICKNESS.
!!
I'VE READ ABOUT IT IN BOOKS.
IT'S FAR MORE AGONIZING AND SEVERE THAN ANY DISEASE.
BUT...
...IT'S EVERY BIT AS PRECIOUS AS IT IS PAINFUL.
AND THAT'S...
ZAA (FSSH)

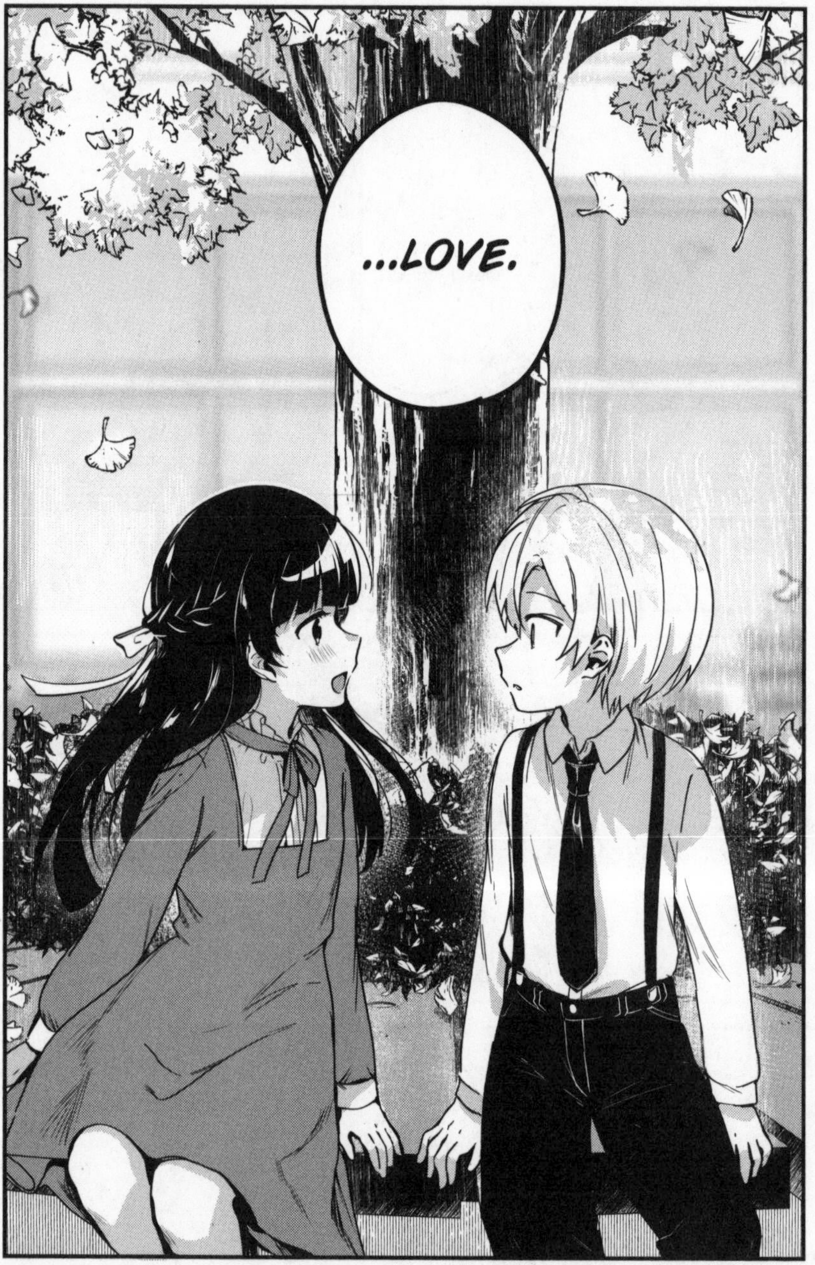
...LOVE.

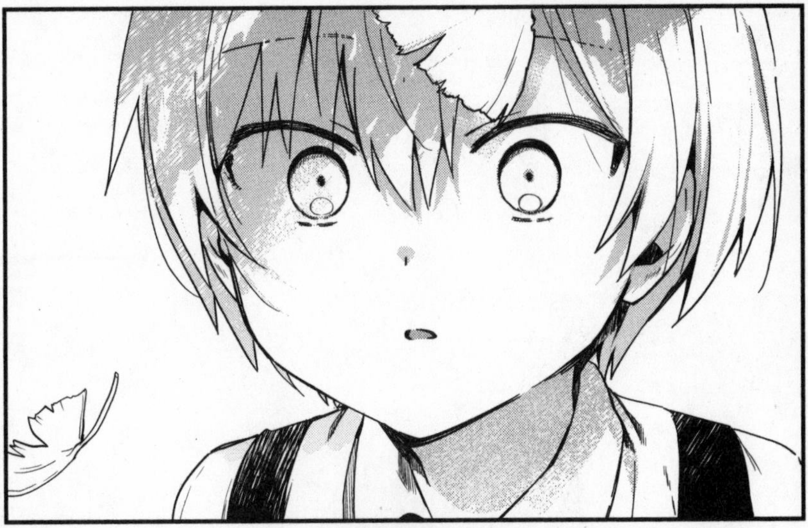

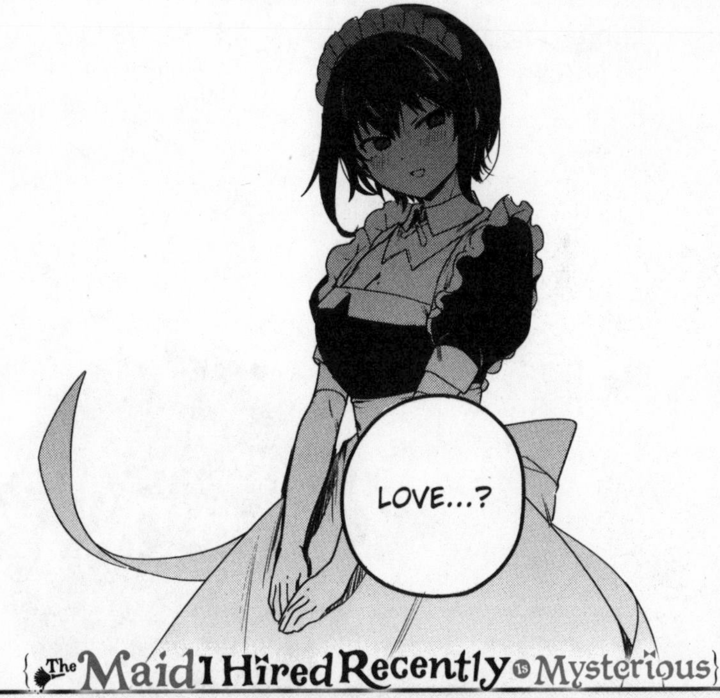
LOVE...?

The Maid I Hired Recently is Mysterious

VOLUME 3 END

The Maid I Hired Recently Is Mysterious

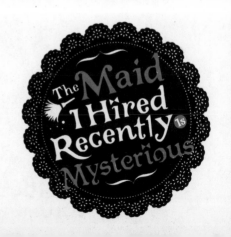

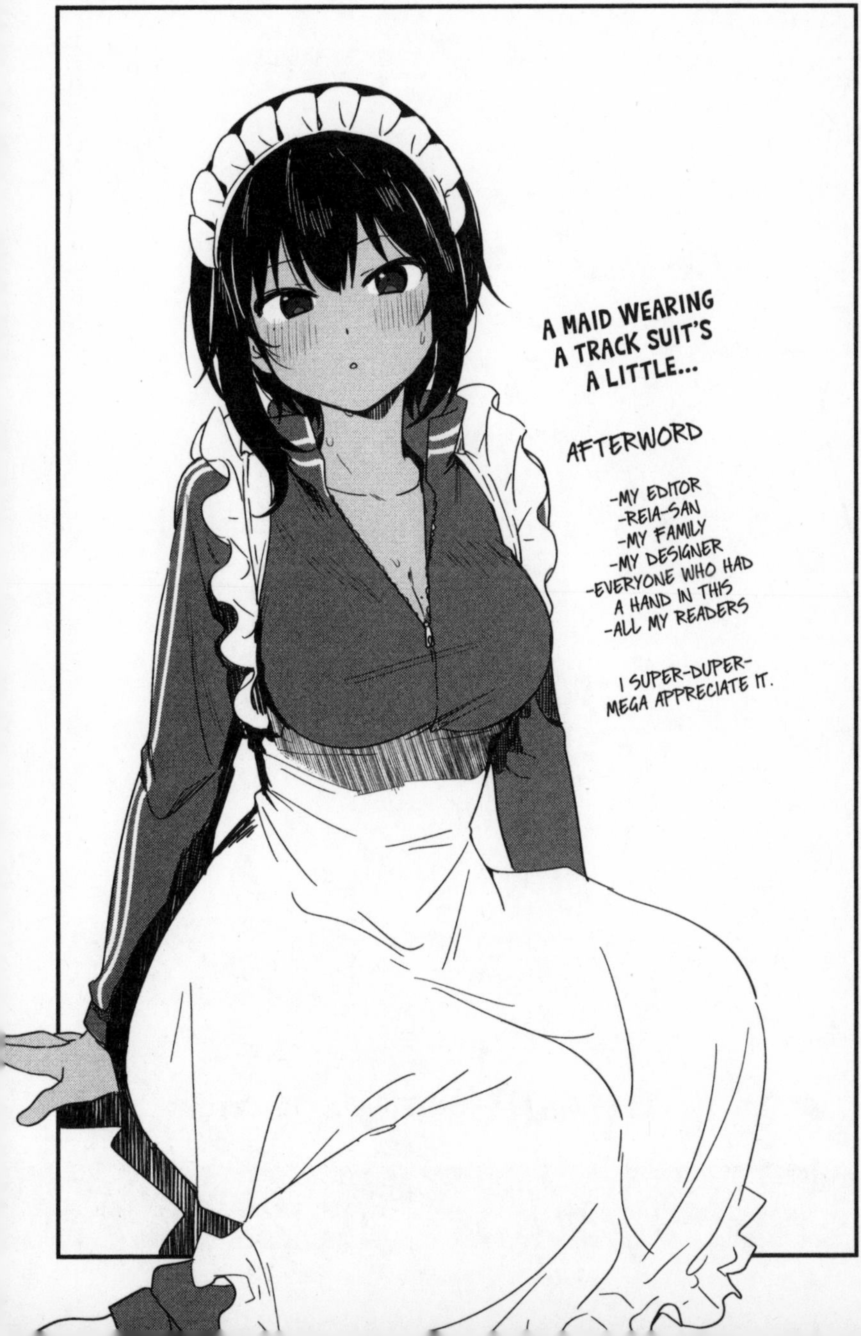
A MAID WEARING A TRACK SUIT'S A LITTLE...
AFTERWORD
-MY EDITOR
-REIA-SAN
-MY FAMILY
-MY DESIGNER
-EVERYONE WHO HAD A HAND IN THIS
-ALL MY READERS
I SUPER-DUPER-MEGA APPRECIATE IT.

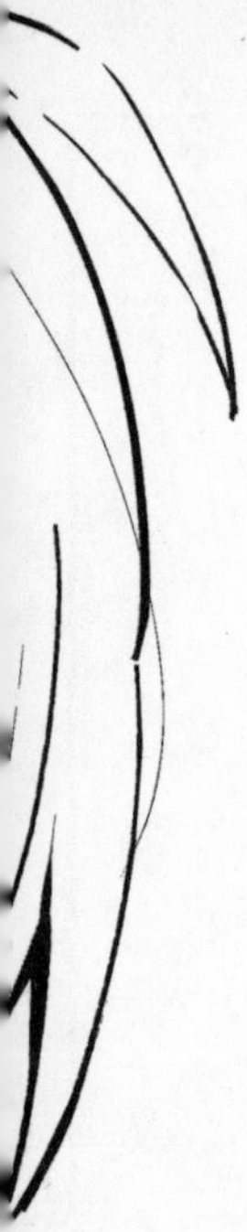

NEXT VOLUME PREVIEW

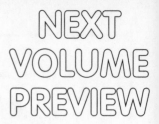

A RACING HEART. A FUZZY HEAD. WHAT IS THE TRUTH BEHIND THESE MYSTERIOUS FEELINGS...!?

The Maid I Hired Recently Is Mysterious 4

ON SALE IN FALL 2022!

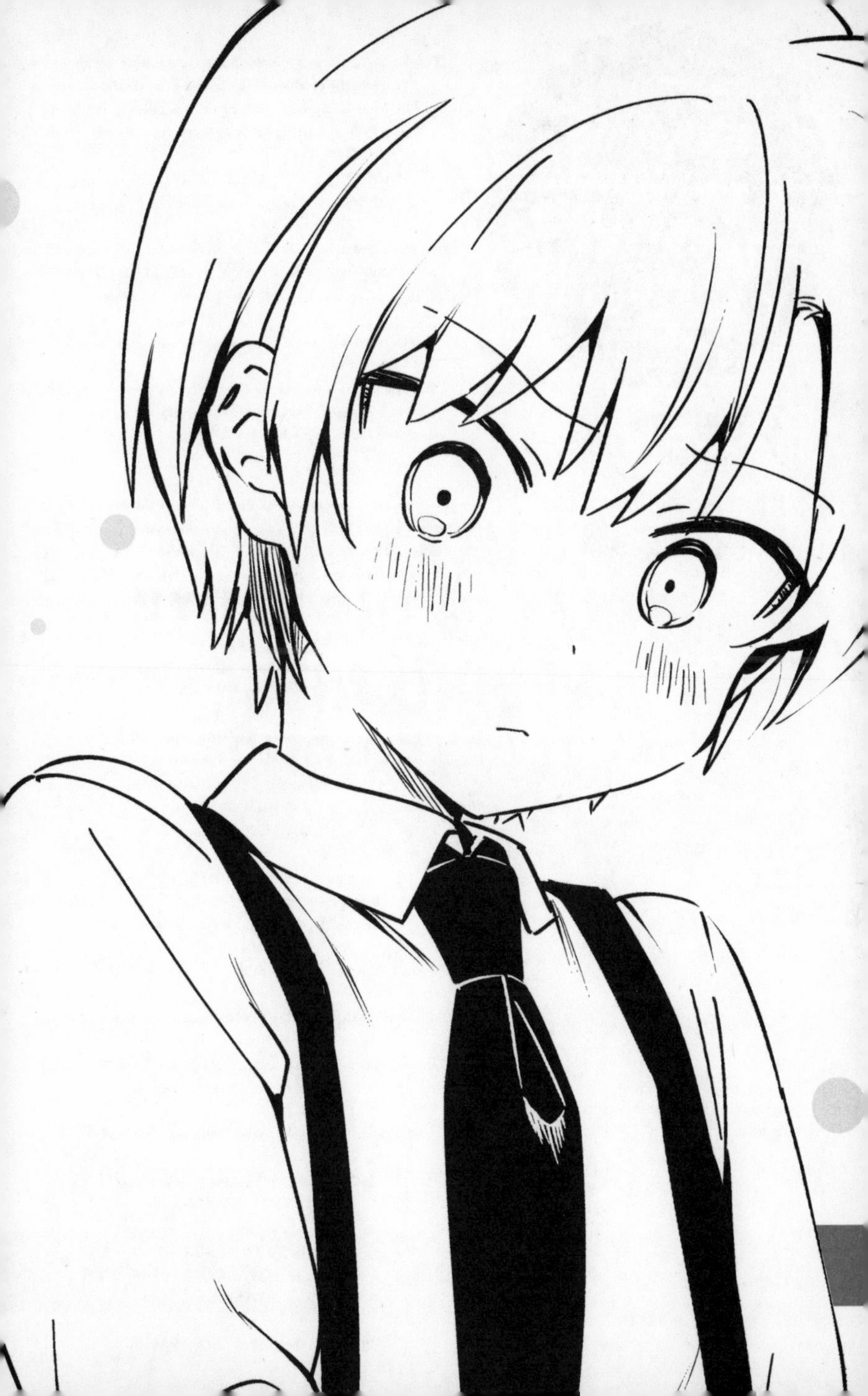

3 Wakame Konbu

Translation: Christine Dashiell

Lettering: Brandon Bovia

SAIKIN YATOTTA MAID GA AYASHII, Vol. 3
©2021 Wakame Konbu/SQUARE ENIX CO., LTD.

First published in Japan in 2021 by SQUARE ENIX CO., LTD.
English translation rights arranged with SQUARE ENIX CO., LTD. and Yen Press, LLC through Tuttle-Mori Agency, Inc.

English translation ©2022 by SQUARE ENIX CO., LTD.

Yen Press
150 West 30th Street, 19th Floor
New York, NY 10001

Visit us at yenpress.com
facebook.com/yenpress
twitter.com/yenpress
yenpress.tumblr.com
instagram.com/yenpress

First Yen Press Edition: June 2022
Edited by Yen Press Editorial: Liz Marbach, Riley Pearsall
Designed by Yen Press Design: Wendy Chan

Yen Press is an imprint of Yen Press, LLC.

Library of Congress Control Number: 2021935580

ISBNs: 978-1-9753-4464-1 (paperback)
978-1-9753-4465-8 (ebook)

10 9 8 7 6 5 4 3 2 1

WOR

Printed in the United States of America